THE LEGACY OF BENEDETTO CROCE

THE LEGACY OF
Benedetto Croce

CONTEMPORARY CRITICAL VIEWS

Edited by Jack D'Amico, Dain A. Trafton,
and Massimo Verdicchio

UNIVERSITY OF TORONTO PRESS
Toronto Buffalo London

© University of Toronto Press Incorporated 1999
Toronto Buffalo London
Printed in Canada

ISBN 0-8020-4484-0

Printed on acid-free paper

Toronto Italian Studies: Major Italian Authors

Canadian Cataloguing in Publication Data

Main entry under title:

The legacy of Benedetto Croce : contemporary critical views

(Toronto Italian Studies. Major Italian authors)
Includes bibliographical references.
ISBN 0-8020-4484-0

1. Croce, Benedetto, 1866–1952 – Criticism and interpretation.   I. D'Amico,
Jack.   II. Trafton, Dain A.   III. Verdicchio, Massimo, 1945–   .   IV. Series

B3614.C74L43 1999   195   C99-930761-4

University of Toronto Press acknowledges the financial assistance to its
publishing program of the Canada Council for the Arts and
the Ontario Arts Council.

This volume was published with the financial assistance of Canisius College
and the University of Alberta.

Contents

ACKNOWLEDGMENTS   vii
CONTRIBUTORS   ix
CHRONOLOGY   xi

1 Introduction   DAIN A. TRAFTON AND MASSIMO VERDICCHIO   3
2 Croce, Philosopher of Naples   MASSIMO VERDICCHIO   16
3 Croce and the *Commedia dell'arte* of Naples   JACK D'AMICO   31
4 *È stata opera di critica onesta, liberale, italiana*: Croce and *Napoli nobilissima* (1892–1906)   THOMAS WILLETTE   52
5 Croce's Theory of Historical Judgment   RENATA VITI CAVALIERE   88
6 Political Doctrine in Croce's *History of the Kingdom of Naples* DAIN A. TRAFTON   103
7 Croce and Mosca: Pluralistic Elitism and Philosophical Science   MAURICE A. FINOCCHIARO   117
8 Croce and Collingwood: Philosophy and History   MYRA MOSS   145
9 Croce on Vico   GIUSEPPE MAZZOTTA   163
10 The Impact of Croce's *Aesthetics* of 1902 and Today's Revolt against Modernity   EDMUND E. JACOBITTI   174
11 History as Thought and Action: Croce's Historicism and the Contemporary Challenge   DAVID D. ROBERTS   196
12 Croce's *Taccuini di lavoro*   RITA MELILLO   231

SELECTED BIBLIOGRAPHY   239

Acknowledgments

The editors wish to thank Kerry Mulvaney for the excellent assistance she provided in the preparation of the manuscript, made possible with a grant provided by Canisius College in Buffalo, NY, and the Hearst family and also the Cheek Fund at Rockford College in Rockford, Ill.

Contributors

Massimo Verdicchio is professor of Italian at the University of Alberta in Edmonton and author of the forthcoming *Naming Things: Aesthetics, Philosophy and History in Benedetto Croce.*

Jack D'Amico is professor of English at Canisius College in Buffalo, NY, and author of the forthcoming *Shakespeare's Italy: The City and the Stage.*

Thomas Willette is visiting associate professor of the history of art at the University of Michigan in Ann Arbor and co-author of *Massimo Stanzione.*

Renata Viti Cavalieri is professor of philosophy at the University of Naples – Federico II.

Dain A. Trafton is professor emeritus of English at Rockford College in Rockford, Ill., and co-author of *Torquato Tasso's Dialogues.*

Maurice A. Finocchiaro is distinguished professor of philosophy at the University of Nevada – Las Vegas and author of *Beyond Right and Left: Democratic Elitism in Mosca and Gramsci.*

Myra Moss is professor of government and philosophy at Claremont McKenna College in Claremont, Calif., and author of *Benedetto Croce Reconsidered: Truth and Error in Theories of Art, Literature, and History.*

Guiseppe Mazzotta is Charles C. and Dorothea S. Dilley Professor of Italian Literature at Yale University in New Haven, Conn. His latest book is *The New Map of the World: The Poetic Philosophy of Giambattista Vico*.

Edmund E. Jacobitti, professor emeritus at Southern Illinois University at Edwardsville, is author and editor of the forthcoming *Composing Useful Pasts: History as Contemporary Politics*.

David D. Roberts is professor of history at the University of Georgia in Athens, Ga., and author of *Nothing But History: Reconstruction and Extremity after Metaphysics*.

Rita Melillo teaches philosophy at the University of Naples – Federico II and is editor of *Ka-Kanata*.

Chronology

1866   25 February, born in Pescasseroli, Abruzzi, where his family possesses estates. Brought up and educated mainly in Naples

1875–82   Early education at the Collegio della Carità and Liceo Genovese in Naples

1883   Death of parents and sister in earthquake in Casamicciola, Ischia

1883–6   With brother Alfonso resides in Rome at home of uncle Silvio Spaventa, parliamentary leader and brother of neo-Hegelian Bertrando Spaventa. Enrolls in jurisprudence at University of Rome but does not take a degree

1886   Returns to Naples to administer family affairs and begins study of the city and its culture

1887–92   Travels to Germany, Austria, France, Holland, Spain, and Portugal

1891   Publication of *I teatri di Napoli alla fine del secolo decimottavo*

1892   Founds the journal *Napoli nobilissima: Rivista d'arte e di topografia napoletana*

1893   Studies Vico's *Scienza nuova*; publishes *La storia ridotta sotto il concetto generale dell'arte*

1895   Introduced to the work of Marx by A. Labriola; a period of enthusiasm is followed by a critique of Marxist doctrine

1898   Opposes the government's proclamation of the state of siege and expresses solidarity with Filippo Turati, the Socialist leader

1900   *Materialismo storico ed economia marxistica: Saggi critici*

1901   Meets publisher Giovanni Laterza of Bari

1902   *Estetica come scienza dell'espressione e linguistica generale*

1903   20 January, with Giovanni Gentile, founds the bi-monthly *La critica, rivista di letteratura, storia e filosofia*
1904   *Lineamenti di una logica del concetto puro*
1906   Laterza begins to publish *La critica*, published until then at Croce's expense. *Ciò che è vivo e ciò che è morto nella filosofia di Hegel*; the first work of Croce to be published by Laterza
1909   *Filosofia della pratica: Economia ed etica*
            Logica come scienza del concetto puro
1910   26 January, appointed senator of the kingdom
            Problemi di estetica e contributi alla storia dell'estetica italiana
1911   *La filosofia di Giambattista Vico*
            Saggi sulla letteratura italiana del seicento
            La rivoluzione napoletana del 1799: Biografie, racconti, ricerche
1913   *Saggio sullo Hegel seguito da altri scritti di storia della filosofia*
            Breviario di estetica
            Makes public his philosophical disagreement with Gentile
1914   Marries Adele Rossi, with whom he later has four daughters, Elena, Alda, Lidia, and Silvia
1914   Early opposition to Italy's entering war against Germany
            La letteratura della nuova Italia: Saggi critici, vols. I and II
            Cultura e vita morale: Intermezzi polemici
1915   *Contributo alla critica di me stesso*
            La letteratura della nuova Italia: Saggi critici, vols. III and IV
1915–18   Writings on the war, later collected in *Pagine sulla guerra* (1919, 1928), later appearing as *L'Italia dal 1914 al 1918* (1950)
1917   *Teoria e storia della storiografia*
            La Spagna nella vita italiana durante la Rinascenza
1918   *Conversazioni critiche: Serie prima e seconda*
1919   *Storie e leggende napoletane*
            Goethe, con una scelta delle liriche nuovamente tradotte
            Una famiglia di patrioti ed altri saggi storici e critici
            Primi saggi
1920–1   Minister of education in Giolitti's government; proposes educational reforms, supported by Gentile, but defeated in parliament
1920   *Nuovi saggi di Estetica*
            Ariosto, Shakespeare e Corneille
            La poesia di Dante
1921   *Storia della storiografia italiana nel secolo decimonono*
            Goethe, con una antologia della lirica goethiana

1922   Mussolini gains power and selects Gentile as minister of education. Croce a supporter of fascism at first, believing that it will fade after restraining the excesses of the far left

1922   *Frammenti di etica*

1923   *Poesia e non poesia: Note sulla letteratura europea del secolo decimonono*

1925   After the fascist takeover (3 January) writes against Gentile's 'Manifesto of Fascist Intellectuals' (1 May), speaks against the fascist regime in the National Caucus of the Liberal party (28 June)

1925   *Storia del Regno di Napoli*

1926   Home attacked by fascists; though ostracized, Croce too well recognized to be imprisoned or openly censured

1926–42   Croce's banishment from all government-supported academies; though under constant police vigilance, allowed to travel to Berlin, Paris, London, Oxford, and in Belgium and Switzerland

1927   *Uomini e cose della vecchia Italia*

1928   *Storia d'Italia dal 1871 al 1915*

1929   Continues opposition to fascism and speaks against the Lateran Pacts. *La critica* becomes a forum of intellectual opposition to Mussolini's dictatorship
'Aesthetics,' in 14th ed. of *Encyclopedia Britannica*
Storia dell'età barocca in Italia: Pensiero, poesia e letteratura, vita morale

1931   *Etica e politica*
Nuovi saggi sulla letteratura italiana del seicento
Elementi di politica

1932   *Conversazioni critiche: Serie terza e quarta*
Storia d'Europa nel secolo decimonono

1933   *Poesia popolare e posia d'arte: Studi sulla poesia italiana dal tre al cinquecento*

1935   *Ultimi saggi*
Varietà di storia letteraria e civile

1936   *La poesia: Introduzione alla critica e storia della poesia e della letteratura*
Vite di avventure, di fede e di passione

1938   *La storia come pensiero e come azione*

1939   *La letteratura della nuova Italia, vol. V*
Conversazioni critiche: Serie quinta

1940   *La letteratura della nuova Italia, vol. VI*

1941   *Il carattere della filosofia moderna*
       Poesia antica e moderna: Interpretazioni
       Pagine sparse, vol. I
1942   *Aneddoti di varia letteratura* (1st ed., 3 vols., 2nd ed., 4 vols.)
1943   Allied invasion; Croce escapes with family to Capri, which is
       in the hands of Allied forces. Proposes formation of detach-
       ments of Italian volunteers, under the Italian flag, to fight
       Germans alongside the Allies. Proposes abdication of the king
       and his removal from Italy. President of newly formed Liberal
       party
1944   Liberation of Rome by the Allies. Croce a member of the new
       Bonomi cabinet with Togliatti, De Gasperi, and Saragat
1943   *Pagine sparse, vol. II and vol. III*
1944   *Per la nuova vita dell'Italia*
1945   *Discorsi di varia filosofia*
       Poeti e scrittori del pieno e del tardo Rinascimento, vol. I and vol. II
       Pagine politiche: (Luglio–dicembre 1944)
1946   Declines to be temporary president of the republic
1946   *Pensiero politico e politica attuale: Scritti e discorsi*
       Quando l'Italia era tagliata in due
1947   16 February, establishes Istituto Italiano per gli Studi Storici, a
       postgraduate school of historical studies, in a wing of his
       home, Palazzo Filomarino
1948   Made senator in the first Italian parliment; declines offer of
       Luigi Einaudi to be senator for life
1948   *Nuove pagine sparse: Serie I e II*
       Due anni di vita politica italiana: 1946–1947
1949   *Filosofia e storiografia*
       Varietà di storia letteraria e civile: Seconda serie
       La Letteratura del Settecento
1950   *Letture di poeti e riflessioni sulla teoria e la critica della poesia*
       Storiografia e idealità morale
1952   Suffers stroke in February and dies 20 November
1952   *Indagini su Hegel e schiarimenti filosofici*
       Poeti e scrittori del pieno e del tardo Rinascimento, vol. III
1954   *Anedotti di varia letteratura, 4 vols*
1955   *Terze pagine sparse*
1963   *Scritti e discorsi politici*

THE LEGACY OF BENEDETTO CROCE

1

Introduction

DAIN A. TRAFTON and
MASSIMO VERDICCHIO

[One ought to study Croce] provided one puts aside all the silliness and the commonplaces and wishes really to understand in depth the character of a writer who yesterday was perhaps read too much by too many, and most of the time poorly, and who today is read only by a few and not always well.

Gennaro Sasso[1]

When Benedetto Croce died in 1952 he was one of the most influential philosophers and literary critics not only of his native Italy but also of Europe, and even North America.[2] Today, however, his very extensive work on philosophy, literary criticism, and history seems to many old-fashioned and inadequate and is largely ignored.[3] Only in the last few years, in Italy, has there been a minor revival, with the reprinting of his complete works under the direction of the historian Giuseppe Galasso, who has also written a comprehensive study of Croce's life and works.[4] In North America, Croce has fared somewhat better, largely through the efforts of scholars such as Gian Orsini and Ernesto Caserta, who have made sure that he has remained a critical presence, albeit a solitary one.[5] Moreover, recent studies by M.E. Moss and David D. Roberts suggest that a similar revival may be occurring in North America.[6] The editors hope that this volume will contribute to this trend.

How to explain the sudden decline of interest in Croce? Some of the reasons are to be found in Croce's enormous success during his lifetime and can be explained as a reaction to the authority, even 'dictatorship,' that he wielded for years over Italian intellectual and political life.[7] Croce's authority is very well captured by an epitaph he wrote for himself, in which he makes clear his criticism of universities and their traditional ways of doing philosophy and literature: 'He rescued philosophy and literature from the hands of university professors.' (Tolse la filosofia e la letteratura dalle mani dei professori universitari.)[8] The epitaph, which was never used, is indicative not just of the contempt that Croce had for the establishment, but also of his role as sole arbiter over matters of culture and knowledge in Italy for many years. His works were mandatory reading in schools everywhere in Italy, where they were held up as the last word in all matters of literature and philosophy. Thus Croce unwittingly became a 'cross' to bear – one that students quickly got rid of at the first opportune moment. This was the ultimate irony in the life of a man who had been catapulted unexpectedly to fame after publication of his *Aesthetics* in 1902. Fifty years later, that same fame made him infamous to the point that to talk of Croce, or to be Crocean, was to be outdated and traditional.

Croce's reputation can be said to have been made and unmade more as a result of circumstances than by serious assessment of his work, of what it can still mean to us today, or, as Croce would have it, of what it can mean to our own historical time. The epitaph quoted above holds the key to an understanding of why Croce can still be a voice for us today and why he should still be read. Its bold words can be read with profit as emphasizing above all the importance he placed on philosophy and literature, which he saw as too vital to be taken lightly and left to those who dealt with them as mere university subjects. For us today, Croce's lifelong dedication to the serious study of philosophy and literature constitutes a major part of his legacy.

Croce was born in Pescasseroli, Abruzzo, on 25 February 1866 and died in his adopted city, Naples, on 20 November 1952. His legacy grows out of a vast learning that at first found its focus in erudite studies on the history and culture of Naples, many of which he later collected in *Storie e leggende napoletane* (Neapolitan Histories and Legends, 1919). In this period he was also a contributor to, and later editor of, *Napoli nobilissima* (1892–1906), a journal of Neapolitan art and culture, and wrote the first history of the theatres of Naples, *I teatri di Napoli dal Rinascimento alla fine del secolo decimottavo* (Neapolitan Theatres from the Renaissance to the End of the Eighteenth Century, 1891). From these early years also dates his brief encounter with Marxism, which culminated in and ended with the publication of *Materialismo storico ed economia marxistica* (Historical Materialism and Marxist Economics, 1900). From the historian of Naples and erudite scholar of things Neapolitan, the philosopher of art and history and the logician were born out of necessity. As early as 1893, he reflected on the nature of art and its relation to history and philosophy in *La Storia ridotta sotto il concetto generale dell'arte* (History Reduced under the General Concept of Art),[9] and in 1902 he published his *Estetica come scienza dell'espressione e linguistica generale* (Aesthetics as Science of Expression and General Linguistics),[10] which brought him instant fame.

Estetica defined the aesthetic as intuition, as identical with expression, and differentiated it from other pseudo-aesthetic forms that are often erroneously taken to be art. The aesthetic is also the first moment in the evolution of the theoretical in Croce's three-volume *Filosofia dello Spirito* (Philosophy of Spirit), his attempt, based largely on a refinement of Kant and Hegel, to develop a systematic understanding of human knowledge and activity. Croce argues that knowledge begins in intuition and aesthetic experience and moves on to concepts that, while dependent on aesthetic experssion, are also distinct from it. Croce's theory of the concept was developed in *Logica come scienza del concetto puro* (Logic as Science of Pure Concept, 1905; rev. 1909).[11] The evolution of the practical sphere of the 'Philosophy of Spirit' moves from the Economic to the Ethic in a similar relation of interdependence whereby the former produces actions that have individual ends, the latter actions that have universal ones – a process that Croce described in *Filosofia della pratica: Economia ed Etica* (Philosophy of the Practical: Economic and Ethic, 1909).[12] In contrast to the Hegelian dialectic of opposites, Croce's movement of Spirit is circular. Having reached its last stage in action, Spirit returns to intuition and to thought, and the cycle renews itself as action by becoming once again a moment of intuition and reflection: 'Philosophy ... cannot of necessity be anything but the methodological moment of historiography: an eilucidation of the categories constitutive of historical judgments, or of the concepts that direct historical interpretation. And since historigraphy has for content the concrete life of the spirit, and this life is life of imagination and of thought, of action and of morality (or of something else, if anything else can be thought of), and in this variety of its forms remains always one, the elucidation moves in distinguishing between aesthetic and logic, between economic and ethic, uniting and dissolving them all in the philosophy of the spirit.'[13]

To the three volumes that constitute the *Filosofia dello Spirito* – *Aesthetics, Logic, Philosophy of the Practical: Economic and Ethic* – Croce added a fourth on the theory and history of historiography, *Teoria e storia della storiografia* (1917),[14] which does not constitute another system but is a further elaboration and development of chapters in the second part of the *Logic*.[15] In fact, history was always central to Croce's thought, and in later works, the term 'Philosophy of Spirit' gives way to 'absolute historicism' ('storicismo assoluto'), a more appropriate name for his philosophical system. Croce's preoccupation with history and historiography is also evident in the many historical studies that he penned throughout his career. Among the most important are *Storia del Regno di Napoli* (History of the Kingdom of Naples, 1925),[16] *Storia d'Italia dal 1871 al 1915* (History of Italy from 1871 to 1915, 1928), *Storia d'Europa nel secolo decimonono* (History of Europe in the Nineteenth Century, 1932), and his last and most important theoretical work on history, *La storia come pensiero e come azione* (History as the Story of Liberty, 1938).[17]

All the while Croce never abandoned writing on aesthetics and literature, both Italian and European. He continued refining his definition of art, first in *Breviario di estetica* (The Breviary of Aesthetic, 1913),[18] later by elaborating the lyrical character of art in *Problemi di Estetica* (Aesthetic Issues) and its cosmic character in *Nuovi Saggi di Estetica* (New Aesthetic Essays), and finally by differentiating pure lyric poetry from literature in *La poesia: Introduzione alla critica e storia della poesia e della letteratura* (Benedetto Croce's Poetry and Literature: An Introduction to Its Criticism and History, 1936).[19] Of his literary studies, *La poesia di Dante* (The Poetry of Dante)[20] and *Ariosto, Shakespeare and Corneille*[21] deserve mention because of their impact on the development of his aesthetics. Finally, Croce's seminal essay on Giambattista Vico, *La Filosofia di G.B. Vico* (The Philosophy of Giambattista Vico, 1911),[22] attests to his lifelong interest in Vico's philosophy and to the impact that it had in shaping his own philosophy.

From 1903, moreover, Croce was editor of, and principal contributor to, *La critica, rivista di storia, letteratura e filosofia*, a journal initially meant to survey and assess the temper of the intellectual life of the newly formed Italy, and later the barometer for measuring the cultural and political climate of Europe. Croce also enjoyed a modest political career, occupying various posts, as commissioner of public education for the city of Naples and surroundings, as minister of education for all Italy, and for one year as senator – a title that he was given for his valuable contribution to Italian letters. He refused to be named senator for life. Because of his stand against fascism, Croce became a virtual prisoner in his own house during the years Mussolini was in power. After the war, he was one of the few intellectuals called on to shape, together with the king of Italy and the allies, a new Italian government, and he was instrumental in paving the way for an end to the monarchy and the creation of an Italian republic. In a life that saw him almost perish at a very young age in an earthquake that killed his parents and a sister, Croce lived to complete numerous volumes that influenced the thinking of Italians and Europeans for more than half a century.[23] As a philosopher and critic, Croce had a profound impact on an entire generation of thinkers, and the value of his thought cannot be easily dismissed today.

Croce's questioning in matters pertaining to all spheres of the theoretical and the practical is a key to reading Croce 'well,' as Sasso intimates in the epigraph. This questioning is exemplified by his critical method, which in his lifetime and afterward was often thought to be biased and limited.[24] Croce first applied this method to Hegel in an essay entitled 'Ciò che è vivo e ciò che è morto nella filosofia di Hegel' (What Is Living and What Is Dead in the Philosophy of Hegel).[25] Croce applied a similar method to his reading of literature in order to make a distinction that he referred to variously as that between 'poesia e non poesia' (poetry and non-poetry) or, as in his reading of Dante, between 'poesia e struttura' (poetry and structure).[26] Although these distinctions may appear at first to be sweeping and not very rigorous, they always serve a deeper purpose, since they are symptomatic for Croce of a far more troubling issue that entails the very survival of both literature and philosophy, as well as of his own philosophical system.

Fundamental to Croce's system is the insight that intuition and expression are one and the same or, as he indicates in the subtitle to his *Aesthetics* of 1902, that a theory of aesthetics is also a theory of linguistics, since aesthetic expression is necessarily linguistic expression. One of the far-reaching consequences of this theory is that while it makes possible the utterance of clear and distinct ideas, as a reflection of a clear mind that thinks distinctly, it also facilitates the correction of confused thinking once its confusion has become manifest at the level of expression. Croce's method intervenes whenever a philosophical or a poetic work is found to be in error, when it is no longer capable of clear and distinct utterances – namely, when it is 'dead.'

There are always two moments in a Crocean reading. The first moment identifies the error and isolates it. In a philosophical work such as Vico's *New Science*, for instance, what is at issue for Croce is the disruption of the conceptual expression by the figurative or metaphorical elements that constitute it. In Dante's *Commedia*, Croce finds an error in the confusion between the structural or didactic parts of the poem and the lyric poetry, which, though dependent on the allegorical structure, is also quite distinct from it.

The second moment in a Crocean reading is characterized by an act of separation, which eliminates the error and restores the truth of the aesthetic or philosophical text by clearly distinguishing in philosophy between what is metaphorical and what is conceptual and in poetry between what is simply structure and what is pure poetry. This second moment is seminal in Croce's attempt to re-evaluate what is living and what is dead in art or in philosophy, since on this distinction depends the possibility of survival not only of any philosophical system and poetic work but also of art and philosophy in general.

In reading Croce, one must always differentiate between two stages of critical inquiry, as outlined above, rather than confusing them, as so often occurs.[27] Only in this manner is it possible to assess the pertinence of Croce's critical observations, which may appear arbitrary or superficial but are in fact always profound and worthy of careful consideration. Furthermore, it is essential to keep in mind that for Croce the work of critical intervention is never meant to be final, but has to be performed continuously, since this is the essential characteristic of any critical and philosophical practice. For this reason, no philosophical system, not even Croce's, is meant to be the last word on the subject. Croce did not intend his own philosophy to be accepted uncritically. On the contrary, he expected those who came after him to scrutinize his work and evaluate it according to what was still living or dead for them. Error, according to Croce, can never be completely overcome or erased but only discovered by a constant act of separation that distinguishes pure from impure concepts, poetry from non-poetry.

Outline of This Study

The task of the philosopher, for Croce, lies precisely in clearing up this type of confusion and reducing error – in dissipating the 'clouds, obscurities, and perplexities' (nubi, oscurità, e perplessità) that constantly threaten knowledge. In so doing he also meant to contribute to the progress of culture and the enhancement of a moral life: 'One is a philosopher in the strict or eminent sense if he removes one more of these stumbling-blocks, great or small, if he dispels one of these clouds, or lightens one darkness, so that by the result of his work the activities of civilisation and morality, slowly perhaps but certainly, enjoy increase.'[28] (Filosofo in senso specifico o eminente è chiamato colui che rimuove uno di questi ostacoli più o meno gravi, dissipa una di queste nubi, fuga una tenebra, e della cui opera si godono perciò rapidi o lenti ma sicuri gli effetti nel crescere d'intensità della cultura e della vita morale.)

It is to this Croce – the Croce whose work has the power to remove obstacles, shed light, and deepen our cultural and moral life – that this volume is dedicated. The essays collected here cover the broad range of his development, from his earliest endeavors in the archives and local intellectual circles of Naples to his maturity as a philosopher of world renown and an inspiration to his country during the desperate crisis precipitated by the Second World War. Moreover, the diversity of the contributions represents in itself a confirmation of Croce's enduring relevance. In what follows, eleven scholars from three countries and four academic disciplines demonstrate the rich variety of ways in which Croce remains of value today.

The first three essays explore the shaping of Croce's mature thought through his early study of Neapolitan history. The work of Croce's early period has sometimes been characterized as mere erudition, unphilosophical fact-gathering of the kind that he later repudiated, but this view is superficial and misleading. His critical method, the leading ideas of his 'Philosophy of Spirit,' his conception of history, and his sense of public responsibility as a philosopher all are present, at least in embryo, in his youthful meditations on the history of his chosen city. As Massimo Verdicchio and Jack D'Amico show, Croce exhibits his philosophical predilections from the beginning: in the critical distinctions that he establishes among Neapolitan legends and stories (or histories); in his 'deconstruction' of the assumptions underlying the view of Pulcinella as a represention of Neapolitan ethnicity; in his analysis of the relationship between 'aesthetic' and 'industrial' elements in the *commedia dell'arte*. His *Neapolitan Histories and Legends* and his *Neapolitan Theatres from the Renaissance to the End of the Eighteenth Century* continue to command the attention of scholars and remain a source of fresh speculation, not only about particular historical topics, but also about general questions of aesthetics, logic, and historiography.

Examining another aspect of Croce's early career, Thomas Willette offers an account of *Napoli nobilissima*, the magazine that Croce founded

with a group of friends with the aim of stimulating civic pride and public virtue through local history. By presenting the results of serious historical research in a popular manner, *Napoli nobilissima* cleared away
misunderstandings and laid the foundation for a sound appreciation of
the past. Through accurate description of the historic fabric of the city,
moreover, Croce and his collaborators sought to engage public opinion
in a campaign to preserve the city's ancient monuments against the rav-
ages of the so-called *piano di Risanamento* – Naples's nineteenth-century
version of urban renewal. Willette's essay provides a vivid account of an
episode during which Croce discovered his considerable aptitude for
the polemics of cultural warfare.

As these studies of the early Croce make clear, history was where he
started. And history, as subsequent contributions to this volume emphasize, remained at the centre of his intellectual development even as he
turned to more directly theoretical and philosophical investigations. In
the essay that follows Willette's, Renata Viti Cavaliere focuses on the
theoretical reflections by which Croce put his particular historical studies into a steadily broadening context. She situates the young Croce in
the context of nineteenth-century debates over the question whether history is an art or a science and traces the complicated path by which these
debates led him first to seek a new ground for history and, indeed, all
thought in aesthetic intuition and then to the conclusion that all thought
is the product of history. For Croce, however, this hypothesis did not
preclude a dimension of human freedom, which Cavaliere undertakes
to define as precisely as possible, linking it to Croce's sense that the phi-
losopher-historian has a duty to contribute to the ethical and political
development of his time.

Dain A. Trafton's study of the *History of the Kingdom of Naples* demonstrates how this sense of public duty informs one of Croce's major
historical works. Calling attention to a hitherto unnoticed pattern in
the book, Trafton argues that its main purpose is to alert readers to the
fundamental qualities of political vitality. Thus the work is a form of
political teaching, or doctrine. Like *Napoli nobilissima*, it is addressed
primarily to southern Italians, inhabitants of the territory that was once
the kingdom of Naples, but its message is more general as well; the
political lessons that it presents appear to be applicable to all nations
and perhaps to all historical periods.

Maurice Finocchiaro's examination of Croce's relationship to Gaetano
Mosca pursues the theme of Croce's politics. After his youthful flirtation
with Marx and other forms of socialism, Croce became a liberal – a posi-

tion that he maintained against temptations and attacks from both left and right throughout his life. Finocchiaro describes the main features of Croce's liberalism and situates them in the context of his actual political activity in the 1920s, including his brief attraction to fascism and his part in founding the Liberal party in 1924–5. Like Mosca, Croce developed a form of liberalism that was elitist but also pluralistic, that was moderate and practical, and that sought a middle ground between radical egalitarianism and authoritarianism that would preserve human freedom and ensure the progress of the human spirit. As Finocchiaro suggests, Croce's goal as well as the means by which he hoped to achieve it still deserve our careful examination.

Croce's relations with such eminent contemporaries as Mosca constitute a chapter in his intellectual biography. In her essay on Croce and R.G. Collingwood, Myra Moss reveals how problematic these relations could be. Although Collingwood did much to advance Croce's reputation among readers in England and North America, his grasp of Croce's thought was not always either accurate or sympathetic. Unfortunately, moreover, his misunderstandings have in some cases been accepted by scholars, thus distorting and diminishing Croce's reputation. Moss illustrates this point by analysing the mistakes in Collingwood's criticism of Croce's categorial theory of error and by demonstrating how a proper understanding of Croce's theory remains useful as a way of evaluating the truth or falsity of historical judgments.

Of the great philosophers of the past, none looms larger in Croce's intellectual biography than Giambattista Vico, whom Giuseppe Mazzotta identifies in his essay as 'a steady point of reference' for Croce's thought. Nevertheless, Mazzotta argues, Croce misread Vico, and in a way that reveals a central epistemological difficulty in Croce's own thought. Rejecting both religion and science as grounds for knowledge, looking to history as the source of whatever truth is available to human beings, Croce none the less sometimes wrote – wittingly or not is unclear – as though he possessed access to transcendent or scientific certainty. But this tension between Croce's historicism, which denies transcendence, and his rhetoric, which makes a claim to truth even as it denies the validity of such a claim, might be said to be characteristic of a general predicament of philosophy since Nietzsche. The epistemological difficulty that Mazzotta reveals in Croce can be seen as emblematic of our time.

Croce's role as one of the founders of a peculiarly modern mode of philosophy – a theme in many of the contributions to this book – is the focus of the essays by Edmund E. Jacobitti and David D. Roberts that open the concluding section of the book. Returning to Croce's decisive turn towards aesthetic intuition as the ground for all thought, Jacobitti places this move within the broad context of twentieth-century intellectual development, showing how Croce prepared the way for, or foreshadowed, many developments of philosophy in our time: its emphasis on language, for example, and its interest in paradigms and in chaos theory. Pursuing a different but parallel line, Roberts focuses on Croce's 'absolute historicism' and the political liberalism that he derived from it, comparing them with the alternatives offered by fascism and Marxism and the thought of such thinkers as Gadamer, Kuhn, Rorty, Foucault, and Derrida. Calling attention to Croce's limitations as well as his strengths, Roberts makes a compelling case for seeing in his 'non-ironic' view of history a 'new cultural middle ground' that speaks to our condition at the end of the twentieth century.

Fittingly, given Croce's emphasis on the individual as an agent of freedom and responsibility within the context of history, the book concludes with an essay by Rita Melillo on Croce the man. Relying on the *Taccuini di lavoro* – the working diary that Croce began in 1906 and continued until just two years before his death in 1952 – Melillo stresses the simple, human discipline that made possible Croce's enormous productivity in so many fields. It was the example of his committed life as much as his work, Melillo argues, that exerted such a powerful influence on several generations of his countrymen. Thus the *Taccuini*, which have only recently begun to attract critical attention, direct our attention behind the work to the man, where we may also find inspiration to guide a scholarly and philosophical life.

NOTES

1 From Gennaro Sasso's study of Croce's notebooks, *Per invigilare me stesso. I Taccuini di lavoro di Benedetto Croce* (Bologna: Il Mulino, 1989), 30, translation by the editors. Sasso's words refer to the *Taccuini*, which, he says, 'occorre conoscere, sempre che, lasciando finalmente da un canto le sciocchezze e i luoghi comuni, s'intenda davvero cercar di capire in profondità la fisionomia di uno scrittore che, ieri, forse, fu letto troppo, e talvolta male, da troppi, e oggi soltanto pochi [e non sempre bene] leggono.' We have taken the liberty, which we hope Sasso would find appropriate, of applying his injunction to Croce's work as a whole.

2 See, for instance, René Wellek's essay on Croce in *Four Critics: Croce, Valéry,*

Lukacs, and Ingarden (Seattle: University of Washington Press, 1981). Also see Wellek's account of Croce's literary theory and criticism in 'La teoria letteraria e la critica di Benedetto Croce,' in *Letteratura Italiana*, vol. IV, *L'Interpretazione* (Torino: Giulio Einaudi editore, 1985). Croce's influence has been very well documented by David D. Roberts in 'Croce in America: Influence, Misunderstanding, and Neglect,' *Humanitas* 8 no. 2 (1955), 3–34.

3 Antonio Prete's *La distanza da Croce* (Milan: Celuc, 1956) can be taken almost as a manifesto of young Italian critics who rebelled and 'took their distance' from Croce. See also works cited in note 2.

4 Giuseppe Galasso, *Croce e lo spirito del suo tempo* (Milan: Mondadori editore, 1990). Croce's works were previously published by Laterza in Bari. Galasso is now publishing Croce's main works with Adelphi Editions of Milan.

5 See Gian N.G. Orsini. *Benedetto Croce Philosopher of Art and Literary Critic* (Carbondale: Southern Illinois University Press, 1961). Caserta has dedicated much of his scholarly life to making Croce known in North America. For one of his best studies of Croce, which unfortunately remains available only in Italian, see *Croce critico letterario (1882–1921)* (Napoli: Giannini editore, 1972).

6 M.E. Moss. *Benedetto Croce Reconsidered: Truth and Error in Theories of Art, Literature, and History* (Hanover, NH: University Press of New England, 1987). See also Moss's translation of some of Croce's major literary essays, *Benedetto Croce: Essays on Literature and Literary Criticism*, annotated and translated from the Italian with an introduction by M.E. Moss (New York: State University of New York Press, 1990). David D. Roberts, *Benedetto Croce and the Uses of Historicism* (Berkeley: University of California Press, 1987) and *Nothing but History: Reconstruction and Extremity after Metaphysics* (Berkeley: University of California Press, 1995).

7 See 'Croce critico "dittatore"' in René Wellek, 'La teoria letteraria e la critica di Benedetto Croce,' in *Letteratura Italiana* (Torino: Giulio Einaudi editore, 1985).

8 Quoted by Alfredo Parente, in 'Rapsodia delle celebrazioni e un inedito epitaffio del Filosofo,' in *Rivista di Studi Italiani* anno XIX, fasc III (luglio–settembre 1982), 217–20.

9 The essay is now collected in *Primi saggi*.

10 Part I of the *Estetica* was translated by Douglas Ainslie as *Aesthetic and Science of Expression and General Linguistic* (London: Macmillan, 1909), and later republished with a translation of Part II (London: Macmillan, 1922). A more recent translation by Colin Lyas, *The Aesthetic as the Science of Expression and of the Linguistic in General* (Cambridge: Cambridge University Press, 1992), contains only Part I; Part II is to follow.

11 English translation by Douglas Ainslie (London: Macmillan, 1917).

12 English translation by Douglas Ainslie (New York: Biblo & Tannen, 1967).

13 From *History: Its History and Practice*, trans. Douglas Ainslie (New York: Russell & Russell, 1960), 151.

14 See the newly revised edition by Giuseppe Galasso (Milan: Adelphi, 1989). For the translation see note 13.

15 See the Editor's Note by Giuseppe Galasso to the Adelphi edition of 1989. Galasso believes that *Teoria e storia della storiografia* is much more than a simple continuation of the *Logic*. He quotes Gramsci, for whom the work 'contains, besides a synthesis of the entire Crocean system, also a fundamental revision of the same system' (oltre che una sintesi dell'intero sistema filosofico crociano, anche una vera e propria revisione dello stesso sistema), 414–15.

16 English translation by Frances Frenaye (Chicago: University of Chicago Press, 1970).

17 English translation by Sylvia Sprigge (New York: Noonday Press, 1955).

18 *Guide to Aesthetics*, trans. Patrick Romanell (Indianapolis: Bobbs-Merrill, 1965). This is the most recent translation of *Breviario di estetica*.

19 English translation by Giovanni Gullace (Carbondale: Southern Illinois University Press, 1981).

20 English translation by Douglas Ainslie (London: 1922).

21 English translation by Douglas Ainslie (London: 1920).

22 English translation by R.G. Collingwood (1913), reprint (New York: Russell & Russell, 1964).

23 Corrado Ocone in his *Bibliografia ragionata degli scritti su Benedetto Croce* (Napoli: Edizioni Scientifiche Italiane, 1993) counts four volumes of *Philosophy of Spirit* (Filosofia dello Spirito), fourteen of *Philosophical Essays* (Saggi filosofici), forty-four of *Writings on Literary and Civil History* (Scritti di storia letteraria e civile) and twelve of *Miscellaneous Writings* (Scritti vari). To these we should add the enormous correspondence, which, Ocone estimates, amounted to about thirty letters a day, and the six volumes of Croce's working diaries, the *Taccuini di lavoro*.

24 See Wellek, *Four Critics*, 18

25 In *Saggio sullo Hegel seguito da altri scritti di storia della filosofia* (An Essay on Hegel with Other Writings on the History of Philosophy), 5th ed. (Bari: Laterza, 1967). English translation of 'What Is Living and What Is Dead in the Philosophy of Hegel,' by Douglas Ainslie (New York: Russell & Russell, 1969).

26 See *La poesia di Dante*, 11th ed. (Bari: Laterza, 1966).

27 See, for instance, the analysis by Mario Sansone in his *Storia della letteratura*

italiana (History of Italian Literature), 13th ed. (Milano: Casa Editrice Giuseppe Principato, 1970).

28 Croce, 'My Philosophy,' in *My Philosophy and Other Essays on the Moral and Political Problems of Our Time*, selected by R. Klibansky, trans. E.F. Carritt (London: George Allen & Unwin, 1951), 12. Translation of *La mia filosofia*, ed. Giuseppe Galasso (Milan: Adelphi, 1993).

2

Croce, Philosopher of Naples

MASSIMO VERDICCHIO

By 'Croce, philosopher of Naples,' I am referring not only to the fact that
Benedetto Croce is rightly considered a Neapolitan philosopher, though
born in Pescasseroli in Abruzzo, but also to those early years between
1882 and 1892 when, not yet taken by philosophical concerns, he
devoted most of his time to 'reconstructing' the history and culture of
Naples. I am alluding to Croce 'erudito,' the erudite or learned, whose
work forms a separate chapter from the later historian/philosopher.[1] In
this paper, however, I want to address the continuity that I believe exists
between the two Croces and to show not only that the later work on history and philosophy commences in these early studies but that the
method that Croce used later did not change significantly from that of
those earlier inquiries.

History

Croce's early work on the history and culture of Naples shifts constantly
between two types of legends, one popular and the other learned or historical, between one that should be appreciated for the pleasure that it
provides without question of authenticity, the other, which must be
examined closely to ensure that truth is respected and adhered to as
much as possible. Popular legends, according to Croce, should be read
for amusement and even nostalgia while the historical ones must be
analysed carefully and even rewritten. Popular legends, because they
are the product of the collective spirit of a people, should not be
subjected to scientific scrutiny but only appreciated for what they really
are – 'humble truths' (umile verità), which endear themselves to us because they 'bring back our childhood impressions' (riportano alle im-

pressioni della fanciullezza) (*Storie e leggende napoletane*, 297).[2] Learned legends, in contrast, require scientific scrutiny, since they deal with history and the issue of truth becomes relevant.

However, on closer scrutiny one realizes that the collective spirit supposed at the origin of popular legends is really the result of personal conjecture that has been accepted as truth. The same is the case with learned legends, which most of the time are the product of documents or artefacts that have been poorly interpreted or understood. Their common character stems from the fact that both popular and learned legends share a common origin in 'some kind' of history. Just as at the basis of any history there is a legend, underlying legend there is history. In either case, Croce writes, all we need to do is re-examine the sources and re-interpret them 'differently' (altrimenti) 'by substituting a better story to the older one' (sostituendo una migliore storia alla storia innanzi posseduta) (296).

Thus, for Croce the difference between popular and erudite legend is really quantitative ('di quantità') and depends on the degree of fiction, or misreading, at the source.[3] At the origin of every popular legend there is always some kind of history, some truth, even if only in the form of a physical or material sign such as an image, an inscription, or a place that stands as the guarantor of its truth (297).[4] Unlike fairy tales, which belong to the world of poetry, popular legends, however conceived, always refer us back to some kind of physical reality and lead us eventually to the world of history. Both popular and learned legends create an emotion, an interest linked to a certain spiritual condition, however naïve, that we once enjoyed and as such can always be recaptured by memory. The possibility of recapturing this feeling, radically rooted in the past or in some kind of artefact or monument, makes all the difference between poetry and history, between something completely invented or forged *ex novo* and something that functions as an individual's spiritual link to the past.

An example of popular legend provided by Croce is that of Niccolò Pesce, which had held a special importance for him since his early years in Naples. This is the story of a young man who loved swimming so much that his mother cursed him to become a fish. From that day on Niccolò Pesce lived in the water as if he were a fish and learned the trick of letting himself be swallowed by a big fish and letting it take him wherever he wanted. When he reached a given destination, he cut the fish open and went on with his search. The king heard of Pesce and asked him to search the bottom of the sea and report on what he found there. He told the king that the ocean floor was a garden of coral, that the entire surface was full of precious stones, and that one could find treasures, weapons, human remains, and even sunken ships. At the king's bidding, he descended into the mysterious caves of the Castel dell'Ovo and brought back precious gems. Another time the king wanted to know what kept the island of Sicily standing. Pesce reported that it stood on three enormous columns and that one of them was broken. Finally the king wanted to know how far Pesce could descend into the sea and ordered him to retrieve a cannon ball thrown in the strait of Messina. Although Pesce feared that he would never return from such a mission, he obeyed. When he reached the ball, he realized that he could not return to the surface and died.

According to Croce, the reason that this legend cannot be called a fairy tale is because of its grounding in history – namely, in the 'portrait' that his family coachman, whom Croce calls 'a speaking document' (documento parlante) (299), used to point out to him when he was a young man. The portrait of Niccolò Pesce was sculpted in bas-relief on a house near the port. When the building was demolished, the portrait, with its inscription dating back to the eighteenth century, was placed on the walls of a newly built house.

When Croce first investigates the origins of the legend, he dismisses the scholarly interpretations that see it as an effigy of Orion. He lends more faith to the views of the local populace, who had always seen in it the image of one of their own. Years later, however, Croce discovered that Niccolò Pesce was not after all a 'famous Neapolitan swimmer and sailor' (300), as he had believed, but a young man from Messina, where the legend of his deeds still existed and whence it had passed to Naples, finding its place in that bas-relief near the port (301).

Croce also discovers that the legend had been the object of many literary and musical compositions. Cervantes refers to it in *Don Quixote*, Schiller deals with the subject in *Der Taucher*, and it is mentioned even in Giovanni Pontano's *Urania*, where Niccolò Pesce is described as the brother of Hercules, Theseus, and Perseus (304). As to the genesis of the legend, even though it is established that it was already well known by the end of the twelfth century as a legend of the Faro di Messina, based possibly on some famous local swimmer or diver, its historical origins are a subject for speculation. Every ancient writer who deals with the legend, says Croce, wants to appropriate its historicity, saying that it occurred in his own time or thereabouts, or that he was told about it by someone who had known Niccolò personally (302–3). Croce dismisses these attempts to ground the legend in historical certainty as far-fetched and speculative. One can be sure, he writes (297), only of the motive that gave it long life and popularity and of the feeling that we once had and lost, which is renewed every time the legend is retold. 'We preserved in our souls not only a feeling for the legends we once heard, but also an interest in all legends, in the legend, in that naive spiritual condition that we once enjoyed and lost, and which in our memories becomes naive once again.' (E allora non solo inserimmo nei nostri animi l'affetto per le leggende una volta ascoltate, ma anche l'interessamento per le leggende tutte, per la leggenda in genere, per quella condizione ingenua di spirito che godemmo e perdemmo, e che ingenua ridiventa nel ricordo.)

The legend of Niccolò Pesce makes it possible for the reader to recapture that 'naïve spiritual condition' of his youth or past, which otherwise would be lost for ever. Pesce's story, according to Croce, leaves the reader free to speculate and to believe in the impossible – namely, that people can possess extraordinary abilities as the result of being half-man and half-fish, half-human and half-animal, or even half-human and half-god, as told in the myth of Orion. The story also stimulates the reader's curiosity for the unknown, the greed for riches that the sea may conceal, as well as the fear of the sea that makes people imagine stories that overcome these obstacles. Last but not least in a series of possible motives, Croce adds popular belief in the effectiveness of a mother's curse. These different motives endear legends to us, making possible a mode of thinking that, though 'naïve,' addresses our innermost fears, our needs and desires, while at the same time providing satisfaction and pleasure. These personal experiences are the reason why legends should be regarded as more than just works of fictions or fairy tales and should be thought of instead as history.

The work on the legend of Niccolò Pesce, together with the numerous other erudite investigations conducted by Croce during these early years, published mostly in *Napoli nobilissima*, are formative of a conception of art and history that Croce first formulated in a 'memoria' read at the Accademia Pontaniana, 'La storia ridotta sotto il concetto generale dell'arte' (History Subsumed under the General Concept of Art) and published in a short monograph in 1893.[5] Croce's pronouncements, radical for those times because they challenged a conception of history as science, entail a redefinition of Art as knowledge of the individual, whether imagined or simply possible. While history can be defined as knowledge of the 'real individual' – that is, of the 'historically interesting' (35) – history can also be described as that type of artistic production whose object of representation is what really occurred (36). Just as the artist cannot represent falsehoods but must research his material scrupulously, so the historian must research his material in order to avoid having to invent it, to avoid 'falling in the imaginary' (cadere nell'immaginario) (36). Once the preliminary work is done, the tasks of the artist and of the historian are similar, as both rely on narrative (38). For Croce, however, only the artist can completely fulfil this task, since a complete narrative remains an ideal for the historian, who is limited by 'human imperfection and the limitations that fate places on his activity' (38).

Within the framework drawn by these definitions of art and history, the legend of Niccolò Pesce, as well as others collected and narrated by Croce, are early examples of a genre that subsumes history under the category of Art. They are, in a sense, extreme cases of 'history,' since the documentation is at best based on general hearsay that can never be verified. What is verifiable is the 'evidence' from different sources of the possible existence of someone named Niccolò Pesce, even though one will never be certain of his historical existence. Even so, the legend fulfils an even more primary function, to which Croce does not allude in his monograph – namely, that this type of 'history' allows us to recapture a past now long gone and forgotten, by making it present to us.

As is well known, Croce's definition of history subsumed under the general concept of art was later followed by another view of history in the *Logica* that seemed to contradict it – namely, that history and philosophy are one. In a note added to the 1909 edition (Part II, chap. IV), Croce attempts to explain the apparent discrepancy between the two conceptions of history: 'I now maintain, sixteen years after, that, on the contrary, history is philosophy and that history and philosophy are indeed the same thing' (Dopo sedici anni, sostengo invece che la storia è filosofia, anzi che storia e filosofia sono la medesima cosa).[6]

This formulation, Croce claims, follows on the footsteps of the former 'without discontinuities or jumps' (senza discontinuità e salti) (210). The discrepancy is only apparent and is the result of Croce's former confused view of philosophy, which had led him to identify it with the false universality of science. When he finally understood the true relationship of science and philosophy – that philosophy was not a privileged form of the Spirit independent of history (i.e., that philosophy was not an abstraction) – he was able to arrive at the 'concrete character of philosophy' (il carattere di concretezza della filosofia) (195), which meant that the concreteness of history and that of philosophy were one.

Croce meant neither to reiterate nor to refute his former views on the relation of history to art. He intended his new assessment of the identity of history and philosophy to be a step forward in his investigations on the nature of history, which began with his erudite research in the legends of Naples and culminates, at least theoretically, in the volume *Teoria e storia della storiografia*, published later, in 1917. In this work, which Croce considered the 'fourth' part of his *Filosofia dello spirito*, he expounds on many of the statements made in the *Logica* on the relation between history and philosophy and on the concept of contemporary history: 'Every *true* history is contemporary history' (ogni *vera* storia è storia contemporanea) (emphasis added, 12). Croce wants to claim that the act of historical writing, as any act of the Spirit, is not bound by time and is at one with the act of writing. Furthermore, any history that has meaning for us or that vibrates in the soul of the historian can similarly be said to be contemporary. It matters little, he says, if to these documents are added one or more stories to make the history richer and more effective. In fact, these added stories and narratives themselves become 'facts,' 'documents' (12), which in their turn must be interpreted and judged. In this version of history, not only do narratives and stories take the place of documents, or can be taken for documents, but the very notion of history is predicated on the relevance of the past for the present, which makes it not only 'contemporary' but also 'true' (12). 'Thus if contemporary history springs straight from life, so too does that history that is called non-contemporary, for it is evident that only an interest in the life of the present can move us to investigate past fact. Therefore this past fact answers not to a past interest, but to a present interest, in so far as it is unified with an interest of the present life.' (E se la storia contemporanea balza direttamente dalla vita, anche direttamente dalla vita sorge quella che si suol chiamare non contemporanea, perché è evidente che solo un interesse della vita presente ci può muovere a indagare un fatto passato; il quale, dunque, in quanto si unifica con un interesse della vita presente, non risponde a un interesse passato, ma presente.)

This conception of history erases all distinctions between present and past, chronicle and history, including those between popular and learned legends, legends and history. What matters most is the human spirit, which alone is historical, which alone makes history, 'the spirit itself is history' 'lo spirito stesso è storia' (25). Collecting the fragments of the past, or even the legends of Naples, becomes 'an act of life that serves life' (un atto di vita che serve alla vita) (24). It becomes an act that the spirit relives, with or without its supporting documents, and in which it renews itself by making present and contemporary the memories of the past. The real and only historical sources are in our 'breasts,' says Croce, where ultimately the Vichian synthesis of the certain and the true, philology and philosophy, is achieved and History is produced (26).[8] For it is in our own breasts alone that is to be found that crucible in which the *certain* is converted into the *true*, and *philology*, joining with *philosophy*, produces *history*.' (E il nostro petto, esso soltanto è il crogiuolo in cui il certo si converte col vero, e la filologia, congiungendosi con la filosofia, produce la storia.) This is also the process that makes it possible to produce from Neapolitan legends the history of Naples.[9]

Philosophy

The common origin of popular and learned legends undermines the epistemological validity of history when what is at issue is the authority of a given history and a given *modus operandi*. As I have indicated, at their origins there is hearsay, but at worse there may be fraud, which is hardly ever eradicated or vanquished. At best it is replaced with an equally acceptable falsehood or fraudulent lies:[10] 'After all, legends are nothing more than hearsay or even frauds, not unlike those created by visionaries, muddlers, jokers, the naive and the crafty that find credence with the many or with most people, and that disappear in the face of acknowledged genuine truth or, more often, *solely because they are forgotten*, they are supplanted by new rumors' (emphasis added). (In fondo, le leggende non sono altro che dicerie o anche imposture, non dissimili da quelle che vediamo nascere quotidianamente intorno a noi per opera di visionari, confusionari, burloni, gente candida e gente furba, e trovar credito presso i molti o presso i più, e poi sparire innanzi alla riconosciuta genuina verità, e, più spesso, unicamente *perché vengono messe in dimenticanza*, soppiantate da nuove dicerie.)

While in the case of popular legends, such as those concerning Naples (as with Niccolò Pesce), epistemological validity is not at stake, in the case of history, including literary or even artistic history, their character as legends undermines their credibility.[11] 'Even within so-called literary or learned circles, it happens that lies or ambiguities are sometimes accepted and repeated for centuries. For this reason they are often called "learned legends."' (Anche nella cerchia che si dice più particolarmente letteraria o erudita accade che invenzioni ed equivoci siano talora accolti e ripetuti per secoli; onde a ragione si parla di 'leggende erudite.')

To confront this type of error, Croce suggests a critical method that can deal with the problems plaguing both popular and erudite legends and that would also make it possible to determine the validity of the claims made by each. The problem, as I indicated above, is that both types of legend are usually based on documents, or on simple works of art or monuments, that have either been poorly studied or are not well known. By examining the sources, whenever possible, and by reinterpreting them, one can, Croce believes, replace the lies with the proper story. In other words, Croce believes that it is possible to distinguish popular legends from learned ones, lies or frauds from history, truth from error.

One place where Croce's scrutiny of learned legends is clearly at work is in the pages of *Napoli nobilissima*, a journal of Neapolitan art and topography published by the Società Storica Napoletana (Neapolitan Historical Society), where Croce, with other influential Neapolitan intellectuals, historians, and writers, wrote from 1892 to 1906 and was editor from 1921 to 1924.[12] The journal intended initially to draw attention to the neglected historical and artistic monuments of the city, with the added objective of generating interest in local and southern Italian art and of making it better known.

In the first volume, Croce begins an investigation of southern Italian art from its origins to the thirteenth century under the title *Sommario critico della storia dell'arte nel Napoletano* (Critical Outline of the History of Art in Southern Italy). The task, however, required that Croce first clear the field of previous misconceptions about this type of history, and this meant coming to terms with a work on a similar topic, *Vite dei pittori scultori ed architetti napoletani* (Lives of Neapolitan Painters, Sculptors, and Architects), by Bernardo De Dominici. In a series of articles aptly titled 'il Falsario' (The Forger),[13] Croce wastes no time in venting his dislike for this author: 'It is not possible to attempt a correct treatment of the history of art in our province, without first *getting out of the way the work and authority of that forger, poisoner of the sources of this history, Bernardo De Dominici, the author of "Lives of Neapolitan Painters, Sculptors and Architects."'*[8] (Non è possibile tentare una trattazione esatta della storia dell'arte nelle nostre provincie, senza prima *togliersi dai piedi l'opera e l'autorità del falsario, dell'avvelenatore dei fonti di questa storia, di Bernardo De Dominici, l'autore delle 'Vite dei pittori scultori ed architetti napoletani.'*)

Croce's initial task exposes this work and denounces the authority of its author and his forgeries, before reconstructing the true history of

Neapolitan and southern art, and this process produced Croce's historical method. Let me briefly summarize the crime of which De Dominici is accused. The story begins with Giorgio Vasari, who in 1544 lived and worked in Naples. When he published his *Lives of the Artists* he not only dedicated very little space to Neapolitan art but attributed all major artistic works in Naples to Tuscan artists. To add insult to injury, he not only denigrated Neapolitan art but also claimed to be the only painter of stature after Giotto to have gone to Naples 'to awaken the talent of that city and to accomplish great and honourable works' (123). His visit, Vasari contended, had inspired the creation of many beautiful works and had contributed to a new renaissance in Neapolitan arts, 'and this is perhaps the reason that from that day on there emerged beautiful paintings and sculptures' (123).

One can easily imagine the anger and resentment of Neapolitan artists and local writers who accused Vasari of wanting nothing more than to diminish the glory of Neapolitan art by enhancing that of Tuscan artists to whom he had attributed all the local masterpieces. One writer, Celano, tried to guess how Neapolitans could have offended Vasari to make him behave in such an odious manner and conceal the virtues of Neapolitan artists: 'Not only did he take away Sannazaro's sepulchre from Santacroce, but he also had the gall to attribute the most ancient works of our city to his countrymen, saying that the head of the bronze horse in Count Maddaloni's yard is the work of Donatello.' (Non solo ha tolto quest'opera al Santacroce (il sepolcro del Sannazaro); ma ancora ha avuto cuore d'attribuire l'opere antichissime della nostra città a' suoi compatriotti dicendo che la testa di bronzo del cavallo che sta nel cortile de' signori Conti di Maddaloni sia del Donatello.) At the time no one challenged Vasari's claims. The reply came only in 1742, when Bernardo De Dominici, after seventeen years of 'hard work,' as Croce adds emphatically, published *Vite dei pittori*. De Dominici undertook the work, he wrote in his treatise, to redress the neglect with which Neapolitan artists had been treated and in particular the injustice done to them by Vasari.

De Dominici's account of Neapolitan and southern art was even more glorious than could have been expected. According to him, the first recorded Neapolitan artist, Tauro, dated as far back as AD 335 and was so famous that the Emperor Constantine preferred him even to Greek artists. For the ninth and tenth centuries, he listed the sculptors Fiorenza and Cosentino, and around the year 1000 the architects Masullo and Iacobello. From 1250 to 1739 the list of Neapolitan painters, sculptors, and architects is endless. Most of these artists are related to each other, and their ties are reflected in the schools that are handed on from generation to generation. De Dominici seems to know every work done in Naples and the author of every work. His study contains very detailed information on every contemporary artist and on every work. Of every artist he gives the dates of birth and death, his family relations, his loves, and his every adventure. About everyone, says Croce, he knows 'many curious and appetizing anecdotes' (126).

Croce also traces the fortune of De Dominici's work and how it influenced later art historians, Neapolitan and others, such as Lanzi, Signorelli, Cicognara, D'Agincourt, Kugler, Perkins, and Salazaro, who accepted his findings unquestioningly. Croce tells how even the anecdotes on artists and important figures of the time became very popular, in some cases inspiring dramas and historical novels. De Dominici's work was reprinted in 1846 in four volumes at the expense of Don Antonio Statella, prince of Cassaro. The Preface (141) commended the work for two reasons: 'First for *respecting the truth;* second for its love of country' (in primo, *per rispetto della veridicità;* secondo, per un caldissimo amor di patria).

Before setting out on a critical survey, Croce believed it necessary to free it of any vestiges of De Dominici's work, which he felt was still corrupting many histories of the subject, even though critics had disproved many of his findings. In fact, it had become more and more clear that although Vasari had been somewhat presumptuous in suggesting that he had contributed to a renaissance of the arts in Naples, he had been correct in attributing the authorship of many Neapolitan works to Tuscan artists.

As for De Dominici – the 'Neapolitan Vasari,' as Croce calls him ironically – critics had demolished many of his spurious arguments, including the anecdotes. Bartolommeo Capasso, the famous Neapolitan topographer and contributor to *Napoli nobilissima,* disproved even one of De Dominici's stories about a Calabrese artist who, condemned to death, was pardoned on condition that he paint images of saints and Madonnas on the city gates. The story was only partly true. Not only had the artist not committed any crimes, but he had been paid for the work.

The list of De Dominici's misdeeds is long. Not only had he falsely attributed the works of others to Neapolitans, but he had invented many of the early artists, together with the sources for his documentation. For the modern period, he instead made up many biographical data, including authorship and number of works. In some cases the artist's name is all that is true; the long biography is an invention (142).

Besides the lies, the overall study is full of incongruities and contradictions, as an artist (Andrea Ciccione) is described as having equal virtuosity in two styles: the gothic and the classical. The work of a Bolognese artist (Antonio Rimpatta) is attributed to a Neapolitan (Zingaro). The birthplace of one artist may be substituted for that of another, as when Mormando, a Calabrese, is said to be Florentine, while Naccherino, a Florentine, is said to be Neapolitan (143). To one artist (Andrea da Salerno) is attributed (143) works that he could not have produced, since he was long dead: 'Every new study demonstrated that De Dominici not only accepted and exaggerated the mistakes of previous writers, but also circulated a mass of information entirely without documentation or simply false. The substance of his work is discredited.' (Ogni studio che si va pubblicando prova che il De Dominici non solo accettò ed esagerò gli errori degli scrittori che l'avevano preceduto, ma mise fuori una folla di notizie tutte senza riscontro o false. Il contenuto della sua opera è screditato.) But even if art critics had discredited De Dominici's work, Croce still was not satisfied. He was not entirely happy with the accusations of 'gullibility,' 'daydreaming,' and 'lies' (142) that had been used to criticize De Dominici's work over the years. For Croce, De Dominici is above all a 'falsario' – a forger – a fact of which only a few people besides himself were really aware.

Croce's major quarrel is with the forgery of manuscripts that De Dominici claims to have been his sources. One of these is by the painter Marco Pino da Siena, who, evidence shows, barely knew how to write. In De Dominici's version, however, Pino da Siena not only possesses a very good grasp of grammar but is also a very able rhetorician. Furthermore, the document at issue is supposed to date many years before 1568 and yet addresses the second edition of Vasari's *Lives* (1568), the only one that speaks of Neapolitan art.

De Dominici also falsified the memoirs of Giovan Angelo Criscuolo, notary public and painter, who makes reference to Pino da Siena and for whom Criscuolo is supposed to have done extensive research. Croce takes pain to quote many of the inconsistencies in style and argument from these memoirs to demonstrate the 'self-evident lie' of De Dominici's allegations. But the clincher in Croce's argument is Criscuolo's supposed mention of the bell tower of Santa Chiara's monastery, which is described in the condition to which it was reduced after 1600, while Criscuolo is supposed to be writing in 1569.

Another forged source is the memoir of Massimo Stanzioni. If the originals of Pino da Siena and Criscuolo can no longer be found, those of Stanzioni are preserved in the National Library of Naples. What Croce cannot explain is how they got there, but he supposes that the forger had made sure that the manuscripts would be found in a public library to serve as evidence for his allegations (144). In his discussion of Stanzioni, Croce does not quote the usual inconsistencies but rather comments on the forger's skills and his ability ('finezze di falsario') to produce an almost perfect forgery. Nothing gives the forger away, he writes, except that 'certain *ostentatious* air of sincerity that arouses one's suspicions' as when on the cover page of the documents one finds written *'imo Stantione'* (these are Stanzioni's papers).

Another example quoted by Croce could well be used to argue for the authenticity of Stanzioni's manuscript. There are scribbled notes on money that Stanzioni was paid for work done in Regina Coeli and in San Lorenzo, and the latter note can even be verified by existing documents in the convent of San Lorenzo. But Croce adds that De Dominici himself tells us that he did research in the archives of San Lorenzo and asks: 'Is there anything to stop us from thinking that he discovered those details and transcribed them to give greater semblance of sincerity to his forgery?' (144) The supposition of authenticity is further undermined when Croce, in comparing the two banknotes, questions why a note from 1639 precedes the one from 1628 and asks why both were written on with the same ink and calligraphy. But for Croce, the clinching argument is that in the whole document there is not one line in Stanzioni's hand.

In conclusion, the documentation that supposedly comes from Marco Pino da Siena, Criscuolo, and Stanzioni presents us with evidence that no other Neapolitan writer knew and which De Dominici alone was able to collect and provide. 'The doubt,' says Croce, 'that he had forged the documents comes naturally (144).

The main purpose of Croce's denunciation of De Domenici's forgeries is not only to warn others against the more treacherous, because less obvious, falsehoods hidden in his work but to advise the less experienced reader not to read the work at all: 'Those who are not critics would do better not to touch it, and to place it in the *Index librorum prohibitorum.*' But even the experts, it seems, cannot tread safely in this work. 'There are still many people who believe in him, and many who, though believing he is not to be trusted, have no clear idea of the extent of his forgery. Then there are those who, against their will, are still deceived, indirectly.' (Veggo ancora i moltissimi credenti in lui, i molti che pur ritenendolo uno scrittore malfido, non hanno un chiaro concetto della portata di quella sua falsificazione; i non pochi che, senza volerlo, ne sono ancora ingannati, per vie indirette.) One of these experts is Prince Filangieri, a fine critic and scholar, who, though aware of the fasehoods in De Dominici's text, was himself deceived. 'The excellent Prince Filangieri, in his recent and seminal *Index of the Artists*, provides much documentation which he borrows from Lanzi, without being aware, however, that Lanzi copies from De Dominici. Thus, after being thrown out of the door, he [De Dominici] returns by the window.' (Ed è l'ottimo Principe Filangieri, che nel suo recente ed importantissimo *Indice degli artefici*, parecchie notizie riferisce desumendole dal Lanzi, e non s'accorge che il Lanzi copia il De Dominici, il quale, per tal modo, cacciato dalla porta, rientra per la finestra.) De Dominici remains very much a danger for writers on Neapolitan art, like Prince Filangieri, because most are still unable to distinguish what is true from what is false in his work. Although critics have disproved many of his arguments, they continue to quote from his study, even unaware that what they may be quoting is a falsehood. The threat is so great that it cannot be countered even by someone such as Croce, who believes that he knows the difference between what is and is not a forgery, between what is true and what is false. In fact, Croce too admits to having been deceived: 'And "*I too among them.*" It happened to me too, once. I borrowed an item from a very authoritative writer and later I discovered that it came from De Dominici.' (E *'di questi cotai son io medesmo'* al quale è capitato, una volta, di attingere da un nostro per altro autorevole scrittore una notizia che poi m'avvidi derivar dal De Dominici.)

Croce's philosophical calling of distinguishing truth from error is born in these early years in the attempt to expose De Dominici and denounce his work as forgery or at best as 'learned legend,' not as a valid history of Neapolitan art. His war against De Dominici, against the treacherous spread of fraudulent lies that have the look of truth, is just the beginning of a life of struggle against similar foes, as he himself says fourteen years later in the last issue of *Napoli nobilissima*, in bidding farewell to his readers: 'And the present writer who has moved over to philosophy to pursue the De Dominicis in this new field just as he pursued them in the field of the history of southern Italian art.'[14] (Chi [come il sottoscritto] si è dato alla filosofia, e perseguita nel nuovo campo i De Dominici, che perseguitava già in quello della storiografia artistica meridionale.)

Croce's war against the De Dominicis of philosophy reappears in many forms and in many texts as the struggle between truth and error, which received its more famous, or infamous, characterization in the title of his study on Hegel's philosophy, Ciò che è vivo e ciò che è morto nella filosofia di Hegel (What Is Living and What Is Dead in Hegel's Philosophy).[15] As for Bernardo De Dominici, Croce knew that he would never be able to expose him completely – 'that he would never reach a full result' (123). He knew that he and other historians could never determine the extent of his lies, where the rumour and fraud of popular legend ended and the truth of learned legend begun. 'Surely,' Croce concluded, 'he must be laughing at us in the other world.'

Conclusion

The above analysis of the origins of history and philosophy in Croce's early writings on popular and erudite legends stems, not surprisingly, from a common root. Croce's preoccupation with legends leads us first towards an understanding of the historical, because even popular legends, which contain elements that endear themselves to us, have some meaning for us and so are present to us. At the same time, the corruptible nature of legends – their uncertain origins and their easily falsifiable data – gives rise to a philosophical method aimed at distinguishing and resolving the error inherent in any epistemological endeavour. History and philosophy – a thesis and a method – are at the heart of Croce's philosophy of absolute historicism.

NOTES

1 Although the relevance of these early studies for Croce's later writings on history and philosophy has often been remarked by critics (see, for example, Giuseppe Galasso, Croce e lo spirito del suo tempo [Milan: Mondadori, 1990], the specific terms of this relation have not been analysed before.
2 Croce, Storie e leggende napoletane, 5th ed. (Milan: Adelphi, 1991), 297. All further page references appear in the text. Here as elsewhere the translation from this work is mine.
3 In the Laterza edition of 1967, which conforms to earlier editions, the distinction is said to be of 'quantity' (la distinzione tra le due è di quantità); in the Adelphi edition, the distinction is said to be of 'quality' (la distinzione tra le due è di qualità). The discrepancy no doubt results from the zeal of the editor, who felt that the difference should be qualitative.

4 For Croce this distinction is important, since it differentiates between popular legends and fairy tales. The latter, which begin 'Once upon a time,' are
   clearly fictions and belong to the world of poetry.

5 Now in *Primi saggi*, 3rd ed. (Bari: Laterza, 1951). All page references are given
   in the text.

6 *Logica come scienza del concetto puro*, 9th ed. (Bari: Laterza, 1963), 210. The
   English translation is from the 2nd edition of 1909 translated by Douglas
   Ainslie as *Logic as the the Science of the Pure Concept* (London: Macmillan,
   1917), 327.

7 *History: Its History and Practice*, trans. Douglas Ainslie (New York: Russell &
   Russell, 1960). All page references are to this edition and are indicated in the
   text.

8 The allusion here is to the philosophy of Giambattista Vico and to the principle of the *verum factum* – that the true and the fact are convertible. See Benedetto Croce, *La filosofia di G.B. Vico* (Bari: Laterza, 1973), *The Philosophy of
   Giambattista Vico*, trans. R.G. Collingwood (New York: Russell & Russell,
   1964).

9 I am referring especially to Croce's *Storia del Regno di Napoli* (Bari: Laterza,
   1965), *History of the Kingdom of Naples*, trans. F. Frenaye and edited with an
   introduction by H. Stuart Hughes (Chicago: University of Chicago Press,
   1970).

10 *Storie e leggende napoletane*, 295.

11 Ibid.

12 *Napoli nobilissima* lasted fifteen years, from 1892 to 1906, and was briefly
    revived from 1920 to 1922.

13 See *Napoli nobilissima* 1(1893), 122. The article, 'The Forger,' which serves as
    introduction to *Sommario critico della storia dell'arte nel Napoletano*, is in two
    parts: I, 122–6 and 140–4. All quotations appear in the text.

14 See 'Commiato' (Farewell) in 'La Società storica napoletana e la Napoli nobi-
    lissima,' *Pagine Sparse*, vol. I (Bari: Laterza, 1960, chap. 1.)

15 See *What Is Living and What Is Dead of the Philosophy of Hegel* (New York: Rus-
    sell & Russell, 1969). Similar distinctions are at the basis of each of Croce's
    four moments or distinctions of his Philosophy of Spirit: the aesthetic, the
    conceptual, the practical and the historical. On this point see also chapter 1
    above.

3

Croce and the *Commedia dell'arte* of Naples

JACK D'AMICO

The overall purpose of this essay is to examine the origins and the consequences of Croce's definition of the *arte* in *commedia dell'arte* as a professional, industrial art, rather than as a purely aesthetic, or poetic art. A major element of Croce's contribution to theatre history emerges from his careful examination of the documentary evidence relevant to a study of theatre in Naples and in particular to commedia dell'arte during the fifteenth and sixteenth centuries. Croce's definition of commedia dell'arte and his critique of the cultural assumptions related to Pulcinella have informed twentieth-century theatre criticism in certain fundamental ways.

In his *Contributo alla critica di me stesso* (1950) Croce described the period 1885–92, after the loss of his parents and sister in the 1883 earthquake at Casamicciola, as a time when he turned his intellectual energy outward and devoted himself to research. He recounts that for his spiritual development the negative aspect of this work was in its own way useful because it led to the realization that science must have a form and value quite distinct from what he calls 'these extrinsic erudite and literary exercises' (quelle estrinseche esercitazioni erudite e letterarie).[1] In a more positive sense, this early work, which was undertaken in Naples and focused on various aspects of the literary and cultural history of the city, provided both an outlet for his imaginative love of the past and the formal discipline that characterized, for Croce, scientific research. In his work on commedia dell'arte we can trace the movement from what Croce calls the narrow, 'gossipy' confines of the city to the more general, philosophical study of the relationship between history and art.

I teatri di Napoli (1891), chapter 3, identifies the origins of commedia dell'arte in Naples with the formation of 'compagnie comiche di mestiere' in the second half of the sixteenth century.[2] Croce makes a distinction between professional companies of actors who share a craft and the 'esercizi dilettanti,' comprising 'amateur' actors drawn from the upper class. Croce, the scientific researcher, focuses on a date and a document relevant to commedia dell'arte in Naples – a 1575 contract for the formation of a company composed of five *commedianti* (two from Naples, the others from Siena, Milan, and Lucca) organized to create and perform comedies in Naples ('per far et recitare commedie'). In his treatment of this document Croce singles out certain odd clauses that reflect the historical climate of Counter-Reformation Italy, such as the fact that these most profane *istrioni* take care to exhibit their spiritual devotion by agreeing to denounce one another to the Inquisition should the need arise.

Croce's earliest work on theatre makes a distinction between the occasional, amateur theatre of *dilettanti* and the contractual/commercial character of commedia dell'arte. The professional company has as its objective the presentation of theatre before a public that will pay to see a performance. This distinction, to which Croce returns in the opening of his *Intorno alla 'Commedia dell'Arte'* (1993), forms the basis of his assertion that modern theatre, theatre as we know it, is an Italian creation (il teatro moderno, in quanto teatro, è creazione italiana).[3]

As Ferdinando Taviani remarks, 'Paraphrasing what Croce said, we must return to an element that often eludes our thought: to sell theatre meant, in a sense, to create it, that is, as it exists for us, in its ideological form and in its material existence.'[4] Taviani distinguishes performance based on the calendar of festivity from performance that responds to the needs and demands of the marketplace.[5]

Croce uncovers evidence that theatre had become public and popular enough to be banned in 1581 because the performers continued to be identified with mountebanks. This brush with the law opens many important questions that have subsequently occupied critics. Taviani distinguishes the actor as itinerant mountebank who has little social status, but may enjoy the protection of the aristocracy in his role as court buffoon, from the actor who enjoys the contractual status of artisan but is subject to governmental or ecclesiastical censorship. In his early work Croce examines the places of performance, such as the *ospedale degl'Incurabili* where the commedia dell'arte resumed in 1589 after eight years of prohibition, or the *teatro fisso*, on the grounds of what would later become the church of San Giorgio dei Genovesi. The theatre in the area of the Duchesca used by the company of Marco Antonio Masiello and Ciommo de Manso was closed in 1626 by Giuseppe Calasanzio, founder of the convent of the Duchesca, who took over the very place where lewd comedies once were heard and then proceeded to convert the actors (*I teatri di Napoli*, 49–55). Public performance also took place in rented rooms and open spaces, the area near Largo del Castello being particularly suited to the performance of what Croce refers to as buffoons and mountebanks of every kind ('buffoni e cerretani d'ogni sorta' [53]).

Croce identifies Carlo Fredi (died 1615/16) as a Neapolitan *impresario* and actor who formed his own company (50).[6] As an administrator and organizer of performances, he was the creator of a permanent theatre ('un teatro fisso per commedie'), which stood where the church of San Giorgio dei Genovesi would be built (53). Croce suggests a movement from itinerant theatre and performance in open spaces to the quasi-independent status of actors who could rent their own spaces for performance and achieve enough respectability to enjoy the protection of the court. Similarly, Taviani identifies theatre as *mercato* with the urban space that an impresario such as Fredi could use at any time to attract a circle of regular spectators.[7]

In his early study, Croce focuses on documents found in Naples, on some anecdotal evidence, on the role of comedy within the city, and on the tensions between Counter-Reformation censorship and the support for the theatre that emanated from the Spanish court in Naples. He characterizes the legal status and reputation of the actors without saying much about the nature of their performance techniques, aside from alluding to the fame attached to the physical *lazzi* depicted by Callot in *I balli di sfessania* (47).[8] The performers are professionals defined by their legal status, but they are also the 'buffoni e cerretani' whose mimetic skill, rather than verbal artistry, places them in the popular tradition of charlatans and mountebanks, who are very much at odds with the spirit of the Counter-Reformation. Croce the researcher finds no documentary evidence of what one might call their aesthetic art; he concentrates on their existence as an *arte*, or guild. An intriguing and often frustrating problem for the researcher is the very evanescence of commedia dell'arte, a form of theatre that does not leave a performance document to study. Evidence that a company existed and of where it may have performed, indirect comments on the character of the performers, perhaps a visual image of costume or gesture – such traces constitute the kind of evidence that young Croce examined.[9]

The elusive character of theatre does not prevent Croce from returning to the figure of Pulcinella in 'Pulcinella e la commedia dell'arte' (1898).[10] Although he begins by admitting that Pulcinella, like all of the commedia figures, eludes definition, Croce provides the basis for a definition by examining linguistic variations on the word *pulcino*, or chicken helper, by reviewing use of the cognomen *Cetrulo*, and by identifying Pulcinella with Ponteselice. He concludes with a symbolic identification of the mask with the animal-like stupidity of the bumpkin-clown-peasant who carries his *corno* of fertility as a good luck charm. However, Croce hesitates to generalize and rejects the argument that belief in ethnic continuity will lead one to possible Roman antecedents (196–213), a point that I consider in greater detail in the second part of this essay.

Croce explains the popularity of the actor's mask outside Italy in the context of historical circumstances such as the influx of visitors to Vesuvius after the eruption of 1632, the revolution of 1647, the discovery of Pompeii and Herculaneum, and the notoriety of the *lazzari* after the revolution of 1799. The mask as an aesthetic form is always available to the artist, who may or may not use it and may or may not succeed artistically. Croce concludes that the mask was popular not as an expression of common folk values but as a reflection of how cultivated city spectators ('classi colte') viewed their foolish country cousins. The tendency to see popular customs in the mask reveals, for Croce, an underlying hypocrisy implicit in the laughter of those who forget the poverty, ignorance, and corruption of human life in their enjoyment of the type. He relates this laughter to the medieval enjoyment of dwarfs and hunchbacks, something he deems no longer acceptable (238).

In his conclusion Croce makes two judgments that reveal a movement towards theory – he notes that Pulcinella no longer functions in the world of art as anything other than an example of what one might call secondary creations ('creazioni reflesse' [239]). Comparing the Italian people to an individual who is no longer a child, he maintains that the Italians no longer produce great mythological fantasies but enjoy seeing the myths and legends of the past represented in works of art. This characteristic, which was particularly strong in Germany and in Italy during the Romantic period, has come up against what Croce calls realism and balance within the modern Italian spirit. He implies that Pulcinella and commedia dell'arte should be seen as the product of a particular historical period – the Renaissance – but he now adds a theory of cultural evolution that identifies a period of myth-making and fantasy in the life of a people and limits the role of myth within the world of modern art to a reflexive creation, a self-conscious look backward by those who can no longer enter into the spirit of their cultural origins.

Croce notes that Pulcinella has not survived in any noteworthy literary works and has not been transformed by some Rabelais of Naples – myth and fantasy have not become that great work of art that would survive in a literary text. He does, however, end with the suggestion that a surrogate for this missing work of literature could be supplied by the scholar who reconstructed the artistry of Pulcinella from documents and from a study of surviving theatrical traditions.

In summary we can see in this early work of Croce's a research method grounded in documents and a sense of history, a method that is wary of making assumptions about ethnic-Neapolitan character but willing to see the commedia dell'arte as part of the period of myth-making in the history of the Italian people, with its implied notion of a development from the child-like stage to the adult.

These observations anticipate Croce's brief but influential remarks in *Intorno alla 'Commedia dell'Arte'* (1933) where he takes up the question of whether commedia dell'arte is popular *or* artistic and considers whether the popular tradition had its origins in the practices of Roman theatre and entertainment.[10] His answer takes one back to the formative period of his early research, as we can see when he defines the arte of commedia as the art of a guild, an organization that is professional or industrial (i.e., having to do with what is made or manufactured). The phrase used to characterize the actors, 'gente di professione e di mestiere,' recollects the 'compagnie comiche di mestiere' whose contractual relationship Croce had examined in his early work on theatre in Naples. As we saw above, Croce identifies the industrialization of performance in the Renaissance with a shift from the theatre of nobles, amateurs, students, and confraternities to professional companies. What is new in Croce's approach is evidence of his work on Marx, as can be seen in the emphasis on the economic character of the Renaissance as that which defines its modernity.[11] The commedia dell'arte actors succeeded because they could satisfy the new social needs of a middle-class urban audience that enjoyed laughing at the popular Pulcinella. The success of the genre did not result from its aesthetic/poetic quality but was rather the result of a historical conjunction of social need and a new industrialization of theatre. Fixed theatres provided the economic advantage of controlled access and hence better management of the fees charged to an audience constituted on the basis of its ability to pay, not by social class. The very different social and economic conditions of performance set this marketable theatre apart from the amateur theatre of the church or the court. Attendance at a court performance was by invitation only, while the sacred representations were open to one and all. Croce also cites the introduction of actresses, Baroque developments in scenic design, the formation of acting schools, and the popularity of musical theatre as elements in the movement of theatre from the Renaissance court to the early modern professional company.

Croce does not identify commedia dell'arte with either Roman antecedents or the popular folk tradition, nor does he see it as essentially literary or poetic. Though he concedes that actors may have used elements of both the popular and the erudite traditions, for Croce (*Interno*, 510) the substance or nucleus of their art is to be found elsewhere: 'The theory that *commedia dell'arte* is popular comedy, or popular comedy grafted on the trunk of erudite comedy, is one of the usual imaginative creations of philologists, who write the history of literature, and every other history, from their studies.' (La teoria che la commedia dell'arte sia commedia popolare o innesto della commedia popolare sul tronco della commedia erudita è una della solite immaginazioni e combinazioni dei filologi, che fanno la storia della letterature, e ogni altra storia, nei loro gabinetti.) Croce does not favour the line of research represented by Paolo Toschi, who maintains that commedia dell'arte can be understood only in the context of the popular festivals from which it originates.[12] The essential question for Croce is not whether actors made use of elements of the tradition but whether the popular tradition defines commedia dell'arte. This approach has been continued by Taviani, who argues that the spirit of the actor's persona comes from the theatrical context that gives the character life in performance.[13] Croce observes that performers were so identified with a mask that they seemed to become Brighella, Pulcinella, or Pantalone, and he asserts that the mask became the genius or demiurge of allegria.

An overly nostalgic sympathy for the mask of commedia dell'arte leads some critics to exaggerate both its folkloric antiquity and its aesthetic value (515). The arte of the actor must be understood with reference to the mode of theatrical production that characterizes this particular form of theatre. In his interpretation of the relationship between improvisation and printed texts, Croce suggests that the centre of gravity shifted from word to mime: the word became an accompaniment and was delivered in the spirit of improvisation, created and adapted in the heat of performance (512). Another metaphor that Croce uses equates all the printed material on which the actors could draw with a libretto, while mime and improvised speech become the music.

Once again Croce hits on a notion that Taviani redefines as a central component in his own study of commedia dell'arte. Taviani locates the unique character of commedia not in the mask, or in the art of improvisation, but in the relationship between texts, or parts, and the scenic action. Drawing an analogy with the role of a screenplay in film production, Taviani argues that the particular concatenation of spoken parts, set speeches, and pieces of action was controlled by the actors who had mastered certain roles and who had gained control of the theatre. This theatrical repertoire could be recombined in a variety of ways to meet the shifting demands of the marketplace. What Croce calls the libretto Taviani calls the action, which could be altered to generate a new set of relationships between the parts. The Italian companies developed repertoires that could quickly produce different kinds of plays: 'The Italians were tied to the process of producing dramatic literature *and they adapted it, outside the conventions of writing,* to other professional practices of theatrical production' (gli italiani si legarono al processo di produzione *e lo adattarono, fuori dalla pratica della scrittura,* ad altre pratiche professionali di produzione di teatro).[14] Taviani is suspicious of modern evocations of a theatre of popular roots characterized by the use of the mask for improvisation; like Croce, he focuses on the historical conditions of production. The insight of Croce's that Taviani feels must form the basis of any investigation into commedia dell'arte is that this theatre was created by actors who came from the middle class.[15]

Individuals of conventional beliefs, not rebels, these actors joined in typically middle-class contractual relationships to market theatre, and for Taviani it was their ability to organize productions in a new way that accounted for their commercial success. The unique character of this theatre and its innovative use of printed texts posed problems for those who would control or censor performance and who did not have a printed text that could be relied on to mirror performance, as is evident in Giovan Domenico Ottonelli's observations on improvisation, 'If the actors improvise in performance, what can we say or do to revise the language in accordance with the proper moderation?' (Se i comici recitano improvisamente, noi che dobbiamo dire o fare intorno alla revisione verbale secondo la debita moderazione?)[16] But it is this flexibility, rather than the improvisational genius of any one actor, that for Taviani explains both the success of commedia dell'arte and the fact that as historical conditions have changed its allure has been lost. Thus the secret

of the commedia resides in a practical mode of production that generated a different relationship to the printed word.

Croce sees commedia dell'arte as firmly planted in the economic and
social conditions of the Renaissance. The triumph of the agile, flexible
professional companies over the academic theatre disproves the theory
that commedia derives from Roman theatre, because its success derives
from its ability to satisfy a new social need (508).[17] A theatre that drew
its essential spirit from ancient Rome would have been unable to
respond to this need.

Croce also anticipates the Marxist focus on a conjunction of the erotic
and the theatrical as central to the creation of modern theatre in Italy
when he remarks that the erotic too has its own history (509). The figure
of the actress/singer becomes a cultural sign of desire ('attrazione amo-
rosa'), an important component of the industrialization of theatre. For
Croce, as Marxist theatre critic, commedia dell'arte is located at the
meeting place of a new social need and the social mechanism that could
manipulate that need. The 'teatro buffonesco' is part of a lost cultural
nexus of pleasure and performance: 'Also laughter, like love, has its history and, like love, one cannot rekindle it and make it take flame when it
is out' (Anche il riso, come l'amore, ha la sua storia, e, come l'amore, non
si può riattizzarlo e farlo rifiammeggiare, quando si è spento, [514]). The
historical conditions that shape laughter and love can be studied, but
the unique character of the comic or the erotic as a reflection of social
history cannot be rekindled. Croce implies that commedia dell'arte created a theatre that satisfied desire and aroused laughter in ways that we
can intellectually understand but no longer respond to as spectators.
Laughter and desire are thus part of the industrialization of arte. There
is an art in the ability to arouse laughter that depends for its success on
an understanding of what appeals to a particular society. But this arte is
quite distinct from poetry, which, for Croce, is definitely not subject to
social conditions. The lack of a great text, created by a great poet (an Italian Rabelais, Shakespeare, or Molière) signals for him the difference
between professional/theatrical arte and a poetic art of the theatre that
would transcend historical conditions.[18]

For Croce commedia dell'arte emerges as the poetic spirit in Italy
declines. What he calls 'teatro buffonesco' (510) never rises to the level
of poetic art. According to Croce, the industrialization of theatre, its success as erotic commodity, and the popularity of the mask – a kind of
demi-urge that takes over the actor – have caused critics to confuse the
quality of buffo with true poetry (515). Here Croce seems to have aban-

doned the notion of a critical approach that might recreate commedia's spirit from its documented history. Although some of the individual actors may have risen from low buffo to a more elevated and cultured form of humor ('all'umoristico e all'umano'), in general the performance leaves no more than the fame attached to certain actors, the echo of vanished laughter and applause (515).

Roberto Tessari questions both Croce's denial of aesthetic value and the opposite tendency of Allardyce Nicoll to compare commedia dell'arte to the creative genius of a Shakespeare. According to Tessari, 'Harlequin is not Hamlet, but nor is he a lifeless piece of ceramic statuary.'[19] Tessari examines the arguments used by Flaminio Scala in the prologue to his *Il finto marito* (1619) and of Niccolò Barbiere in *La supplica* (1634) in defence of the aesthetic value of an art form that had a unique relationship to both the spectator and the printed word. Since aesthetic judgments have traditionally been tied to the analysis of a text, commedia dell'arte is apt to be undervalued because the theatrical tradition did not produce a printed text that might rival *Hamlet* or conversely to be overvalued as a form of improvisational theatre dear to those critics who champion performance as a neglected area of research and critical study. Whether its performance drew on a vast repertoire of texts, or eventually led to publication of a text that might give commedia canonical status, the art cannot be separated from a tradition of performance that was alive (not inert) and effective.

Croce sees commedia dell'arte as a theatrical phenomenon attached to particulars – a city, a mask, actors, theatres, contracts, costumes, the lazzi, bits of dialogue, and the plots and gestures that can be reconstructed and studied in the context of cultural history. But he finds no aesthetic arte of the commedia to measure with the kind of theoretical concepts that he developed in his study of history as art, there is only the echo of a lost act, of a gesture that remains the coin of cultural exchange. To be sure, the performers used printed or written texts as a source of material and might look to print as a means of enhancing their reputation.[20] But whether studying sources, printed *scenarii*, or the printed text of plays, the modern critic must imagine a performance tradition that cannot be fully circumscribed by the written or printed word. The unique combination of spoken words, gestures, and *canovacci* (if this word can indicate the plot or action in Taviani's sense) is not a variation on some Ur-text – it is, in each of its manifestations, the artistic creation of a group of professional actors whose training, skill, and instinct shaped the spoken text in performance.

Thus Croce maintains a clear distinction between aesthetic art and the arte of commedia dell'arte, and in his treatment of the Neapolitan mask Pulcinella he makes an equally important distinction between a theatrical type and a cultural stereotype. Croce began his early essay on Pulcinella by warning that Pulcinella cannot be defined ('Pulcinella non si definisce'), and he rejects any attempt to identify the mask with the supposed character of Neapolitans or southern Italians.

In *I teatri di Napoli* (1891), Croce had derived evidence of the vitality of commedia dell'arte in Naples from the multitude of comic types and Neapolitan masks that emerged in the city during the sixteenth century, most notably *Coviello* and *Pulcinella*, the latter identified with the great actor Silvo Fiorillo. To this Croce added the evidence of Neapolitan actors such as Fabrizio de Fornaris, the *capitan Coccodrillo*, Aniello Solden as *Dottore Spaccastrummolo*, and Tiberio Fiorilli, *Scaramuzza*, all of whom exhibited the proverbial versatility reflected in the expression 'Lazzi napoletani e soggetti lombardi' (45–9).

The study 'Pulcinella e il personaggio del napoletano in commedia' was first published in the *Archivo storico per le province napoletane* (vol. 23) in 1898 and subsequently appeared as a pamphlet in 1899; with revisions and additions, it was included in Croce's *Saggi sulla letteratura italiana del seicento* (1911) as 'Pulcinella e la commedia dell'arte,' along with another essay entitled 'Il tipo del napoletano nella commedia.' We should view Croce's work on Pulcinella in the context of his early reflections on something larger than this one theatrical personage – the question that he takes up very directly is whether the commedia mask can or should be used to characterize Neapolitans or southern Italians.

The dates are useful as a reminder of the turn-of-the-century intellectual and political climate in which the young Croce wrote. In his *Storia d'Italia dal 1871 al 1915* (1928) Croce characterizes the period as a prosaic age, in contrast to the poetic era of revolution and unification.[21] Croce was particularly sensitive to the so-called southern question – to the debate over the real and perceived differences between north and south in Italy.[22] As Trafton demonstrates in his essay (chapter 6, below), Croce's *Storia*, despite the undeniable failure of the Kingdom to fulfil its political and economic promise, Croce flatly rejected the positivist identification of racial inferiority as a contributing factor.[23]

In the 1899 monograph, Croce makes reference to Francesco De Sanctis to introduce the question of how or whether one can define Pulcinella. Serious critics, such as De Sanctis, failed in their attempts to define the comic ethos of Pulcinella because the mask is the focal point for various personages.[24] By drawing the reader's attention to the teaching of De Sanctis at the University of Naples and to the period of the Risorgimento, Croce provides context for his discussion of the mask, particularly regarding the ethnic definition of a characteristically southern type. The lectures and seminars that De Sanctis organized aroused considerable emotion and optimism because they encouraged the intelligentsia in Naples to inaugurate a period of intellectual and political renewal. Croce, however, takes issue with a provisional statement that De Sanctis made to his students in 1872 about the identification of Pulcinella with the foolish, lazy populace ('Pulcinella rappresenta il popolano sciocco ed ozioso'). Croce promptly raises objections: Pulcinella is not always the stupid, lazy popolano, and, as he points out, De Sanctis did not repeat the statement when he published an article based on the seminar later in 1872.[25]

In 1872 De Sanctis had asked his students to paint a verbal portrait of Pulcinella ('Fatemi un ritratto di Pulcinella'). He designed this exercise to counter a tendency towards abstract disputation that he had observed in his students, especially the Neapolitans, whom he describes as eloquent and intellectually subtle, born lawyers ('tutti avvocati nati' [*Libro*, 312]). This particular assignment was part of the pedagogical reform that De Sanctis envisioned, which would stimulate genuine intellectual curiosity. This moral and intellectual risorgimento would replace pedantry and over-generalization and require greater attention to particulars. With the Pulcinella of Goethe's *Faust*, Part II, in mind, De Sanctis set a theme designed to stimulate and challenge the class. One of his students, Giorgio Arcoleo, responded with a Pulcinella who represents the Neapolitan populace – braggart, street urchin, lazy trifler, the product of popular instinct: 'Pulcinella, to conclude, is the Neapolitan populace proud of its empty and sad heredity [i.e., the old dynasty]' (Pulcinella in somma è il plebeo napoletano che va superbo di una vacua e triste eredita).[26] Domenico Scafoglio sees in Arcoleo's treatment of Pulcinella a reaction of the Italian intelligentsia against the limitations of Neapolitan society under the *Regno*.[27]

De Sanctis, in a passage alluded to by Croce in the revised 'Pulcinella e la commedia dell'arte' (190), in fact criticizes Arcoleo for both representing Pulcinella as the over-generalized symbol of the comic spirit and making him the too-particular offspring of popular instinct. In either case Pulcinella becomes the symbol of some 'other' for Arcoleo, who focuses on the populace while speaking of Pulcinella.[28] Despite the correction offered by De Sanctis, the way in which the question was framed by the professor and pursued by the pupil tells us a good deal about how the Puclinella–*meridionale* equation fed and was in turn fed by ethnicity, particularly for those who sought to identify something reactionary, child-like, lazy, or superstitious in the Naples of Pulcinella or in the Pulcinella of Naples.

In 'Pulcinella' (195–6) Croce rejects ethnic assumptions and instead pursues a method that concentrates on Pulcinella as the purely theatrical type introduced by Silvio Fiorillo during the period 1616–18. He works from the specific references to Pulcinella in Pier Maria Cecchini's *Frutti delle moderne comedie* (1628), Crotese's *Viaggio del Parnasso* (1621), Callott's *I balli di Sfessania* (1622), and Fiorillo's play *La Lucilla Costante con le ridicolose disfide e prodesse di Policinella* (1632).[29] Croce asks whether Fiorillo was truly the inventor of Pulcinella or was rather an actor who lent his artistic talent to a pre-existing, popular tradition 'and with his art gave worth to the figure of Pulcinella that he took from more vulgar actors, humble village entertainments and an obscure pre-existent theatrical tradition?' (e fece valere con l'arte sua, la figura di Pulcinella, ch'egli tolse a comici più volgari, a umili divertimenti di villaggio, a una oscura tradizione teatrale preesistente?) (202).

Arcoleo had identified the Neapolitan ethos of Pulcinella with a lower class ('classe infima') huddled in the narrow, filthy streets that snake about the grand edifices of high culture. For Arcoleo, the art, wealth, and industry of high culture was to be studied at Pompeii or in the Museo Nazionale, but the essence of that other, subterranean world he looked for in the populace and its representative, Pulcinella.[30] The assumptions revealed in his juxtaposition of the fragments of high culture with the serpentine customs inherited by the populace and represented by Pulcinella help one understand Croce's cautious approach to the Roman antecedents of commedia dell'arte. While granting the possibility of some indirect influence, Croce finds no evidence to support Arcoleo's suggestion of a direct line leading from the figure of Maccus in Roman *atellan* farce through popular medieval traditions to the commedia of the Renaissance.[31] Resemblances of the kind that the German anthropologist and classicist A. Dieterich saw between the figure of Maccus and Pulcinella are, for Croce, suspect because Dieterich assumed that the same soil and the same people that gave birth to the Roman personage also produced Pulcinella (208).[32] Croce warns that the critic must guard against transforming figures of speech into what appear to be historical realities, as when one thinks of Pulcinella as an indigenous plant suited to the southern climate or when one says that the germ of commedia is to be found in ancient civilization (212). He is more interested in specific historical conditions than in metaphorical 'germe.'

Croce concludes that these questions of ethnic continuity, of the persistence of ancient customs and dispositions, must be resolved in other fields of study (213). In a slightly different context, he seems willing to admit an identity of sorts between Pulcinella and the Neapolitan populace ('dei lazzari e della plebe napoletana') (235)) but only after the fact of artistic creation. The identification is created by us, says Croce, not by artistic representation, which is always free of 'intentionalism and allegorisims' (sempre scevra d'intenzioni e di allegorismi) (235) .

At this point in his essay, Croce introduces Goethe as an example of an astute observer ('osservatore accurato e sennato') who made the connection between Pulcinella and the 'southern' temperament of the Neapolitan populace in the following noteworthy passage from Goethe's *Italian Journey* (19 March 1787): 'Yesterday at the Molo, one of the noisiest corners in the city, I saw a Pulcinella on a wooden platform, fighting with a little monkey, while on the balcony above them a rather pretty girl was offering her charms for sale ... Painted by Gerrit Don, it would have made a picture worthy of delighting both contemporaries and future generations ... Pulcinella is now: a truly calm, composed serving man, somewhat indifferent, almost lazy, and yet humorous. And waiters and porters of that type are found everywhere. Today I was especially amused by our man, and it was merely a matter of sending him to fetch paper and pens. Partial misunderstanding, hesitation, good will, and roguishness created the most charming scene, one that could be produced with good success on any stage.'[33]

Goethe, the observer, connects the street performance of Pulcinella and the activity of an attractive prostitute within a frame that is itself like a picture, a way of seeing or representing a world that is picturesque. Croce's reluctance to accept any easy definition of the mask, or of a regional temperament that lies behind it, is itself a reaction against the natural tendency of the observer to assimilate details and to create a consistent, coherent definition of typically 'southern' behaviour. Cultural preconceptions undoubtedly shape observation. The northern visitor finds southern, Mediterranean life picturesque, lively, and roughish, and the southern temperament childlike, passionate, and irresponsible. One does not often stop to ask what social or political conditions determine the behavioural patterns that take shape in the streets.

Goethe will, however, correct his own perspective when he examines his friend Volkmann's reference to the existence of 'thirty to forty thousand idlers in Naples.' Goethe, drawing on his powers of observation – for he is very much the traveller as naturalist and social scientist – concludes that this 'might well be the Northern way of thinking' but that after careful observation he is prepared to advance the paradox that 'in Naples, comparatively speaking, perhaps the greatest industriousness is to be found among the lowest classes' (263–5). By the time we reach Goethe's *Faust*, as Croce notes, the poet's imagination has transformed Pulcinella from an ethnic type into a purely human personage (236).

Goethe does not, however, entirely abandon the 'naturalist-ethnic' perspective that recurs in many traveller's accounts of the South: 'Nature compels the Northerner to make provisions and preparations ... On the other hand, Heaven has dealt very leniently with Southern peoples, and it is too severe of us to judge them from our viewpoint' (265). Hence the people of the south, less compelled to meet urgent and elementary needs, can enjoy life; unlike the northerners, they 'work not merely to *live*, but to *enjoy*' – and these humble people, like children, 'make play out of their work.' Significantly, Goethe ends his long discussion of industriousness with a return to the question of antecedents: 'Without exception this class of people has a very lively temperament and a candid, straightforward gaze. Their speech is said to be metaphorical, their wit very quick and caustic. Ancient Atella was located not far from Naples, and just as their beloved Pulcinella still carries on those farces, so the very common class of people still keeps that humour alive today' (266–7). Goethe follows with a quotation from Pliny's *Natural History* on the character of the people of Campania.

Thus the link between Atellan farce, the common people, and Pulcinella continues. Assumptions about natural disposition and abiding cultural traits can be drawn on, Croce would say, to give order and continuity to experience, especially the visitor's baffling, sometimes disturbing experience of Naples. Croce suggests a related approach to the identification of Pulcinella with the Neapolitan populace when he remarks that the personage was created for the specific amusement of the upper class. A member of the intelligentsia, such as Arcoleo, or a traveller, such as Goethe, might be inclined to see Pulcinella as the 'other' precisely because the personage was originally created as the social 'other,' not so much a representative figure as a representation, a way of seeing the lower class that tells us more about the preconceptions of the observers than it does about the character of the populace. Building on his dry, erudite research, Croce resists the tendency to detach Pulcinella from very specific historical conditions. This historical approach forces us to think of Pulcinella as a theatrical figure whose traits reflect specific social and historical conditions.

To whatever extent Pulcinella may be said to mirror certain characteristics of the Neapolitan populace, rather than the conditions that shaped his distinctive character, Croce insists that the figure is definitely not meant for caricature or satire.[34] He traces the origins of the satirical treatment of the Neapolitan in Renaissance theatre to the Florentine merchant class resident in Naples. Its observations of certain Neapolitan characteristics, particularly among the nobility, provide the basis for the stereotypical boastfulness, ceremoniousness, and exuberance of speech and gesture of the Neapolitan, as depicted in Renaissance erudite theatre (255).[35]

As a student of theatre, Croce adheres to the theatrical definition of Pulcinella as 'secondo zanni' – the foolish servant who plays the clown in tandem with the clever intriguer or first *zanni* Brighella, a basic pattern that can be observed in the relationship between Pulcinella and Volpone in *La Lucilla costante*. Andrea Perrucci provides a convenient definition, 'In this way the part of the second servant comprises a fatuous person, stolid, simple, whose gestures and words will move laughter.' (Di sì fatta maniera consistendo la parte di secondo Servo in persona fatua, stolida, e semplice, e ne i gesti e nelle parole potrà movere il riso).[36] Croce notes that Pulcinella does not conform to the usual contradistinction between the clever first zanni, which Cecchini calls 'un servo astuto ed ingegnoso,' and the foolish second zanni, who is totally opposite to the first and, like the servant whom Goethe describes, purposely exploits equivocation. Croce (214) paraphrases Cecchini, who tells us that 'Capitan Mattamores' (i.e., Silvio Fiorillo) invented Pulcinella 'to make one believe that simplicity could be found even among Neapolitans' (per far credere che anche la semplicità abbia loco d'albergare fra napoletani) and that he 'introduced a studied simplicity at whose first appearance melancholy would flee or at least be kept away for a long period of time' (ha introdotto una disciplinata goffaggine, al quale, al primo suo apparire, conviene che la melanconia se ne fugga, o almeno si concentri e stia rilegata per longo spazio di tempo).[37] The interplay of art and reality changes in this equation because Pulcinella's simplicity is from its very inception a way of playing against the stereotype of the *furbo* – the clever, street-wise Neapolitan.

Croce, concentrating on the difficulties encountered by anyone who attempts to define Pulcinella, quotes Cecchini, who must explain the paradoxical phrase 'disciplinata goffagine': 'I say studied simplicity because he [Fiorillo] spares no pains to outgo Nature in presenting a simpleton who is almost an imbecile, and an imbecile whose dearest wish is to be thought a wise man' (Dissi disciplinata goffagine, poschia ch'egli fa uno assiduissimo studio per passar i termini naturali, e mostar un goffo poco discosto da un pazzo ed un pazzo che di soverchio si vuol accostar ad un savio) (214). These words, Croce comments, would describe an absurdly contradictory character if it did not seem that they either reflect Cecchini's failure to define the character he had in mind or indicate that he had in mind many personages who could not be reduced to one character. As second zanni, Pulcinella should conform to Perrucci's prescription that the type be entirely given to foolishness and flee cleverness.[38] However, as Croce tells us (215): 'The incoherent mixture of cleverness and foolishness was, to be sure, so frequent that Riccoboni was moved to say that in Neapolitan comedies the roles of Brighella and Harlequin were played by two Pulcinellas, one clever and the other stupid.' (Il miscuglio incoerente di furberia e di sciocchezza era, anzi, così frequente che il Riccoboni ne fu tratto a dire che nelle commedie napoletane i posti di Brighella e di Arlecchino erano occupati da due Pulcinelli, *un fourbe et l'autre stupide*.) Croce explains this apparent contradiction by returning to his premise – there is no one Pulcinella. There are rather a multiplicity of theatrical manifestations projected through the one mask, some foolish, others clever, and thus the traditional theatrical distinction is undercut, as is the ethnic identification of Pulcinella with a certain Neapolitan, or southern character type.

It is precisely this contradictory quality that has become the focal point of recent studies, such as Domenico Scafoglio's *Pulcinella: Il mito e la storia* and Franco Di Bello's 'Bianco e nero, doppiezza di una maschera dimezzata.'[39] Modern critics return in a sense to the union of the clever and foolish servants and to the definition of Pulcinella as the 'other' – the kind of definition that was anticipated by Giorgio Arcoleo when he says of Pulcinella: 'His home is outside the walls of the household, it is in the street; his faith is outside religion, in liturgy; his love outside the soul, in the senses; his life outside self-consciousness, in formality' (La sua casa è fuori delle pareti domestiche, è sulla strada; la fede è fuori della religione, nella liturgia; l'amore fuori dell'animo, nel senso; la vita fuori della coscienza, nella forma).[40] Arcoleo defines the 'other' from the point of view of the middle class, identifying Pulcinella with those characteristics of the populace that set it apart from the intelligentsia. While Croce asserts that Pulcinella cannot be defined, critics such as Scafoglio and Di Bello take a typically modern approach and see contradiction as the very essence of Pulcinella. From this point of view, the mask becomes a symbol of the universal other who comes from the countryside to the city, a figure whose unresolved ambiguity constantly tests the very distinctions between primitive and sophisticated, ignorant and clever, wise and foolish. For Croce, contradiction has more to do with Pulcinella's theatrical role as comic zanni, as we can see in his treatment of the comedy *La Lucilla costante* (200).[41] In his study of the play, Croce remains focused on the theatrical role of Pulcinella the zanni rather than Pulcinella the Neapolitan. In this particular instance and throughout his work on Pulcinella and the commedia dell'arte Croce develops his ideas from a clearly defined historical context. For Croce the contradictory quality of Pulcinella results from the varied responses of professional entertainers to the demands of the marketplace. Wary of making over-generalized assumptions, Croce does not pursue the duality of Pulcinella in the direction of some unique and elusive quality produced by the soil of Naples.

As Willette demonstrates in his essay on Croce and *Napoli nobilissima* (chapter 4, below), when Croce looked back on his early work he characterized those studies as in many ways 'estrinseche esercitzaioni erudite e letterarie,' in the sense that these erudite, literary exercises were outside the main philosophical concerns that he considered his most important contribution to modern thought. But that work is not outside the sphere of his philosophical thought. It provides the grounding for his personal and moral reflections, the point of reference that Croce may have found frustrating but that tested his philosophy. Croce as man of letters was in many ways centred in Naples, not only because he resided in the heart of that city but because he engaged the particulars of its rich history with sympathy and critical acumen. His erudite studies of commedia dell'arte and Pulcinella are not extrinsic to our understanding of the history of theatre in Naples or to our more general understanding of the unique 'art' of improvisational performance and of the relationship between the conventions that shape theatrical types and the cultural stereotypes that colour our understanding of theatre. In his ability to combine detailed research with more theoretical speculation, Croce provides a striking example of the living union of critical erudition and philosophical imagination.

NOTES

1 *Contributo alla critica di me stesso*, in B. Croce, ed., *Filosofia, poesia, storia* (Milan: Riccardo Ricciardi, 1951), 1148. In addition to the studies cited below, see Allardyce Nicoll, *Masks, Mimes and Miracles* (London: G.C. Harrap, 1931); Kathleen M. Lea, *Italian Popular Comedy*, 2 vols. (New York: Russell & Russell, 1934); Roberto Tessari, 'La commedia dell'arte come forma di un'embrionale industria del divertimento,' *Il Ponte* 34 no. 3–4 (1978), 408–23; Ferdinando Taviani, 'La composizione del dramma nella commedia dell'arte,' *Quaderni di teatro* 4 no. 15 (1982), 151–71; Louise George Clubb, *Italian Drama in Shakespeare's Time* (New Haven, Conn.: Yale University Press, 1989), 249–80; and Frank Fata, 'Understanding Pulcinella,' *Italian Culture*, 8 (1990), 87–105.

2 *I teatri di Napoli dal Rinascimento alla fine del secolo decimottavo*, ed. Giuseppe Galasso (Milan: Adelphi, 1992), 42; first published (Bari: Laterza, 1916), abbreviation and revision of material previsouly published in *Archivo storico napoletano* (1889–91), and in extracts (Naples, 1891). On Croce's subsequent evaluation of this work, see Galasso's 'Nota del curatore,' in *I teatri*, 357–78. Parenthetical references are to this edition.

3 *Poesia populare e poesia d'arte: Studi sulla poesia italiana dal tre al cinquecento* (Bari: Laterza, 1933), 508.

4 'L'ingresso della Commedia dell'Arte nella cultura del Cinquecento,' in Fabrizio Cruciani and Daniele Seragnoli, eds., *Il teatro italiano nel Rinascimento* (Bologna: Mulino, 1987), 324.

5 See Ferdinando Taviani and Mirella Schino, *Il segreto della Commedia dell'Arte* (Florence: Casa Usher, 1982), 359: 'The production of comedies and tragedies passed from a festive economy to a market economy.'

6 Ferdinando Taviani sees Fredi as an important figure who fulfilled the dream of many actors to stop wandering but not to stop acting, see ibid., 396.

7 Taviani notes the importance of Vassari's observations on theatre in his life of Battista Franco (Semolei): 'Vasari identifies not theatres of the same *genre*, but theatres in the same condition: he places every form of commercial theatre in the same category.' Taviani insists on the middle-class rather than popular origins of commedia dell'arte, because of the organizational skill of the middle class that lies behind the innovative mode of selling theatre. See ibid., 358 and 398.

8 On these illustrations as representations of traditional dances, see Marco De Marinis, 'Appunti per uno studio diacronico della recitazione nella *commedia*

dell'arte,' in Domenico Pietropaolo, ed., *The Science of Buffoonery: Theory and History of the Commedia dell'Arte* (Toronto: Dovehouse, 1989), 241.

9 See Ferdinando Taviani, 'Sulla sopravvalutazione della maschera,' in Donato Sartoni, direzione artistica, *Arte della maschere nella commedia dell'arte* (Florence: Casa Usher, 1983), 105.

10 *Intorno alla 'Commedia dell' Arte'*, in *Poesia populare e poesia d'arte* (1933), 507.

11 See Ernesto Caserta, *Croce critico letterario (1882–1912)* (Naples: Giannini, 1972), 392–5, and *Croce and Marxism* (Naples: Morano, 1987), 125–51.

12 Paolo Toschi, *Le origini del teatro Italiano* (Turin: Boringhieri, 1955), 118; see also Ludovico Zorzi, 'Intorno alla commedia dell'arte: Due lezioni,' *Forum italicum*, 14 no. 3 (1980), 439.

13 See Roberto Tessari, 'Maschere barocche,' 102, and Ferdinando Taviani, 'Sulla sopravvalutazione,' 105–18, in *Arte della maschera nella commedia dell'arte* (Florence: Casa Usher, 1983).

14 Taviani and Schino, *Il segreto*, 329.

15 See Croce on the 'borghesia letterata o dall'artigianato' (511) and Taviani and Schino, *Il segreto*, 360.

16 *Della christiana moderatione del theatro* (1646) in Ferdinando Taviani, *La commedia dell'Arte e la società Barocca: La fascinazione del teatro* (Rome: Bulzoni, 1969), I, 521.

17 See Taviani and Schino, *Il segreto*, 483–4 no. 43; cf. 375 on Roman antecedents and classical imitation.

18 On the special universality of poetry and its ability to fuse the particular and the universal, the individual and the cosmic, to produce beauty, see Croce's *La poesia: Introduzione alla critica e storia della poesia e della letteratura* (Bari: Laterza, 1936), 56 and 81–4; cf. Caserta, *Croce critico*, 316 and 248, and Edmund E. Jacobitti, *Revolutionary Humanism and Historicism in Modern Italy* (New Haven, Conn.: Yale University Press, 1981), 78.

19 Roberto Tessari, *Commedia dell'arte: la maschera e la ombra* (Milan: Mursia, 1981), 50: 'Arlecchino non è Amleto, ma non è neppure una inerte statuetta di ceramica.' See Allardyce Nicoll, *The World of Harlequin* (Cambridge: Cambridge University Press, 1963), 1–8 and 88.

20 'Però fu la stampa la carta di credito più autorevole a disposizione degli attori,' as Siro Ferrone writes in his introduction to the two-volume anthology of texts, *Commedia dell'arte* (Milan: Mursia, 1985), I, 14.

21 *Storia d'Italia dal 1871 al 1915* (Bari: Laterza, 1928), 2. See Jacobitti, *Revolutionary Humanism*, 47, on Croce and De Sanctis.

22 Christopher Seton-Watson, *Italy from Liberalism to Fascism 1870–1925* (London: Methuen, 1967), particularly the discussion of Francesco Saverio Nitti's *Nord e Sud* (1900), 306. See also Croce's *Storia d'Italia*, 60 and 82.

23 *History of the Kingdom of Naples*, ed. H. Stuart Hughes, trans. Frances Frenaye (Chicago: University of Chicago Press, 1970), 245.
24 *Pulcinella* (Rome: E. Loescher, 1899), 1: 'Pulcinella non designa un determinato personaggio artistico; ma una *collezione di personagi.*' (Pulcinella refers not to a fixed artistic character, but rather to a variety of characters.)
25 '*Libro della scuola*' *di Francesco de Sanctis, 1872*, in Francesco De Sanctis, *L'arte, la scienza e la vita: Nuovi saggi critici, conferenze e scritti varii*, ed. Maria Teresa Lanza (Turin: Einaudi, 1972), with Giorgio Arcoleo's *Pulcinello dentro e fuori di teatro*. Arcoleo's essay was republished (Naples: Morano, 1897) and re-edited by Croce in his *De Sanctis, scritti varii inediti e rari* (1898) while Croce was at work on 'Pulcinella e il personaggio.'
26 Arcoleo, *Pulcinella*, in '*Libro della scuola*,' 503.
27 Domenico Scafoglio and Luigi M. Lombardi Satriani, *Pulcinella: Il mito e la storia* (Milan: Leonardo, 1990), 88: 'La società patriottico-risorgimentale rifiuta di farsi rappresentare da una maschera che sembra compromessa da antiche connivenze coi despoti e appare cresciuta all'ombra della protezione borbonica; il puritanesimo della nuova morale borghese genera disprezzo per un personaggio che di certo non incarnava i valori del lavoro, della famiglia, dell'ordine e del sacrifico.'
28 See De Sanctis, '*Libro della scuola*,' 314: 'Perchè su questa via ciò che è innanzi al suo spirito non è Pulcinella, ma il popolo, e si avvezza in quello a guardar questo. Anche qui Pulcinella non è un individuo vivo e libero, ma la figura di un altro.' Parenthetical page references are to *Saggi sulla letteratura italiana del seicento*, 3rd ed. (Bari: Laterza, 1948).
29 See Lea, *Italian Popular Comedy*, I, 91–3.
30 Arcoleo, *Pulcinella*, 502.
31 See Toschi, *Le origini del teatro italiano*, on the 'comune culla etnologica,' 214.
32 See A. Dieterich, *Pulcinella* (Leipzig: Teubner, 1897), and Scafoglio, *Pulcinella*, 54.
33 Johann Wolfgang von Goethe, *Italian Journey*, ed. Thomas P. Saine and Jeffrey L. Sammons, trans. Robert R. Heitner (New York: Suhrkamp, 1983), 174–5.
34 *Saggi*, 'I Toscani e la satira contro i Napolitani,' 253.
35 On gesture and Pulcinella, see A.G. Bragaglia, *Pulcinella* (Rome: Casini, 1952), 124; cf. A Perrucci, *Dell'arte rappresentativa premeditata ed all'improviso*, ed. A.G. Bragaglia (Florence: Sansoni, 1961), 122, and Andrea De Jorio, *La mimica degli antichi investigata nel gestire napoletano* (Naples: Fibreno, 1832).
36 Perrucci, *Dell'arte*, 224.
37 Pier Maria Cecchini, *Frutti delle moderne comedie et avisi a chi le recita* (1628), in Ferruccio Marotti and Giovanna Romei, eds., *La commedia dell'arte e la società*

barocca: La professione del teatro (Rome: Bulzoni, 1991), 85 and 90. Cf. Scafoglio, *Pulcinella*, 607ff. Cf. Lea, *Italian Popular Comedy*, I, 91.

38 Perrucci, *Dell'arte*, 221: 'Ogni Paese ha il suo linguaggio grazioso tolto dal Plebeo, e così ogn'uno può formarselo a suo capriccio ... Tutti però devono dare nella sciocchezza, e fugire l'arguzie.'

39 Di Bello's essay appears in Franco Carmelo Greco, ed., *Pulcinella: una maschera tra gli specchi* (Naples: Edizioni Scientifice Italiane, 1990), 235–58.

40 Arcoleo, *Pulcinella*, 502–3.

41 *La Lucilla costante e le ridicolose disfide di Policinella*, in Laura Falavolti, ed., *Commedie dei comici dell'arte* (Turin: Classici UTET, 1982).

4

È stata opera di critica onesta, liberale, italiana: Croce and Napoli nobilissima (1892–1906)

THOMAS WILLETTE

The many pages of essays, reviews, and notes that Benedetto Croce wrote for the first series (1892–1906) of the journal *Napoli nobilissima* span what is certainly the most complex and interesting period of his intellectual life. Within these fifteen years Croce concluded his intense engagement with historical materialism, launched his new journal of literature and philosophy *La critica*, and sketched out his major philosophical system, the *filosofia dello spirito*. For students of Croce's historicism, this is also the period of his deepest ambivalence about *metodo storico* and the moral, political, and intellectual merits of regional historiography. Thus it is a little surprising that the *Napoli nobilissima* project, as I call it, to which he devoted so many years of his early maturity, has rarely been treated as one of his intellectual and cultural endeavours.[1]

Certainly the journal was a collaborative enterprise, to a much greater degree than was Croce's partnership with Giovanni Gentile in the first years of *La critica*. Moreover, the pages of *Napoli nobilissima*, devoted variously to municipal preservation efforts and documentation of historical places, monuments, and works of art, have proved uninteresting to most scholars who happen to be interested in Croce. Despite its lively, at times polemical engagement with the intellectual, cultural, and political issues of post-Unification Italy, the journal rarely spoke the languages of philosophy, literary criticism, or political theory. The fifteen volumes of the first series are still consulted by historians of visual art, architecture, and urbanism, but chiefly as repositories of documents and bibliography. These historians are by and large indifferent to the aesthetic, critical, and political content of the journal, even though Croce himself would later have considerable influence on Italian and German art history, particularly in the period between the world wars.[2] Thus it seems that Croce's lifelong sense of being divided uncomfortably between 'concrete history' and philosophy is reproduced in the scholarship devoted to his work, in such a way that *Napoli nobilissima* has fallen between the cracks. Nevertheless, the main reason why this journal tends not to be considered a Crocean endeavour may be the fact that Croce himself all but repudiated the project and, in his autobiographical *Contributo alla critica di me stesso* of 1915, greatly diminished both the political-cultural character of its mission and the importance of his friendship with the men who collaborated with him during those years.[3] In what follows I try to throw some light on this neglected activity of Croce's, in a way that clarifies both the details of his involvement and the broad cultural goals of this journal in the political and intellectual context of post-Unification Naples. I conclude with a discussion of Croce's retrospective presentation, in the *Contributo*, of his relations with the regional historical movement that was led by Bartolomeo Capasso (1815–1900), to which *Napoli nobilissima* was associated as a sort of client organization during Capasso's presidency of the Società napoletana di Storia Patria.

The first series of *Napoli nobilissima* was a large-format monthly journal, physically more similar to illustrated general culture periodicals, such as the Neapolitan *Poliorama pittoresco*, than to the austere and imposing organs of regional historical societies.[4] Its tone was in fact both popular-izing and scholarly, something like that of *Giambattista Basile*, the monthly review dedicated to Neapolitan folklore and dialect literature.[5] According to Croce's account of the founding of *Napoli nobilissima* – written nearly sixteen years later for the *commiato* or farewell address of the final issue of the first series – the idea for the journal was born in October 1891 in the palace of the duca di Maddaloni, when Croce's close friend Salvatore Di Giacomo proposed that they do something to benefit the historic and artistic monuments of Naples by cultivating public awareness and knowledge of the city's material cultural heritage. A few evenings later, according to this account, Croce gathered some friends at his own house and announced the *programma* of the new review, for which he also devised a title, drawn from the frontispiece of Domenico Antonio Parrino's late-seventeenth-century description of the city, *Napoli città nobilissima*. Di Giacomo himself wrote out Croce's program in the form of a preface to the first issue, published early in 1892 and col-lectively signed by the seven co-founders.[6] As Croce would later emphasize, this was a diverse group of friends: *artisti, letterati, eruditi, dilettanti*, united by love of art and the cult of historical memory.[7] However, they were all men of high-bourgeois or aristocratic origin and all of the same generation. As a mark of their corporate spirit, their names appeared below Di Giacomo's text in egalitarian alphabetical order: Riccardo Carafa, duca d'Andria (b. 1859), Giuseppe Ceci (b. 1863), Luigi Conforti (b. 1854), Croce (b. 1866), Di Giacomo (b. 1860), Michelangelo Schipa (b. 1854), and Vittorio Spinazzola (b. 1863).

In fact, the group had no official *direttore*, as we learn from a letter that Di Giacomo wrote to Croce in December 1892, near the end of the first year of publication. However, from the same letter we also learn that Croce, despite his being the youngest member of the group, assumed the authority (in what remains a murky incident) to relieve Di Giacomo of his administrative duties without advance notice.[8] It is, in any case, quite clear that an effective hierarchy was soon established, with Croce in charge and Ceci, his close friend and former schoolmate, as his chief collaborator.[9] For most of the period 1892–1906 it was Croce's vision and editorial voice that guided the project, and his vigorous involvement as co-director, editor, and contributor does not seem to have flagged noticeably until 1903 (the first year of his new journal *La critica*), when Croce shifted most of the editorial responsibilities for *Napoli nobilissima* to his protégé Fausto Nicolini, but even then he insisted on reading the final proofs himself.[10]

In Croce's 'unofficial' autobiographical narrative 'Curriculum vitae,' written in 1902 and apparently never intended to be published, he reported that in late 1891 and early 1892 (precisely the period in which *Napoli nobilissima* was founded) his increasing dissatisfaction with erudite research and local history, together with his growing intellectual ambition, had reached a sort of crisis, 'manifested, among other things, by doubt about the *value* of history and of *historical methods*' (esso si manifestò, tra l'altro, col dubbio sul *valore* della *storia* e dei *metodi storici*).[11] However, there is no evidence from the time that Croce ceased his erudite studies of regional history; nor does the essay of 1893, *La storia ridotta sotto il concetto generale dell'arte*, often described as Croce's first 'philosophical' essay, represent an abandonment of either metodo storico or regional history.[12] However, with the founding of *Napoli nobilissima* there was a significant change in orientation, in that Croce's commitment to erudite historical scholarship expanded decisively into the public sphere. In the 'Curriculum vitae,' Croce wrote that '1892 signified for me the beginning of a more intense life,' as he developed his ideas about the influence of Spain in Italian culture and began to find a voice in the current debates over the conceptual status of historical (as opposed to scientific) knowledge.[13] In January of that year Croce was admitted into the membership of the Accademia Pontaniana, and in the very same month he began attending meetings of the Circolo filologico, a civic organization founded by Francesco De Sanctis in 1876 (on the model of similar groups in Florence, Genoa, Milan, Palermo, Rome, and Torino) with the purpose of promoting discussion of art and literature among young Neapolitan aristocrats and bourgeois.[14] The larger goal of De Sanctis's strategy for defeating factionalism among local elites was to create a society of intellectuals, sufficiently versed in modern languages and current publications in science and literature to enter into communion with the high culture of civil Europe. He was convinced that Neapolitans could have a place in the new national culture of Italy only if they became a collective force as an intellectual society united in a civil purpose. 'In Naples,' he affirmed in a public speech in the spring of 1876, 'we are divided, we do not know ourselves, each branch of culture is organized as a closed field. It is necessary, for a people so much alive, to have a meeting place, to have a house where studious men gather ... Thus we will have means to obtain that unity of strengths that has always been lacking in Naples, where we have a strong sense of individuality but are divided and dispersed by the wind' (In Napoli siamo divisi, non ci conosciamo, ciascun ramo di cultura è organizzato come un campo chiuso. È necessario, per un popolo così vivo, avere un luogo di convegno, avere una casa dove convengano gli uomini studiosi ... Così avremo mezzo di ottenere quella unione di forze, che è mancata sempre a Napoli, dove abbiamo grandi individualità, ma divise e disperse dal vento).[15] Croce was an energetic vice-president (and de facto president) of the Circolo filologico from 1894 to 1896, as Toni Iermano has recently documented, pursuing the old dream of De Sanctis, whose writings Croce had begun to reread by this time, organizing readings and lectures by leading Italian intellectuals and tending to the publicity of the Circolo's activities as editor of its first *Annuario*.[16] Many of the men who contributed to *Napoli nobilissima* attended events organized during Croce's tenure, including the co-founders Carafa d'Andria, Ceci, Di Giacomo, and Spinazzola. This meshing of interests is further attested by the fact that Carafa and Ceci served with Croce on the Circolo's directorial board.

The cultural work of *Napoli nobilissima* shared at least one major goal with the Circolo filologico, and that was the development of what might be called a discourse of Neapolitan identity in the public sphere, a shared

set of beliefs and conventions that would rise above the multiple contrasting private-sphere interests of old nobility, wealthy middle class,
and lesser nobility that typically divided the higher social strata along
countless fractures, inhibiting both civic loyalty and the formation of a
broad ruling elite.[17] The use of art and history to create such a discourse
was fundamental to De Sanctis's work as a political educator, journalist,
and 'cultural organizer,' and his unity of *letterato* (or *studioso*) and *cit-
tadino* became Croce's vision (a vision not well suited to the circumstances of modernity, as Fiammetta Rutoli has reminded us) and one of
his escape routes from the narrow world of the library and archive.[18]

Raffaele Ajello has recently described *Napoli nobilissima* as 'the official
organ of *napoletanità*' (l'organo ufficiale della napoletanità) in this
period, and indeed its largest claim was to speak for the broad-based
interests of the citizenry.[19] However, the true measure of its ambition lay
in the intention of its designers to ground Liberal *napoletanità* in material
historical culture, to posit this 'spirit' in the phenomenal *evidentiae* of
places and things, as well as in their literary remains. Croce's *programma*,
as we have it in the text of Di Giacomo's salute *Ai nostri benevoli lettori*, is
a fairly explicit scheme 'to revive the past' as an object of patriotic and
civic feeling.[20] The text of the program outlines purposes both *spirituali*
and *pratici* for this reconstruction of history. The 'spiritual' activity of the
journal would be accomplished through the collection and dissemination of the latest erudite scholarship, to be presented in a form accessible
to everyone, so that the research of scholars could become part of the
general culture. It is predicted that the didactic labour of summarizing
and synthesizing the raw data of historical research would, after three or
four years, result in the compilation of a patriotic book of artistic and
topographic history for the citizens. The 'practical' activity of the journal, however, would be directed towards interventions in policy, as a
public mouthpiece calling for the conservation and improvement of historical material culture, 'of all that represents our ancient patrimony,
scattered throughout the streets of the city, but not lovingly looked after
and never cultivated.' As an advocate for the preservation of historic
monuments and artworks, *Napoli nobilissima* would assist the official
work of the existing provincial and municipal commissions for the conservation of monuments, whose proposals were not as effective as they
should have been, thanks in part to the silence of the newspapers. By
amplifying the proposals of such official commissions, the journal,
working unofficially, would encourage the papers to take up proposals
for conservation and improvement, so that 'a beneficial reawakening of

public interest could follow, concerning that which regards the gentle study of art, our paternal memories.'

The use of words such as 'revive' and 'reawaken' in the text of the *programma* reveals the inspiration of Risorgimento ideology in this post-Unification cultural project, and indeed the patriotic name of the journal was deliberatley old-fashioned, meant to evoke 'un lieve sapor antiquato' of times of greater glory.[21] The emphasis on art as an instrument of moral unity is much in line with Luigi Settembrini's decidedly Romantic faith in the redemptive power of art to create a spiritual common ground for politically and socially divided peoples.[22] Nevertheless, the project directly engaged problems of modernity in *la nuova Italia*, and its nostalgic appeal to the culture of the old regime, *la vecchia Napoli*, was not merely an effect of reactionary *municipalismo*. On the contrary, the 'practical' mission that *Napoli nobilissima* shared unofficially with the official Commissione municipale per la conservazione dei monumenti was nothing less than protection of the material fabric of civic life, specifically through attentive monitoring and informed criticism of the massive demolition work of the *piano del Risanamento* then in progress. This highly disputed 'plan of reclamation,' begun in the 1880s in the name of hygienic and economic improvement, was wiping out many old quarters of the city with what seemed to be reckless disregard for the historical values that the leaders of the Risorgimento had worked so hard to create and on which many Liberals counted for the success of their plans for local political and cultural unity across middle and upper classes. In Naples, as in the Paris of Baron Haussmann, for every proponent of modernization there was someone who mourned the loss of history.[23] The disputes around the piano del Risanamento might be described as struggles over the material foundations of urban life, carried out between two politicized forces of modernization – one essentially economic and the other essentially cultural (or in the language of the time, 'spiritual') – both attempting to control the image of the city.

Already in 1890 Croce had laboured to preserve the names of old streets then being destroyed under the plan of reclamation. This became one of the first 'practical' interventions of the *Napoli nobilissima* project, making a broader public issue out of what had been the concern of scholarly historians in long, heavily documented articles on the old streets and monuments for the journal of the Società napoletana di Storia Patria.[24] As secretary of a commission on street names created by the Giunta municipale di Risanamento in collaboration with the Società (and directed by Bartolommeo Capasso, supporter and mentor of the *Napoli nobilissima* group), Croce drew up a detailed plan to preserve forty-seven old street names of historical value, while deriving the new street names that were needed from local traditions or from the names of historical persons associated with the places in question.[25] Croce's proposals for new names were generally ignored, and his criteria for saving historic names, laboriously justified by historical research, were ignored entirely, while the report he produced as secretary of the commission was apparently never acknowledged by the city council members to whom it was addressed.

Commentary on, and eventually sharp criticism of, the Giunta's indifference to cultural heritage and historical memory was supplied in the pages of *Napoli nobilissima* by the acerbic pen of 'Don Fastidio' – a pseudonym employed by both Croce and Giuseppe Ceci, in this case certainly Croce, for their more pointed cultural commentary, often having to do with the functioning of public offices and institutions, under the monthly rubric *Notizie ed osservazioni*.[26] The name Don Fastidio was borrowed for this rubric, as is known, from an eighteenth-century comic character in Neapolitan theatre, a pedant whose pompous discourse freely mixed Neapolitan dialect and Tuscan with entirely made-up words. The character was a perfect mask for Croce's haughty satire and habitual ironic self-deprecation (as a young man playing the role of an old-fashioned *erudito*) in the many shorter essays that he contributed. Don Fastidio's constant companion in the back pages of *Napoli nobilissima* was the milder 'Don Ferrante' (another pseudonym used by both Croce and Ceci), who presided over the rubric *Da libri e periodici*, dedicated to book reviews and to summaries of historical, literary, and critical-methodological scholarship.[27] It must have been obvious to Croce's contemporaries, although it seems to have gone unrecorded, that the name Don Ferrante was borrowed from the bibliophile husband of Donna Prassede, whose famous library is described in chapter 27 of Alessandro Manzoni's *I promessi sposi*. Indeed, Don Fastidio and Don Ferrante make a fine pair as ironic characterizations of the twin spirits of the journal (local history and Liberal politics), for the latter has all the vices of the libertine letterato of an earlier age – impracticality, excessively heterogeneous interests, false modesty, doctrinaire attitudes – while the former has those of the backward provincial erudito, a figure also associated with the past, even though, as Croce remarked in 1891, 'Even now each one of us knows many Don Fastidios!' (Anche ora, ognun di noi conosce tanti Don Fastidii!)[28]

Many contributions to the journal took the form of philological reve-
lations of lost communal meanings hidden in the names of urban
places.[29] Others, such as Ceci's article on the old churches slated for
demolition under the piano di Risanamento (a companion to his lengthy
treatise for the journal of the Società), appealed to civic spirit in the hope
of endowing endangered buildings and places with historical meaning,
thus transforming into monuments (sites of communal memory) ordinary things that might not otherwise have been considered as elements
of a shared cultural heritage.[30] Similarly, the chief political and ethical
purpose of Croce's (unsuccessful) appeal on behalf of the old via di
Porto neighbourhood, in his essay 'L'agonia di una strada,' was to discover, in the history of the place itself, a means by which to focus the
diverse cultural identities that, despite national unification, were pre-
venting bourgeoisie and aristocracy alike from uniting behind their
common interests on the regional level. The Porto was a neighbourhood
of the 'popolino,' but Croce argued that it was valuable to all citizens for
the 'intensa e caratteristica' expression of this life that it contributed to
the fabric of the city, especially for its past glory as one of the illustrious
streets of la vecchia Napoli, the 'biografia' of which could be reconstructed, from as far back as the early fourteenth century, in documents,
literature, and the spoken language of the people who lived there.[31]

A later controversy that further illuminates the cultural politics of
Napoli nobilissima in the 'practical' sphere is the case of the little
Baroque church of Santa Croce di Lucca, one of the buildings that was
threatened by the construction of the new university clinics on via dei
Tribunali. Over several years, Croce collaborated in an effort to save
the structure, writing articles defending its historical significance while
exposing the private motives of those (in his view, a group of Masonic
medical doctors) who would selfishly have deprived the citizens of one
of the 'monumenti che connettono la nostra vita a quella del passato.'[32] The decision to level the edifice, to make room for a regular and
spacious piazza in front of the new clinics, was attacked in newspapers on 6 July 1903 by 'un gruppo di amici dell'arte,' whose protest,
signed by Ceci, Croce, Schipa, Spinazzola, and others, was subsequently reprinted in a longer article written by Croce and collectively
signed 'La *Napoli nobilissima*.'[33] This was followed, again in the pages
of *Napoli nobilissima*, by a scholarly article from Alfonso Miola on the
history of the church's construction and interior decoration, and
another by Ceci that employed archival documents to establish more
precisely the names and activities of the various artists responsible, as

well as the relation of their work on this site to other *monumenti* in the city.[34] While these historians were in effect creating historical culture by weaving a net of relationships linking historical events and persons to contemporary urban spaces, Croce, in the guise of Don Fastidio, disseminated various journalistic and official statements supporting the cause. As the critical voice of *Napoli nobilissima*, and by extension, of the citizens of Naples, Don Fastidio proclaimed the success of their effort to give form and purpose to public consciousness, affirming that, despite their remaining enemies, the 'protest of the group of friends of art aganist the demolition of the Croce di Lucca has found a large consensus in the Neapolitan citizenry' (il più largo consenso ha trovato nella cittadinanza napoletana la protesta del gruppo di amici dell'arte contro l'abbattimento della Croce di Lucca).[35]

If the urban plan of reclamation seemed to be guided by forces indifferent to public interests (or at least could be represented that way), Croce's most heated polemic emerged from his profound distrust of the new official state institutions created for the administration and care of the regional artistic heritage. Croce thought that the Museo Nazionale di Napoli and two successive directors had failed in their public duties and had, out of negligence or perversity, served private interests instead. In 1900 he reported the 'scandalo' of a museum administration that had mysteriously allowed the removal of frescos from excavations at Boscoreale, thus putting them in grave danger of appropriation by the Italian state or of export out of the country. 'Think for a moment,' Croce satirically observed, 'these would be the first frescos from the Vesuvian region to appear in a foreign museum as testimony to the misery of the Italian resurrection!' (Si pensi un po': sarebbero questi i primi affreschi della regione vesuviana che comparirebbero in un museo straniero a testimoniare della miseria della risorta Italia!) From the same site, Croce complained, the negligence of Director Gilio de Petra's museum staff had already permitted ancient works in silver to escape to the Louvre.[36] De Petra's successor, Ettore Pais, was soon confronted with his own misdeeds against the *patria*, not the least of which was exporting native works of art to foreign museums, and in June 1904, after a year of severe criticism in *Napoli nobilissima*, Pais was dismissed from his post at the conclusion of a formal inquiry.[37]

Croce's contributions to the 'spiritual' history of Neapolitan culture and, more specifically, to the goal of laying the groundwork for a comprehensive history of art in the Mezzogiorno, are based mostly on literature, memoirs, and stories, including popular forms such as songs and legends and, less frequently, inscriptions and manuscript sources. Quite a few of these essays are literary evocations of storied places, such as 'La villa di Chiaia,' 'La tomba di Iacopo Sannazzaro,' and 'L'arco di S. Eligio,' many of which were later revised and republished in Croce's *Storie e leggende napoletane* (1919).[38] Most of his other contributions appeared under one of five rubrics, devoted to summarizing art-historical scholarship, unearthing literary sources for historical research, analysing inscriptions from monuments of the Spanish period, sketching biographies of remarkable persons, and explicating local cultural practices (*costume*).

The first series, *Sommario critico della storia dell'arte nel Napoletano*, was originally meant to be a comprehensive 'exposition of the history of art in the region of Naples, according to the results of the latest research' (esposizione della storia dell'arte nel napoletana, secondo risulta dalle ultime ricerche). This 'critical summary' was to have offered a periodized overview of southern Italian art, illustrated with photographs and drawings, beginning with early medieval times and extending through the eighteenth century, with each of five chronological divisions defined in terms of the foreign influences (such as Byzantine, Islamic, Tuscan, and Flemish) that characterized local artistic production in a given period. For reasons never explained at the time, Croce ended the series abruptly in the third volume, having briefly surveyed sacred architecture in the Mezzogiorno from the eleventh to the thirteenth century, largely on the basis of original research carried out earlier in the century by Heinrich Wilhelm Schulz.[39] It is clear that he intended this unfinished series, projected as a history of art up to the end of la vecchia Napoli (the Republican revolution of 1799), to be the skeleton of the patriotic book of Neapolitan art history envisioned in the programma of the journal.

The second of Croce's major rubrics, *Napoli nella descrizione dei poeti*, was to be the title for a future book that someone might wish to write, making use of the materials that Croce would reprint and annotate, drawn, in no particular order, from the texts of foreign and Italian poets and other writers who have described the appearance of the city and its people.[40] Like the *Sommario critico* series, this column seems to have exceeded the limits of Croce's interest before it produced a large body of results. A partial explanation may lie in the fact that in both rubrics Croce was advocating the study of art (whether visual or literary) as a product of culture, rather than as a primitive act of intuition – the position fully stated in the *Estetica* of 1902 but also anticipated, as is shown briefly below, in earlier writings of an art-historical character published in *Napoli nobilissima*.

The third rubric, *Memorie degli spagnuoli nella città di Napoli*, documented the history of Spanish domination through epigraphy, employing this modern tool of critical historical method to investigate via secondary scholarship (compilations of transcriptions) 'those traces remaining in the city of Naples, or rather in its material part, of the populous Spanish society established here and of its life and customs' (quali tracce restino nella città di Napoli, ossia nella parte materiale di essa, della numerosa società spagnuola che vi si stabilì e della sua vita e delle sue abitudini), from the Aragonese period to the seventeenth century.[41]

A fourth rubric initiated much later (in 1905) had the relatively open-ended title *Curiosità napoletane*. This short series makes no pretense of laying groundwork for any systematic history and consists of just five anecdotal appreciations of persons whose colourful lives intertwined with political and historical events of eighteenth- and (in the case of the first) nineteenth-century Europe and Naples – the Napoleonic historian Michele Cimorelli; the quasi-legendary Monsignor Filippo Perelli; the remarkable Englishwoman Sara Goudar; Carlo Carafa, duca di Maddaloni and friend of Casanova; and the poet and philosopher Onofrio Galeota – all of whom would reappear in Croce's *Anedotti di varia letteratura* (1942) and in one or more of his other collections of historical and biographical sketches.[42]

The fifth rubric, *Nota per la storia del costume*, confined to the final year of *Napoli nobilissima*, consists of three articles on diverse cultural practices: a Neapolitan game of Spanish origin, divorce in the nineteenth century, and the life of an old tavern known as Cerriglio.[43] It seems clear that as time went by Croce's own contributions to the journal, while not declining in frequency, did become less programmatic and more miscellaneous.

Regarding the patriotic book of art history, Croce's most sustained efforts in the *Sommario critico* series consisted of additions to historical knowledge (of the sort mentioned above) as well as strategic subtractions and revisions. In other words, the creation of a cultural heritage for modern Naples required not only dissemination of up-to-date, critically tested art-historical knowledge but also erasure of an obsolete history of art that already existed. The task of eliminating this precedent body of tradition was not directly mentioned in the programma, but the necessity of correcting the old historical record and of purifying art-historical sources of inherited 'falsehoods' emerged almost immediately as a major justification for the journal's work. Croce himself supplied what might be called the enabling argument for the negative side of *Napoli nobilissima's* research project with the opening essay of the *Sommario critico* series. This essay, subtitled 'Il Falsario,' offered a sweeping condemnation of the author of the eighteenth-century *Vite* of the Neapolitan artists, a minor landscape painter and Arcadian poet named Bernardo De Dominici (1683–1759), whose book, patriotically reprinted in the 1840s, had become the first source of art-historical information for virtually all of the politically inspired history writing of the Risorgimento and post-Unification periods.[44] De Dominici's book had originally been written to promote Republican political and cultural goals under the Austrian viceroys and, after 1734, under the administration of Carlo di Borbone, and his strident appeals to local patriotism could only have sounded like reactionary *campanilismo*, or *municipalismo*, or *autonomismo* to Croce's generation of Liberals.[45] De Sanctis, Croce's single most important mentor in matters of cultural politics, had argued that regionalism was the scourge of Italy, and De Dominici's influence among old-fashioned localists was everywhere apparent in scholarly and popular writing alike. As Croce asserted in the opening lines of 'Il falsario,' 'It is not possible to attempt an exact treatment of the history of art in our provinces without first removing from between your feet the work and the authority of the *falsario*, of the poisoner of the sources of this history, of Bernardo De Dominici' (Non è possibile tentare una trattazione esatta della storia dell'arte nelle nostre provincie, senza prima togliersi di tra i piedi l'opera e l'autorità del *falsario*, dell'avvelenatore dei fonti di questa storia, di Bernardo De Dominici).[46] Much of the *Napoli nobilissima* project was hence given over to the authorization of older sources for the history of art, such as guidebooks, descriptions, manuscripts, and archival documents – sources that were far more recondite but demonstrably untainted by De Dominici's distortion of history *ad maiorem gloriam patriae*. Croce himself contributed articles summarizing the contents of the early art-historical sources and published extracts from manuscript sources of (more or less) proven reliability.[47] Modern literature in which De Dominici's history had been unknowingly or uncritically incorporated also received detailed analysis, as with Croce's impressively erudite expurgation of Burckhardt's *Cicerone*, or even ridicule, as in the case of Don Fastidio's rather satirical obituary of Raffaele d'Ambra (1814–1892), one of the old-fashioned historians of Naples whose writing was regarded as too narrowly preoccupied with local events and lacking in rigorous historical method.[48] In a similar vein, Croce attacked the unscientific handling of sources and uncritically Romantic appreciations of historical places and monuments found in the books of popularizing authors such as Carlo Tito Dalbono (1817–1880), another writer of the Risorgimento generation and one who had served on the Commissione municipale per la conservazione dei monumenti but whom Croce's circle dismissed as one of the 'pseudostoriografi napoletani' for his quasi-fictional stories of the past, often claimed to represent the voices of the common people.[49]

What then became of the *Sommario* series, the critical art-historical project that was apparently to have been the basis for the patriotic history of Neapolitan art envisioned at the conception of *Napoli nobilissima*? Years later, in his review of the first volume of Émile Bertaux's *L'art dans l'Italie méridionale* (1904) Croce explained that the project in its short life had soon inspired just the sort of art-historical scholarship for which he had called and having therefore run its course 'passed into the hands of much more competent specialists' (passata nelle mani di specialisti ben più competenti).[50] However, the work of such 'specialists' as the French medievalist Bertaux was not at all comparable to the patriotic historical survey of Neapolitan art that had been one of Croce's initial goals for *Napoli nobilissima*, and it was certainly not art history for the general reader, as the articles of the *Sommario* series had been. Indeed, there must have been other reasons for Croce's abandonment of this major art-historical project of the journal.

The most intellectually ambitious art-historical contributions that Croce wrote for *Napoli nobilissima* are articles conceived in response to recent books. In one of these, printed in 1896 on the occasion of Antonio Filangieri di Candida's publication of the *Diario* of the sixteenth-century sculptor Annibale Caccavello, Croce presented a very conventional account of the artist's surviving works, mainly tomb sculptures, with examinations of their historical contexts, patronage, inscriptions, and iconography. Only at the very end do we find evidence of the Croce who would later write the *Estetica*. Here, Croce very briefly criticized Filangieri for ignoring the 'personalità' and 'valore artistico' of the sculptor, whose work he himself found *practical* but not *artistically* significant.[51] The distinction between the practical and the artistic is of course fundamental to Croce's mature aesthetics, and it is the separation of art, as an autonomous human activity, as a primitive act of intuition, from the externalities of social history, biography, technique, religion, politics, and economics that would eventually make 'art history' a virtual oxymoron from Croce's point of view.

We are indeed much closer to this position in an essay of 1899 titled 'Una questione di criterio nella storia artistica.' In this piece Croce deliberately entered into a polemic then raging between the ecclesiastical historian Baldassarre Labanco and the art historian Adolfo Venturi over whether one could write a proper history of the image of the Madonna in visual art.[52] Venturi had written a book on the Madonna in art, and Labanco had replied that a history of her image could only be a religious history. As Luigi Russo has emphasized, Croce's intervention in this polemic represents an advanced stage of his early aesthetic thinking and is the most notable anticipation of his major methodological study of the visual arts in *La critica e la storia delle arti figurative* (1934).[53] A religious history, Croce argued, *contra* Venturi and in agreement with Labanco, might use paintings of the Madonna, but these could be considered only as documents of religion, not as art. Venturi's book is not a proper history of art, since a chronological survey of such images, made in different epochs by different artists, does not shed any light on art as such. The principle of selection is arbitrary and external to artistic considerations. The topic, the Madonna, is not artistically meaningful, for it is an abstraction that robs the individual works of their concrete reality. Because artistic content, as such, is the form-giving emotion of an individual maker, a Byzantine Madonna, a Madonna by Fra Angelico, and another by Raphael have nothing *artistic* in common, for the animating spirit is different in each case. Although the Madonna is indeed a conventional subject, there is no repetition where *art* as such is concerned, since even a copy would be an interpretation by another artist and hence another work of art. The terms of Croce's argument in 'Una questione di criterio nella storia artistica' may not really allow for a history of Neapolitan art of the kind envisioned in the original program of *Napoli nobilissima*. Here Croce concluded that a proper study of art should be limited to a single work, or to the works of a single artist, or to the art of a particular period, or be cast in terms of a general history of art.

It seems clear that by this time he already doubted the validity of diachronic approaches to the art of a particular region or nation. After all, how could one now write a history of *art* in southern Italy organized around the *influences* of Byzantine, Islamic, Tuscan, Flemish, or North Italian culture? As Croce would later write when commenting on one of the first stylistic histories of Italian art (that of Lionello Venturi, presented in lectures at the University of Turin in 1915), 'art in itself being always individual, universal and supra-national' (essendo l'arte in quanto arte sempre individuale e sempre universale, e perciò sempre sopranazionale), the history of the art of a nation would represent 'not an aesthetic but an ethical development' (uno svolgimento non estetico ma etico).[54] Thus we can see that the doubts about erudite regional history that led Croce to abandon *Napoli nobilissima* at the point when regional studies seemed insufficient for a modern, philosophical historiography must have accompanied doubts about the possibility of a history of Neapolitan art. For, once Croce began to think of art not as something allied with history and distinct from philosophy but rather as something essentially prior to material culture, the art-historical mission of *Napoli nobilissima*, with its emphasis on the external conditions of art, would have seemed intellectually impoverished and bound up with postitivist aesthetics.

If the founding of the journal represented, as I have suggested, the expansion of Croce's commitment to regional history and erudite historical method into the public sphere, beyond the world of the Società napoletana di Storia Patria, it did not diminish his ambivalence about the value of such work, and he continued to feel tension between his developing idealism and his customary practice as a historian. In the context of the same review of Émile Bertaux's *L'art dans l'Italie méridionale* mentioned above, written in 1904, the year after he began to distance himself from the day-to-day affairs of *Napoli nobilissima*, Croce commemorated the journal's leading role in stimulating art-historical scholarship throughout the Mezzogiorno, as well as its civic function of disseminating specialized knowledge while uprooting the prejudices and the falsehoods that grew from De Dominici's *Vite dei pittori, scultori ed architetti napoletani*. This 'small monthly review,' he affirmed, 'still has not lost the favour of the public.'[55] However, only two years later, when he wrote the farewell address for the final issue of *Napoli nobilissima*, Croce declared this very same readership a thing of the past. 'But fifteen years have passed,' he wrote, 'and now the condition not only of scholarship but of souls has changed. The loving, if excessively minute and rather gossipy, investigations of municipal history no longer rouse the interest they did before. We have lost, in this respect, many readers, not because they have deliberately abandoned us, but because ... they are dead and have not been replaced: the young have other interests and inclinations.' (Ma son passati quindici anni; e ora la condizione non solo degli studii, ma degli animi, è mutata. Le amorose, ma troppo minute e alquanto pettegole, indagini di storia municipale, non destano l'interesse di una volta. Noi abbiamo perduto, sotto questo rispetto, molti lettori, non perchè essi ci abbiano deliberatamente abbandonati, ma perchè

... Sono morti, e non sono stati sostituiti: i giovani hanno altri interessi e tendenze.)[56] But as Raffaele Ajello has recently argued, Croce's characterization of *Napoli nobilissima* was hardly accurate, and his disparagement of municipal history reflected his own repudiation of *la storia regionale* more than any change in the interests of younger scholars and readers. This identification of his personal disillusionment with the attitudes of his readers is one instance of Croce's idealist transposition of the details of his own life into universal terms, or of what Ajello has called the 'Crocean exigency to discredit the past in order to give reason to his personal development at the turn of the century and to feel himself fully engaged with Italian and European culture' (l'esigenza crociana di screditare il passato per dare un senso alla sua svolta personale di fine secolo e per sentirsi appieno inserito nella cultura italiana ed europea).[57]

In addition to other instances that Ajello describes, one can find a similar reductionism in the preface of 1918 to the first edition of the *Primi saggi*, in which Croce went so far as to claim that 'the value ... of the writings I now reprint without alteration lies precisely in documenting, I will not say ... a moment of my intellectual life, but a moment of the life of learning in our age, and in Italy' (il pregio ... degli scritti, che ora ristampo inalterati, sta appunto nel documentare, non dirò ... un momento della mia vita intellettuale, ma un momento della vita degli studî nell'età nostra, e in Italia).[58] But what this particular gathering of essays documents far more fully than the complex history of positivism in Italy is the consistency of Croce's own opposition to a whole range of modern ideas that he termed positivistic.[59] To cite one other example, Croce's history of Marxist theory in Italy, 'Come nacque e come morì il marxismo teorico in Italia (1895–1900),' first published in 1938, similarly presents a widespread and diverse cultural phenomenon as if it were reducible – in its chronological dimensions – to the terms of his own personal engagement with the problem, which indeed began in 1895 under the tutelage of Antonio Labriola and definitively ended in 1900 with the publication of his *Materialismo storico ed economia marxistica*.[60]

At least from the beginning of the 1890s Croce was often defensive about his devotion to regional history and to its traditional erudite methods, particularly when this activity conflicted with his ambition to become known as a philosopher. His defensiveness was no doubt sharpened by stinging reviews of his early erudite work in the methodologically advanced journals, such as the *Giornale storico della letteratura italiana*, where in 1892, for example, Michele Scherillo described him as a 'chronicler' 'but not a historian and much less a man of letters' (ma non è uno storico e tanto meno un letterato).[61] It could not have helped either that Labriola, his first mentor in many modern ideas, particularly in German philosophy, chided him (just after Croce had invited him to lecture before the Circolo filologico) for taking irrelevant delight in historical erudition, given that one should be concerned with the present and that 'Il socialismo non ha niente che fare con la erudizione.'[62] When giving an account of his work in the distinguished *Revue de synthèse historique* in 1902, just prior to assigning editorial responsibility for *Napoli nobilissima* to Fausto Nicolini, Croce omitted to mention the essentially erudite, regional character of his earliest studies, claiming that up to the time of his first publications on historical method, beginning with *La storia ridotta* of 1893, he had occupied himself 'with researches on political and literary history' (m'occupant à cette époque des recherches relatives à l'histoire politique et littéraire).[63]

However, we get a good look at Croce's dividedness over the conflicting claims of old-fashioned research topics and method and of more modern and intellectually prestigous endeavours during the bitter aftermath of his polemical theoretical treatise of 1894, *La critica letteraria*. Having been attacked for that work in a pamphlet by Raffaele Trojano, who remarked that he was neither philosopher nor critic, but a mere historian of Naples, Croce apologized for his erudite historical researches: 'I could say that my true studies have always been philosophy and literature. I *have been* a historian, and a historian of Naples, for one reason only: that in Naples, one of the few centres of learning, one of the few living organisms, is the Società napoletana di Storia Patria. Among those dear friends was born my love for the things of Naples' (Io potrei dire che i mei studii veri sono state sempre quelli di filosofia e di letteratura. Io *ho fatto* lo storico, e lo storico di Napoli per una sola ragione: che a Napoli, uno dei pochi centri di studio, uno dei pochi organismi vivi, è la *Società napoletana di storia patria*. Tra quegli amici carissimi mi è nato l'amore per le cose napoletane).[64] This apology reveals the tension that existed between the various forms of Croce's researches in the 1890s while indicating the emotional and social nature of his attachment to the older scholars who represented the ideals of the Risorgimento (the mentors of the *Napoli nobilissima* group), which conflicted with his growing ambition to join the international debates in philosophy and criticism stimulated by his encounter with Labriola and German aesthetics.

In the private setting of the 'Curriculum vitae' written in 1902, Croce's retrospective account of the period 1886–91 (devoted 'quasi esclusivamente ai lavori di storia napoletana') gives the erudite circle of the Società napoletana di Storia Patria centre place in his daily life: 'I was spurred by the welcome received in the Società ... where I found my studies greatly facilitated, and, what is more, dearest friendships with disinterested, enthusiastic, loyal gentlemen' (fui spinto a ciò dalle accoglienze ricevute nella Società ... dove trovai agevolazioni grandi negli studii, e, quel ch'è più, amicizie carissime di galantuomini disinteressati, entusiasti, leali). The closest were Bartolommeo Capasso and Giuseppe De Blasiis, prime movers of the organization; Ludovico de la Ville sur-Yllon (librarian of the Società, to whom Croce dedicated his *Curiosità storiche* of 1919 in memory of their collaboration on *Napoli nobilissima*); and Giustino Fortunato.[65] The tone of Croce's remembrances is distinctly less warm in the more public *Contributo* of 1915. There he described his friends condescendingly as 'worthy, gentle souls, old or middle-aged men for the most part, not much given to thinking' (onesta e buona e mite gente, uomini vecchi o maturi i più, che non avevano l'abito del troppo pensare).[66] The apparent contradiction results largely from the fact that the later autobiographical text is much more concerned with establishing the trajectory of Croce's development as a philosopher of *la nuova Italia* and thus tends to discount the emotional and social values that were inseparable from his life as historian of *la vecchia Napoli*.

In order to understand more fully the interrelated phenomena of Croce's repudiation of erudite regional historiography, his disaffection with the *Napoli nobilissima* project, and his subsequent tendency to minimize the importance of those years, it is helpful to look more closely at Croce's relations with the Società napoletana di Storia Patria and Bartolommeo Capasso. This greatly respected scholar and moral leader in post-Unification historical studies had hailed the advent of *Napoli nobilissima* as the renewal of the patriotic mission of his own generation. In his annual address to the Società in April 1892, Capasso acknowledged the passing of 'la vecchia falange' and proclaimed the new: 'How fortunate that their example does not lie sterile and that young men, tireless and full of patriotic love, are going ahead ... We salute them with joy. We salute – *Napoli nobilissima*' (Fortuna che l'esempio non resta infecondo e che giovani infaticabili e pieni di amor patrio si fanno innanzi ... Noi li salutiamo con gioia. Salutiamo – *Napoli nobilissima*).[67] Eight years later, for this same journal, Croce would write the obituary both of Capasso and of regional historiography in a controversial essay titled 'Il Capasso e la storia regionale' (1900). This was, as Emilio Gabba has recently char-

acterized it, an 'affectionate but certainly reductive evaluation' of
Capasso's work as that of a 'superseded historical phase.'[68] The essay
marks a profound revision in Croce's attitude towards both the study of
the past and his own self-conception as a historian.

In December 1885 the young Croce, not yet twenty, returned to Naples
without having completed his law degree but with the approval of his
guardian and tutor Silvio Spaventa, a cousin of his father and a distinguished Cavourian patriot who had served in the government of the
Destra storica before its collapse in 1876.[69] Very soon after his return,
Croce's name appeared on the roll of *soci promotori* of the Società napoletana.[70] By this time he had already made a name for himself as an *erudito* and been in contact at least once with Capasso, president of the
Società, through the agency of his uncle Giuseppe Ferrarelli (1831–
1921).[71] It is very likely that Ferrarelli, a former official of the Bourbon
government and a man whose soul was divided (like that of many who
came of age during the Risorgimento) between *italianità* and *napoletanità*,
had a hand in shaping Croce's own divided identity, teaching him to
honour local tradition and to feel the burden of the *patrimonio artistico*
while pondering the ethical-political problem of enlarging regional into
national patriotism.[72] An inspiration for Ferrarelli's dual commitment to
national and local patriotism was De Sanctis, whose writings and personal example were fundamental to Croce's own sense of his historical
mission as a politically minded public intellectual.

Having been nominated and promoted to *socio* of Capasso's Società
in 1886, Croce eventually produced long, erudite articles for its journal,
the *Archivio storico per le provincie napoletane*.[73] The first was the mas-
sively documented study of Neapolitan theatres, one of a series of such
reports from the archives later melded into what Croce termed 'la lunga
cronistoria' of *I teatri di Napoli* (1891).[74] In 1890 Croce joined Capasso and
Giuseppe De Blasiis as the third member of the Consiglio direttivo of the
Società and began his long tenure in the office of *Segretario generale*.[75] In
this capacity he read annual reports to the assembled members,
recounted their individual and collective achievements of the previous
year, and announced plans for the next. The *relazione* prepared for
12 January 1901 marked the twenty-fifth anniversary of the founding of
the Società, and it accordingly sets forth a short history of the institution,
which Croce used as the context for one of his more important statements about the intellectual and political status of regional historiography.[76] It is at best an ambivalent defence of historical method and

regional history and something of an apology for the repudiation of Capasso's school of history he had written the year before in 'Il Capasso e la storia regionale.' There Croce had declared, in rather summary fashion, that, along with the mortal frame of Capasso, 'con lui è morta per sempre la storia regionale della vecchia Napoli e del vecchio Regno,' presenting his former mentor as the symbol of la vecchia Napoli, as the embodiment of an obsolete school of history hopelessly mired in promoting the glories of the old order.[77] With a rather sweeping gesture, Croce virtually equated regional history with *municipalismo*, ignoring the broader national and European scope of much of Capasso's work as well as his international reputation. Giuseppppe Galasso has suggested that this essay points to a gulf that had grown between Capasso, the man of la vecchia Napoli, and Croce, the man of la nuova Italia – a separation that Galasso nevertheless thinks was bridged by solidarity of feeling and communion of memory.[78] With equal justness, Angelo Russi has argued that Croce was trying to distance himself from both regionalismo and municipalismo by lumping all forms of regional history together and declairing them collectively dead, whereas Raffaele Ajello, as mentioned above, has taken the position that Croce, by now an Idealist, was rather aggressively translating the facts of his own personality, his own turn towards the history of the 'spirit' of the Nation, into universal terms, at the expense of Capasso and regional historians.[79]

Given Croce's rough treatment of the beloved Capasso and the broad aspersions he had cast on the validity of the group's research, the relazione of 1901 might well have had some patching-up to do. In this paper, Croce touched generally on the regional Italian historical societies and their ability or inability to promote research on the modern periods, which he considered more relevant to contemporary life than their typical investigations of ancient and medieval history. He singled out *Napoli nobilissima* as one of the more successful projects 'indirettamente' promoted by the Società, and reinstates Capasso, buried the previous year, as a 'sort of spirit present in our Società' (egli resta però sempre quasi spirito presente in questa nostra Società).[80] While reviewing the current state of scholarship, Croce did not fail to indicate the criticisms offered by higher forms of *Wissenschaft*: that the arguments of regional history are unworthy of Science, are repetitive, and are motivated by campanilismo and provincialismo. But instead of simply agreeing with this view, Croce now set regional history in favourable opposition to the pretensions of positivist historiography, which assumes 'una *falsa analogia*' between the methods of history and those of the abstract sciences and fails to respect the particularity of historical knowledge. Regional history is justified by virtue of its demonstrable commitment to particulars.[81]

Perhaps the most interesting aspect of the paper is the distinction that Croce restored between culturally backward regionalismo and the politically beneficial brand of regional history practised by the Società and the popularizing *Napoli nobilissima*. Historical methods and subjects of inquiry have changed, he affirmed, 'But it must also be recognized that the work of the Società has always been done on an elevated plain, sheltered from foolish regionalism ... and from gossipy local erudition. It has been honest critical work, Liberal and Italian. This must be granted to us all, Gentlemen – the knowledge that we have not yet joined forces with the timewasters, the more-or-less fanatical collectors of old stuff and curiosities, but like *homines bonae voluntatis* we pursue a civil task' (Ma dovrà riconoscere anche che l'opera della Società si è tenuta sempre in un campo elevato, rifuggente dallo sciocco regionalismo ... e dalla pettegola erudizione locale. È stata opera di critica onesta, liberale, italiana. Questo deve dare a tutti noi, o Signori, la coscienza che non abbiamo già congiunte le nostre forze come dei perditempo, collezionisti più o meno fanatici di anticaglie e di curiosità, ma come *homines bonae voluntatis* che proseguono un'opera civile.[82] In drawing this distinction, Croce seems to have turned once more to the political values of Enlightenment erudition, by borrowing the distinction that Muratori drew in *Della pubblica felicità* (1749) between the dry, sterile kind of erudition that can be poison to the body politic and another that is *onesta* because it serves to promote the advantages of the republic.[83]

None of Croce's autobiographical writings reports very much about his involvement with either the Circolo filologico or the much larger *Napoli nobilissima* project, and it is evident, particularly in the *Contributo alla critica di me stesso*, written in 1915, that he took retrospective pains to construct his personal philosophical destiny at the expense of his life as either an erudite follower of Capasso or as a civic-minded public intellectual in the De Sanctis mould. According to this version, with his return to Naples in 1886 he traded the bitterness and turmoil of Roman political circles for the serene company of librarians, archivists, scholars, and antiquaries, those old or middle-aged men 'not much given to thinking,' and, like theirs, his own activity was given up to antiquarian research, while the 'politics of my country was a mere spectacle which I watched with no intention of active participation and very little in the way of feelings or opinions' (la politica del mio paese

mi stava innanzi come spettacolo al quale non mai mi proposi di parte-
cipare con l'azione, e pochissimo vi partecipavo col sentimento e col
giudizio).[84]

The opposition that Croce created in the *Contributo* between his true
course in life (philosophy) and the almost incidental years of humble,
disinterested *storia locale*, develops further as we read that the 'philosophical questionings of my youth had been driven into a dark recess of
my spirit,' while 'I was for six years, from 1886 to 1892, wholly turned
towards the outer world, I mean toward erudite studies' (Le speculazioni filosofiche della mia adolescenza erano ricacciate in un cantuccio
dell'animo; io per sei anni, dall '86 al '92, fui tutto versato nell'esterno,
cioè nelle ricerche di erudizione).[85] This work, which included his early
studies of the Neapolitan republican revolution of 1799, the chronicles of
the theatres of Naples, the introduction and notes to a projected edition
of Giambattista Basile's *Cunto de li cunti*, and the founding of *Napoli nobilissima*, he reduced to 'the narrow and trivial limits of municipal history'
(ristretto e pettegolo circolo della storia municipale), as if this labour
prevented him from doing something more serious that would 'rise to
the height of national history.' In this account, he described his continuing devotion to regional history as 'tiring myself with learning, with
effort and without meaningful result, lifeless and disconnected facts'
(mi stancai d'imparare, con fatica e senza costrutto, notizie sconnesse e
inanimate), effectively denying the larger cultural and political implications of that research, not to mention *Napoli nobilissima* and the extension
of that work into the public sphere.

In the *Contributo* Croce's aim was rather to give greater significance to
his participation as a young man in the philosophical debate over historical knowledge. Thus he structured the narrative of his intellectual autobiography around the critical moment or turning point that allowed him
to discover this true path. Having found himself 'brought by degrees to
the problem of the nature of history and of knowledge' (mi trovai via via
condotto al problema della natura della storia e della scienza), he was
able to compose his first philosophical essay, *La storia ridotta sotto il concetto generale dell'arte*, read before the Accademia Pontaniana in March
1893. This essay, he affirmed, 'was a kind of revelation to me of my own
self' (fu come una rivelazione di me a me stesso), while the next important one, the polemical booklet of 1894, *La critica letteraria*, confirmed
him in his new path as 'un atto insomma di liberazione personale' from
his training in erudite historical method and philology.[86]

Thus we can see that the story of Croce's intellectual development in the *Contributo* is the 'history of liberty' written on the scale of an individual life, for it presents the awakening and progress of his essential, philosophical nature against the accident of social circumstances that for a time distracted him with superficial interests in archival research, editing, source criticism, and the collecting of folklore and historical anecdotes. The point of this last observation is not that the *Contributo* gives a false history, but only that, as an idealization of Croce's intellectual development, it tends to suppress the complexity and unresolved contradictions of his life.

NOTES

I am grateful to Dain Trafton for his very helpful and extensive comments on an earlier draft of this essay. I also wish to thank Victor Miesel and Tommaso Astarita for their interest in the subject and for the many corrections and elucidations that resulted from their criticisms.

1 Exceptions can be found, for instance, in the writings of Roberto Pane and Giulio Pane. More recently, the Crocean cultural politics of the journal has been considered by scholars such as Giuseppe Brescia, 'Benedetto Croce, studioso di storia locale,' *Nuovi studi politici* 8 (1978), 111–19; Raffaele Ajello, 'Benedetto Croce e la storia "ideale" nel Regno di Napoli,' *Archivio storico per le province napoletane* 110 (1992), esp. 409–14; and Toni Iermano, 'Croce e il "Fanfulla della domenica": Collaborazioni e polemiche (1888–1898),' in his *Lo scrittoio di Croce, con scritti inediti e rari* (Naples: Fausto Fiorentino, 1992), 79–110. My discussion of the journal's civic character takes up several indications offered in Giulio Pane's essay 'Benedetto Croce e Napoli Nobilissima,' *Napoli nobilissima* 3rd series 17 (1978), 14–20.

2 Croce's impact on European art history is only touched on in Udo Kultermann, *The History of the History of Art* (Pleasantville, NY: Abaris Books, 1993). For a summary account of Croce's influence in Italy, see Gilles A. Tiberghien, '*Esthétique critique* et histoire de l'art en Italie,' *Les cahiers du Musée national d'Art moderne* no. 44 (summer 1993), 5–17. Croce's importance for German art history has received still less attention, but see Joseph Gantner, 'Erinnerungen an Heinrich Wölfflin und Benedetto Croce,' *Jahrbuch für Aesthetik und allgemeine Kunstwissenschaft*, 3 (1955–7), 129–52; Otto Kurz, 'Julius von Schlosser, personalità, metodo, lavoro,' *Critica d'arte* 2, nos. 11–12 (1955), 402–19; Sergio Bettini, 'Introduzione,' in Julius Von Schlosser, *Sull'antica storiografia italiana dell'arte*, trans. Maria Ortiz (Vicenza: Neri Pozza editore, 1969), 7–37; Andreas Beyer, '"Pfadfindung einer zukünftigen Kunsthistoriogra-

phie": Julius von Schlosser, Benedetto Croce und Roberto Longhi,' *Kritische Berichte* no. 4 (1988), 24–8.

3 The *Contributo* was written in 1915, first printed in one hundred copies *fuori commercio* in 1918 and reprinted many times. I refer to the latest edition: *Contributo alla critica di me stesso*, ed. Giuseppe Galasso (Milan: Adelphi edizioni, 1989). For all quotations in English I refer, with occasional modifications, to R.G. Collingwood's translation: *An Autobiography* (Oxford: Clarendon Press, 1927).

4 The full title of the latter review is *Poliorama pittoresco: Opera periodica diretta a spandere in tutte le classi della società utili conoscenze di ogni genere e a rendere gradevoli e proficue le letture in famiglia*, published in Naples 1836–60. I restrict my discussion of *Napoli nobilissima* to the contents of the first series (1892–1906), in which Croce and Giuseppe Ceci served as de facto co-directors. The subtitle of the first series, *Rivista di topografia ed arte napoletana*, was modified to *Rivista d'arte e di topografia napoletana* for the brief second series (1920–2), directed by Giuseppe Ceci and Aldo De Rinaldis. Both the third series (1961–86), directed by Roberto Pane, and the fourth series, begun in 1987 under the direction of Raffaele Mormone, employ a subtitle reflecting more recent disciplinary categories: *Rivista de arti figurative, archeologia e urbanistica*. For the 'program' of the modern journal, see Roberto Pane, 'Rinasce Napoli nobilissima,' 3rd series 1 (1961), i–iii; Roberto Pane and Raffaele Mormone, 'Napoli nobilissima: un quarto di secolo,' 3rd series 24 (1985), 2–5; and Raffaele Mormone, 'Napoli nobilissima: Serie quarta,' 4th series 27 (1988), 3, where Mormone reaffirms Pane's interpretation of the mission envisioned by Croce: 'ricerca filologica di prima mano, comunicazione, didattica e impegno civile.'

5 *Giambattista Basile: Archivio di letteratura popolare*, 11 vols. (Naples, 1883–1907). For a few comments on Croce's relations with this journal see Fausto Nicolini, *Il Croce minore* (Milan and Naples: Riccardo Ricciardi, 1963), 66–7. See also Domenico Novacco, 'Appunti su Benedetto Croce studioso delle tradizioni popolari napoletane,' *Belfagor* 5 no. 5 (1950), 563–73.

6 For this account of the journal's origin, see Benedetto Croce, 'Ai lettori, Commiato,' *Napoli nobilissima* 15, nos. 11–12 (1906), 175–6. The main title of Parrino's guidebook (or rather, *descrizione*) is *Napoli città nobilissima, antica, e fedelissima, esposta agli occhi, ed alla mente degli studiosi* (Naples: Parrino, 1700).

7 Benedetto Croce, review of Èmile Bertaux, *L'art dans l'Italie méridionale*, in *La critica* 2 (1904), 204: 'Allorché, tredici anni fa, il recensente con alcuni suoi amici – artisti, letterati, eruditi, dilettanti, riuniti dall'amore dell'arte e dal culto delle memorie storiche – fondò a Napoli una piccola rivista mensile, cui non è mancato finora il favore del pubblico.'

8 Di Giacomo in fact was writing to complain about the summary manner in

which he had been relieved of the job of *amministratore* and to blame Croce for the discourtesy; for the letter, dated 1 December 1892, see Gino Doria, 'Croce e di Giacomo. Lettere e documenti inediti,' *Archivio storico per le province napoletane* 73 (1955), 448. The letter also confirms that Di Giacomo originated the idea of the journal. On their relations, see also Fausto Nicolini, 'Di alcuni amici e frequentatori di Benedetto Croce,' *Bollettino dell'Archivio Storico del Banco di Napoli* 2 no. 7 (1954), especially 245–56; Toni Iermano, 'Un amicizia difficile: Croce e Di Giacomo,' in his *Il melanconico in dormiveglia: Salvatore Di Giacomo* (Florence: Olschki, 1995), 205–24.

9 As Croce would later (in 1902) describe events, 'la direzione dopo un poco cadde interamente su di me e sull'amico Ceci'; see Croce's 'Curriculum vitae' (dated 10 April 1902), published in *Memorie della mia vita. Appunti che sono stati adoprati e sostituiti dal 'Contributo alla critica di me stesso'* (Naples: Istituto Italiano per gli Studi Storica, 1966), 18. On his relations with Ceci, see Nicolini, 'Di alcuni amici e frequentatori di Benedetto Croce,' 256–65; and Giuseppe Brescia, 'Giuseppe Ceci, Benedetto Croce e Giustino Fortunato,' in his *Croce inedito (1881–1952)* (Naples: Società editrice napoletana, 1984), 449–528.

10 See Nicolini's autobiographical remarks in *Il Croce minore*, 17, 194–5.

11 Benedetto Croce, 'Curriculum vitae,' 5–23; see 15 for the quotation regarding Croce's 'bisogno di una vita intellettiva più intensa' in this period. See also the autobiographical comments that Croce included in the overview essay 'Les études relatives à la théorie de l'histoire en Italie, durant les quinze dernières années,' *Revue de synthèse historique* 5 (1902); reprinted in *Primi saggi*, 2nd ed. (Bari: Laterza, 1927), 181. For an instructive comparison of the 'Curriculum vitae' with the more polished *Contributo* of 1915, see Giuseppe Galasso's 'Nota del Curatore' in Croce, *Contributo*, 111–12.

12 Iermano, 'Croce e il "Fanfulla della domenica",' 93. Croce's essay was read before the Accademia Pontaniana on 5 March and published later that year in the *Atti della Accademia Pontaniana* 23 (1893), *memoria VII*.

13 'Curriculum vitae,' 17 ('Il 1892 segna per me il principio di una vita più intensa'); cf. Croce's *Contributo*, 29–31. On this moment in Croce's development, see David D. Roberts, *Benedetto Croce and the Uses of Historicism* (Berkeley: University of California Press, 1987), 36; Charles Boulay, *Benedetto Croce jusqu'en 1911* (Geneva: Librairie Droz, 1981), 90. Croce's retrospective rewriting of his philosophical concerns of the early 1890s, particularly with regard to the Idealist anti-positivism that came later, has been examined recently by Gino Bedani, 'Art, Poetry and Science: Theory and Rhetoric in Croce's Early Anti-Positivist Epistemology,' *Italian Studies* 44 (1994), 91–110.

14 See the valuable study by Toni Iermano, 'Il giovane Croce e il Circolo filolo-

gico di Napoli: Materiali per una storia,' in his *Lo scrittoio di Croce, con scritti inediti e rari* (Naples: Fausto Fiorentino, 1992), 13–77. On De Sanctis's activity as political educator and cultural organizer, see also Luigi Russo, *Francesco De Sanctis e la cultura napoletana*, 3rd ed. (Florence: Sansoni, 1959), 339–82; and Denis Mack Smith, 'Francesco De Sanctis: The Politics of a Literary Critic,' in John A. Davis and Paul Ginsborg, eds., *Society and Politics in the Age of the Risorgimento: Essays in Honour of Denis Mack Smith* (Cambridge: Cambridge University Press, 1991), 251–70.

15 Francesco De Sanctis, 'Il discorso per la istituzione del Circolo Filologico di Napoli (1876),' in *Commemorazione di Francesco De Sanctis nel primo centenario della nascita* (Naples: Università di Napoli, 1917), 91–2.

16 Iermano, 'Il giovane Croce,' 25–34. For the little-known *Annuario del Circolo filologico* (Naples: Tocco, 1894), see also Francesco Bruni, ed., *Benedetto Croce e la cultura a Napoli nel secondo Ottocento* (exhibit catalogue) (Naples: Gaetano Macchiaroli, 1983), 37–8, no. VI.9.

17 On the factionalism of educated and learned culture in Naples, see Guido Oldrini, *La cultura filosofica napoletana dell'Ottocento* (Rome and Bari: Laterza editori, 1973); Paolo Macry, 'La Napoli dei dotti: Lettori, libri e biblioteche di una ex-capitale (1870–1900),' in *Meridiana* no. 4 (1988), 131–61; 'Le élites urbane: Stratificazione e mobilità sociale, le forme del potere locale e la cultura dei ceti emergenti,' in Angelo Massafra, ed., *Il Mezzogiorno preunitario: Economia, società e istituzioni* (Bari: Edizioni Dedalo, 1988), 799–820. For an overview incorporating Macry's work on the conflicted relations of Neapolitan elites, see Lucy Riall, *The Italian Risorgimento: State, Society and National Unification* (London: Routledge, 1994), 29–49.

18 Fiammetta Rutoli, 'Gli scrittori e l'anima antimoderna del Sud,' *Nord e sud* n.s. 41, nos. 7–8 (1994), 96–9; for a different view of Croce's position regarding southern backwardness, see Roberts, *Benedetto Croce*, 8–22.

19 Raffaele Ajello, 'Benedetto Croce e la storia "ideale,"' 411. In thus characterizing the journal, Ajello may exaggerate a bit, but Croce and his colleagues clearly did position themselves as spokesmen for Liberal Neapolitan identity.

20 'Ai nostri benevoli lettori,' *Napoli nobilissima* 1 nos. 1–2 (1892), 1–2. 'Ed ora, ecco i nostri proponimenti. Raccogliere ... le ultime ricerche, quanto s'adatti a metter su un'opera sulla storia topografica ed artistica della città di Napoli: un libro si verrà formando a mano a mano che vedranno la luce i fascicoli di questa rivista ... E però, avendo di mira il libro, che è cosa la quale, per tornare utile e dilettevole a ognuno, ha bisogno d'essere ... accessibile a tutti, ci studieremo d'ottenere ... la maggiore euritmia d'esposizione, con forma che sarà ... lucida e viva. Non pur, fra tanto, riassumeremo pel gran pubblico gli

speciali lavori degli eruditi – poi che crediamo che le ricerche degli studiosi debbano con utile efficacia penetrar nella cultura generale – quanto completeremo, con ricerche e studii affato nostri, quel che ci avverà d'incontrare incompiuto, durante questo lavoro di riassunto e di sintesi. Ma l'opera nostra, in fuori di simili scopi spirituali, ne avrà pur di pratici. È risaputo da quanti amano l'arte nostra antica e i nostri monumenti in che conto gli abbiano, non pur i privati cittadini, ma le autorità del comune, preposte, tra l'altro, per dovere lor sacro, alla conservazione d'ogni umano lavoro che arricchisca ed onori la patria. V'hanno, qui, a Napoli, una commissione provinciale ed una municipale per la conservazione dei monumenti. Ma le proposte loro, quando avviene che ne facciano, non sempre ottengono effetto ... le lor conclusioni son rimaste senza eco; il silenzio ha sepellito, volta per volta, i risultati preziosi di quelle riunioni filopatridi ... Agli scritti nostri illustrativi faranno dunque seguito, sempre, proposte pratiche, come si può immaginare, alla conservazione, al rispetto, al miglioramento di tutto quel che rappresenta il nostro patrimonio antico, disseminato per le vie della città, ma non amorosamente sorvegliato, non coltivato mai. Come noi stessi daremo il posto che meritano ai comunicati, alle proposte che, via via, ci farà avere la commissione pe'monumenti, i giornali cittadini accoglieranno i nostri comunicati, le nostre proposte; forse anco li comenteranno. Così un risveglio benefico potrà seguire nel pubblico interessamento, intorno a quel che riguarda gli studii gentili dell'arte, le patrie memorie nostre.'

21 Ibid., 1; see also the retrospective comments included in Croce's review of Bertaux, *L'art dans l'Italie méridionale*, 204 n 1.

22 See Luigi Russo's pages on 'La cultura arretrata del Settembrini,' in his *Francesco De Sanctis e la cultura napoletana*, 3rd ed. (Florence: Sansoni, 1959), 140–44. Croce briefly discussed Settembrini's advocacy of art as a means to stir regional consciousness in his 'La vita letteraria a Napoli dal 1860 al 1900,' *La critica* 7 (1909), 325–51, 405–23; 8 (1910), 211–21, 241–62. See now Benedetto Croce, *La letteratura della nuova Italia: Saggi critici*, 3rd ed. (Bari: Laterza, 1929), 4, especially 330, 335.

23 On the piano del Risanamento and the watchdog functions shared by *Napoli nobilissima* and the Commissione municipale for the care and study of monuments (established by the Consiglio comunale in 1874 and expanded in 1876), see Giuseppe Russo, *Il Risanamento e l'ampliamento della città di Napoli* (Naples: Società pel Risanamento di Napoli, 1960), especially 402–12; Arnaldo Venditti, 'La tutela del patrimonio d'arte e di natura,' in *Napoli dopo un secolo* (Naples: Edizioni scientifiche italiane, 1961), 235–54; Pane, 'Benedetto Croce e Napoli nobilissima'; Giancarlo Alisio, *Napoli e il Risanamento: Recupero di una struttura urbana* (Naples: Edizioni Scientifiche Italiane, 1981),

especially 78–82; and, more recently, Renata Picone and Marina Rosi, 'La Commissione municipale per la conservazione dei monumenti di Napoli,' in Giuseppe Fiengo, ed., *Tutela e restauro dei monumenti in Campania 1860–1900* (Naples: Electa Napoli, 1993), 161–211.

The group at *Napoli nobilissima* seems to have taken a broader public role in calling for the material preservation of monuments, while the Società napoletana seems to have focused more exclusively on collecting written and photographic documentation. However, it is clear that Bartolomeo Capasso felt that it was the mission of the Società to preserve both the memory and the physical monuments of the past; see his addresses to the annual assembly of the Società read on 21 February 1891 and 9 April 1892, published in *Archivio storico per le provincie napoletane* 16, no. 1 (1891), 258–67; and 17 no. 2 (1892), 520–4. Already by 1885 the piano del Risanamento was deplored as the 'imitazione dell'Haussmann'; see Arnaldo Venditti, 'Breve storia dei piani regolatori,' in *Napoli dopo un secolo* (Naples: Edizioni scientifiche italiane, 1961), especially 211–12 n 4. For the cholera epidemic of 1884 and the official responses that paved the way for the piano del Risanamento, see Frank M. Snowden, *Naples in the Time of Cholera, 1884–1911* (Cambridge: Cambridge University Press, 1995). On the 'Haussmannization' of Paris see T.J. Clark, *The Painting of Modern Life: Paris in the Art of Manet and His Followers* (New York: Alfred A. Knopf, 1985), 23–78.

24 See, for example, Bartolomeo Capasso, 'La Vicaria vecchia: Pagine della storia di Napoli studiata nelle sue vie e nei suoi monumenti,' *Archivio storico per le provincie napoletane* 14 (1889), 97–135, 685–749; 15 (1890), 388–433, 583–635.

25 [Benedetto Croce], *Sulla denominazione delle vie di Napoli risultanti dal piano di Risanamento, Relazione alla Giunta Comunale* (Naples: Giannini, 1890); reprinted in Giuseppe Russo, *Il Risanamento e l'ampliamento della città di Napoli* (Naples: Società per Risanamento di Napoli, 1960), 621–38, appendix 9. For a fuller account of this unsigned work, see Castellano's notes in Benedetto Croce, *Pagine sparse: Serie prima*, ed. Giovanni Castellano (Napoli: Riccardo Ricciardi editore, 1919), I, 49–50. On the collaboration between the Giunta comunale and the Società, see also Capasso's address to the latter group, read 21 February 1891, especially 264.

26 See Don Fastidio, 'Nomi di strada,' *Napoli nobilissima* 1 (1892), 29–30; 'Nomi delle nuove vie,' *Napoli nobilissima* 1 (1892), 127, 160; and 'I criterii della denominazione delle nuove vie di Napoli,' *Napoli nobilissima* 2 (1893), 78–9.

27 The contributions of 'Don Fastidio' and 'Don Ferrante' are attributed to their authors (Croce, Ceci, and less often Ludovico de la Ville sur-Yllon, and from 1903 Fausto Nicolini as well) in the 'Indice generale della collezione' compiled by Antonio Sarno and edited by Ceci for the last issue of the journal;

see *Napoli nobilissima* 15 (1906), 177–93. However, on some occasions more than one person contributed to a given article, and the attribution of particular texts in such cases can be uncertain. On this problem, see Giuseppe Brescia, 'Valdemaro Vecchi,' in his *Croce inedito (1881–1952)* (Naples: Società editrice napoletana, 1984), 103–4. Brescia points out that Silvano Borsari's *L'opera di Benedetto Croce* (Naples: Istituto Italiano per gli Studi Storici, 1964) faithfully follows the attributions in the 'Indice generale' except where the editor thought that he could improve on them, but Brescia suggests that Borsari was not always right.

28 Benedetto Croce, 'I teatri di napoli. Secolo XV–XVIII,' *Archivio storico per le provincie napoletane* 16 no. 1 (1891), 34, for the quotation, and 32–6 more generally for this character invented by the comic actor Francesco Massaro. The political ideals of Manzoni's Don Ferrante are discussed by Giuseppe Mazzotta, 'Manzoni e il barocco: La biblioteca di don Ferrante,' in Guido Publiese, ed., *Perspectives on Nineteenth-Century Italian Novels* (Toronto: Dovehouse Editions, 1989), 65–76.

29 See, for example, Ludovico de la Ville sur-Yllon, 'Tre iscrizioni enigmatiche nelle vie di Napoli,' *Napoli nobilissima* 2 (1893), 27–30; and Vittorio Spinazzola, 'Il nome di Napoli,' ibid. (1892), 33–5, 49–51; 2 (1893), 128.

30 Giuseppe Ceci, 'Per le chiese da demolirsi nel Risanamento della città,' ibid. 1 (1892), 23–35; and Don Fastidio, 'Errata,' ibid., 64. Compare Ceci's 'Le chiese e le cappelle abbattute o da abbattersi nel Risanamento edilizio di Napoli,' *Archivio storico per le provincie napoletane* 15 (1890), 827–41; 16 (1891) 157–73, 398–427, 592–610, 743–72; 17 (1892), 34–70.

31 Benedetto Croce, 'L'agonia di una strada,' *Napoli nobilissima* 3 (1894), 177–80.

32 The quotation is from an account of the controversy that Croce wrote some years later to illustrate what he regarded as the excessive importance granted to specialists in modern society; see his review of Giuseppe Prezzolini's *Leggenda e psicologia dello scienziato*, in *La critica* 6 (1908), 50–1, n 1. Croce's writings on the Croce di Lucca controversy, in several different periodicals, are indicated by Castellano, in Croce's *Pagine sparse*, I, 50–2.

33 'Per la "Croce di Lucca,"' *Napoli nobilissima* 12 (1903), 97–8. For a full account of the events, incorporating a good deal of unpublished material, see Laura Donadio, 'Il risanamento di Napoli e la vicenda della chiesa della Croce di Lucca,' in Giuseppe Fiengo, ed., *Tutela e restauro dei monumenti in Campania 1860–1900* (Naples: Electa Napoli, 1993), 258–80.

34 Alfonso Miola, 'La "Croce di Lucca,"' *Napoli nobilissima* 12 (1903), 99–102; Giuseppe Ceci, 'Gli artisti che lavorarono per la "Croce di Lucca,"' ibid., 145–8.

35 See the two articles by Don Fastidio, 'Per la Croce di Lucca,' ibid., 125 and

144 (for the quotations, see the first article). Thanks in large part to Croce's efforts the church was saved, except for the apse, which was cut off, while the main altar was moved to the church of San Agostino alla Zecca.

36 Benedetto Croce, 'Un nuovo scandalo al Museo Nazionale di Napoli,' ibid. 9 (1900), 145–8; the quotation in the previous sentence is from 145. See also the letters by Croce, De Petra, and others reprinted from various periodicals under the title 'Ancora del Museo Nazionale di Napoli,' ibid., 161–6, as well as Croce's report of De Petra's resignation, in ibid., 177, and the articles by Don Ferrante (Giuseppe Ceci), 'Gli scavi di Boscoreale e gli editi ferdinandei,' ibid., 9 (1900), 166–7; and Don Ferrante (Benedetto Croce?), Review of Giulio de Petra's book *Intorno al Museo Nazionale di Napoli*, in ibid. 10 (1901), 63–4. For a brief account of the larger institutional context of the 'scandel,' see Carmela Dora Gapito, 'I riordinamenti della quadreria del Museo Nazionale di Napoli,' *Bollettino d'arte* 6th ser. 76 (1991), especially 167.

37 The relevant articles in *Napoli nobilissima* alone are so numerous that I give minimum bibliographical data: 12 (1903), 1–3, 17, 28–9, 33, 46–8, 79, 94, 111–12, 113–14, 129, 143, 159–60; 13 (1904), 16, 47, 65, 92, 175–6. Some of Croce's publications in *Marzocco* and *Giornale d'Italia* are reprinted in the articles cited here. See also Castellano's selection of relevant material in Croce, *Pagine sparse*, I, 52–69.

38 The three essays just mentioned appeared in the first volume of *Napoli nobilissima* (1892): 'La villa di Chiaia,' 3–11, 35–9, 51–3; 'La tomba di Iacopo Sannazaro,' 68–76; 'L'arco di S. Eligio,' 147–51. The most recent edition of *Storie e leggende napoletane* is the excellent volume edited by Giuseppe Galasso (Milan: Adelphi edizioni, 1990).

39 For the plan of the *Sommario* series see Benedetto Croce, 'Sommario critico della storia dell'arte nel napoletano,' *Napoli nobilissima* 2 (1893), 6–10, especially 6–7 note; the subsequent instalments follow on 23–7, 35–41, 55–61, 85–9, 130–4, 152–6, 164–7, 179–80; 3 (1894), 39–41, 56–60, 70–2. A pilot article discussed below served as a sort of critical preface to the series and also indicates Croce's intentions. His information regarding medieval church architecture came mainly from Heinrich Wilhelm Schulz, *Denkmaeler der Kunst des Mittelalters in Unteritalien*, ed. Ferdinand von Quast, 4 vols. in 3 (Dresden: Wilhelm K.H. Schulz, 1860).

40 For the plan of this series, see Benedetto Croce, 'Napoli nelle descrizioni dei poeti,' *Napoli nobilissima* 2 (1893), 175–6, especially the opening paragraph: 'Ecco il titolo di un bel libro per chi vuol farlo. A preparare il materiale di esso – che non è di facile raccolta – uno dei nostri redattori apre una rubrica, nella quale verrà ristampando annotando i testi dei poeti e letterati italiani e stranieri, che descrivono l'aspetto della città di Napoli e del popolo napolet-

ano. La raccolta non può avere per ora nessun ordine, neanche cronologico: è una serie d'appunti, e come tale l'offriamo ai lettori.' The subsequent contributions are in ibid. 3 (1894), 78, 159–60, 189–90; and 4 (1895), 47–8.

41 Benedetto Croce, 'Memorie degli Spagnuoli nella città di Napoli,' ibid. 3 (1894), 92–5, 108–12, 122–6, 156–9, 172–6; 92 for the quotation. These essays were reprinted as an appendix to Croce's *La Spagna nella vita italiana durante la Rinascenza* (Bari: Laterza, 1917), 257–76.

42 Benedetto Croce, 'Curiosità napoletane ...' *Napoli nobilissima* 14 (1905), 10–12, 43–6, 121–5; 15 (1906), 74–8. Reprinted in *Anedotti di varia letteratura*, 3 vols. (Naples: Ricciardi, 1942).

43 Benedetto Croce, 'Note per la storia del costume ...' *Napoli nobilissima* 15 (1906), 58–9, 118–22, 140–4, 159–60; variously reprinted.

44 Benedetto Croce, 'Sommario critico della storia dell'arte nel Napoletano: Il Falsario,' *Napoli nobilissima* 1 (1892), 122–6, 140–4; reprinted with revisions in *Aneddoti di varia letteratura*, 2nd ed. (Bari: Laterza, 1953), 2, 323–44. Bernardo De Dominici, *Vite de'pittori, scultori, ed architetti napoletani*, 3 vols. (Naples: Francesco Ricciardi, 1742–5); reprinted in 4 vols. (Naples: Tipografia Trani, 1840–6). Croce's essay includes a sharply biased overview of the fortunes of De Dominici's book up to the late nineteenth century, supporting his assertion that it is virtually without value – an overstatement that Croce would subsequently regret (see Pane, 'Benedetto Croce e la Napoli nobilissima,' 19). On the biographer's supposed falsification of manuscript sources, see Thomas Willette, 'Bernardo De Dominici e le Vite de'pittori, sculturi ed architetti napoletani: contributo alla riabilitazione di una fonte,' *Ricerche sul'600 napoletano* (Milan: Edizioni Lanconelli & Tognolli, 1986), 255–73. For further discussion, see Ferdinando Bologna, 'De Dominici, Bernardo,' in *Dizionario biografico degli italiani* XXXIII (Rome, 1987), 619–28; and see also my two subsequent essays: 'Bernardo De Dominici e la sua *Vita* di Stanzione,' in Sebastian Schütze and Thomas Willette, *Massimo Stanzione, l'opera completa* (Naples: Electa Napoli, 1992), 153–62; and 'Biography, Historiography, and the Image of Francesco Solimena,' in Vega de Martini and Antonio Braca, eds., *Angelo e Francesco Solimena, due culture a confronto* (Naples: Fausto Fiorentino, 1994), 201–8. The current status of post-Crocean studies is measured by Fiorella Sricchia Santoro, 'De Dominici e la storia dell'arte del '500,' in Francesca Amirante et al., eds., *Libri per vedere: Le guide storico-artistiche delle città di Napoli* (Naples: Edizioni scientifiche italiane, 1995), 219–25.

45 The relation of De Dominici's *Vite* to the goals of eighteenth-century republicanism and the problems that his book presented for Liberal Neapolitans in the post-Unification period will be treated at length in a study I am preparing, provisionally titled *Monument/Memory/Identity: Cultural Politics and the*

History of Art in Southern Italy in the Times of Vico and Croce. For an indication of my approach to the earlier period, see Thomas Willette, 'The Image of the Spanish Viceregency in the *Künstliteratur* of the 18th Century,' *Mitteilungen der Carl Justi-Vereinigung* 9 (1997), 52–4.

46 Croce, 'Sommario critico ... Il Falsario,' 122. The particular rhetoric of the anti–De Dominici campaign is further attested by the next lines: 'Tu uccidi un morto – mi avvertirà il colto lettore ... Non morto abbastanza –, rispondo io, che veggo ancora i moltissimi credenti in lui, i molti che pur ritenendolo uno scrittore malfido, non hanno un chiaro concetto della portata di quella sua falsificazione.'

47 See, for example, Benedetto Croce, 'Un innamorato di Napoli: Carlo Celano,' *Napoli nobilissima* 2 (1893), 65–70; 'Scrittori della storia dell'arte napoletana anteriori al De Dominici,' and 'Il manoscritto di Camillo Tutini sulla storia dell'arte napoletana,' both in ibid. (1898), 17–20 and 121–4, respectively. I say 'more or less' proved reliability because Croce and his colleagues were not always very critical of textual sources that antedated De Dominici's *Vite*; see Croce's 'Sommario critico ... Il Falsario,' 122–6, 140–4; and my essay 'Bernardo De Dominici e le Vite, 255–73.

48 Bendetto Croce, 'Per la settima edizione del *Cicerone* del Burckhardt: Lettera aperta al dott. Guglielmo Bode,' *Napoli nobilissima* 6 (1897), 49–56; and Don Fastidio (probably Croce), 'Notizie ed osservazioni: Raffaele d'Ambra,' ibid. 1 (1892), 174. For D'Ambra's work and reputation, see further Paola Fardella, 'L'Ottocento,' in Francesca Amirante et al., eds. *Libri per vedere: Le guide storico-artistiche delle città di Napoli* (Naples: Edizioni scientifiche italiane, 1995), 142–2.

49 For the quotation, see Fausto Nicolini, *Aspetti della vita italo–spagnuola nel cinque e seicento* (Naples: Alfredo Guida, 1934), 71. Croce's unforgiving criticism of Dalbono's popularizing book *Le tradizioni popolari spiegate con la storia e gli edifizii del tempo*, 3 vols. (Naples, 1841–3), may be sampled in his essay 'Leggende di luoghi ed edifizii di Napoli,' *Napoli nobilissima* 5 (1896), 132–5, 172–5; revised under the title 'False leggende popolari,' in Croce's *Curiosità storiche*, 2nd ed. (Naples: Riccardo Ricciardi, 1921), 158–63. On Dalbono, author of tourist guidebooks, popular monographs, and other art-historical writings, as well as plays based on the biographies of artists in De Dominici's *Vite*, see Mariantonietta Picone Petrusa and Magda Vigilante, 'Dalbono, Carlo Tito,' in *Dizionario biografico degli italiani*, XXXI (Rome, 1985), 708–11; and Fardella, 'L'Ottocento,' 150–2.

50 Croce, Review of Bertaux, *L'art dans l'Italie méridionale*, 205: 'quel *Sommario* ... aveva fatto il suo tempo, e perciò ne fu interrotta la continuazione, passata nelle mani di specialisti ben più competenti.'

51 Benedetto Croce, 'Annibale Caccavello scultore napoletano del secolo XVI,' *Napoli nobilissima* 5 (1896), 177–83. On the final page, Croce described Caccavello and the other students of Giovanni da Nola as 'abili *pratici*, più che artisti d'ispirazione.' Cf. *Diario di Annibale Caccavello scultore napoletano del xvi secolo*, ed. with intro. and notes by Antonio Filangieri di Candida (Naples: Pierro, 1896).

52 Benedetto Croce, 'Una questione di criterio nella storia artistica,' *Napoli nobilissima* 8 (1899), 161–3; 'Ancora del libro del Venturi,' ibid. 9 (1900), 13–14.

53 Luigi Russo, 'De lineis et coloribus: Benedetto Croce e la pittura,' *Rivista di studi crociani* 4 (1967), 85–92.

54 Benedetto Croce, 'La critica e storia delle arti figurative e le sue condizioni presenti,' *La critica* 17 (1919), 272. According to this point of view, there can be no 'Italian' poetry or painting as such, since 'Italy' is not an aesthetic category.

55 Croce, Review of Bertaux, *L'art dans l'Italie méridionale*, 204–5: 'Allorché, tredici anni fa [Croce] con alcuni suoi amici … fondò a Napoli una piccola rivista mensile, cui non è mancato finora il favore del pubblico, diretta a raccogliere documenti e a preparare l'illustrazione dei monumenti dell'Italia meridionale, egli fu costretto a non concepirla in modo esclusivo a specialista, e ad unirvi insieme degli scopi di divulgazione: tanto erano poco noti i risultati fin allora raggiunti dalla critica seria, e tanto radicati i pregiudizii e le falsità provenienti dal libro delle *Vite dei pittori, scultori ed architetti napoletani* di Bernardo De Dominici.'

56 Croce, 'Ai lettori. Commiato,' 175.

57 Ajello, 'Benedetto Croce e la storia "ideale,"' 409–14; for the quotation, see 412.

58 Benedetto Croce, 'Prefazione' (1918), in *Primi saggi*, 2nd ed. (Bari: Laterza, 1927), vii–viii. This moment, he continued, is 'il momento, cioè, in cui si cominciò a sciogliere il duro ghiaccio del positivismo, e rispuntarono qua e là, con nuovi atteggiamenti, i problemi filosofici.'

59 H. Stuart Hughes has remarked on Croce's 'tendency … to use positivism as a philosophic catch-all, to embrace under this epithet every doctrine for which he had a dislike,' in *Consciousness and Society: The Reorientation of European Social Thought 1890–1930*, rev. ed. (New York: Vintage, 1977), 37. For commentary on this view, see Roberts, *Benedetto Croce*, 15–16. Some aspects of Roberts's position on Croce's early anti-positivism have been questioned in turn by Bedani, 'Art, Poetry and Science.'

60 Benedetto Croce, 'Come nacque e come morì il marxismo teorico in Italia (1895–1900) da lettere e ricordi personali,' *La critica* 36 (1938), 35–52, 109–24. This was a refutation of Labriola's work and Croce's last word on the subject,

which he did not refrain from reprinting in a new edition of his former mentor's essays: *La concezione materialistica della storia*, 2nd ed. (Bari: Laterza, 1938), 267–312.

61 Michele Scherillo, Review of Benedetto Croce, *I teatri di Napoli, secolo XV–XVIII*, in *Giornale storico della letteratura italiana* 19 (1892), 111. On Croce's early reception in this journal of positivist historiography, see Amedeo Quondam, 'Un "grande emporio d'erudizione": Tradizione settecentesca e metodo storico (1883–1894),' in *Cent'anni di Giornale storico della letteratura italiana: Atti del Convegno* (Torino: Loescher editore, 1985), 418–20. The book under review was the first edition of *I teatri di Napoli* (Naples: Pierro, 1891).

62 See the letter of 14 January 1896 in Antonio Labriola, *Lettere a Benedetto Croce 1885–1904* (Naples: Istituto Italiano per gli Studi Storici, 1975), 93–5. And see the discussion by Iermano, 'Il giovane Croce,' 33.

63 Croce, 'Les études relatives à la théorie de l'histoire,' 181.

64 Benedetto Croce, *Intorno alla critica letteraria: Polemica in risposta ad un opuscolo del Dr. Trojano* (Naples: Pierro, 1895); quoted in Iermano, 'Croce e il "Fanfulla della domenica,"' 92.

65 Croce, 'Curriculum vitae,' 14–15. For the dedication to De la Ville, then recently deceased, see Croce's *Curiosità storiche* (Naples: Riccardo Ricciardi, 1919): 'All'amico Ludovico de la Ville Sur Yllon in ricordo dei tempi della "Napoli nobilissima."'

66 Croce, *An Autobiography*, 45; *Contributo*, 26 (for a fuller quotation, see note 84 below). According to Galasso, the differences between the accounts of the 'Curriculum vitae' and the *Contributo* fit into a pattern revealing Croce's progressive 'distacco' from his early activities, but I see more than a cooling of his passion for minute documentary research in the disdain that he exhibited on other occasions towards the moral and intellectual status of such work. If one were to compare *all* of the retrospective accounts that Croce wrote of the period 1886–91, his attitudes might be seen to vary with less predictable logic. Galasso's comments are found in his illuminating 'Nota del Curatore,' in Benedetto Croce, *I teatri di Napoli dal Rinascimento alla fine del secolo decimottavo*, ed. Giuseppe Galasso (Milan: Adelphi edizioni 1992), 362–5.

67 Bartolomeo Capasso, 'Adunanza annuale,' *Archivio storico per le provincie napoletane* 17 (1892), 523–4.

68 Emilio Gabba, Review of Angelo Russi, *Bartolomeo Capasso e la storia del Mezzogiorno d'Italia*, in *Rivista storica italiana* 110 (1993), 814: Gabba observes that Russi takes as his starting point the 'valutazione affettuosa, ma sicuramente riduttiva che B. Croce aveva dato dell'opera del Capasso all'indomani della sua scomparsa, in quanto legata ad una fase storica superata.'

69 For Croce's stay in Rome with Silvio Spaventa (1822–1893), following the

earthquake at Casamicciola that left him an orphan, see the 'Curriculum vitae,' 12–14; and see Croce's 'Antonio Labriola,' *Marzocco* (14 Feb. 1904), reprinted in *Pagine sparse: Serie terza* (Naples: Riccardo Ricciardi, 1920), 108–14.

70 See the list of 'soci promotori' in *Archivio storico per le provincie napoletane* 11 (1886), 413.

71 Ferrarelli wrote to Croce in Rome (13 April 1884) to send him various pieces of historical information that had been requested from Capasso; see Mario Corsi, *Le origini del pensiero di Benedetto Croce* (Naples: Giannini editore, 1974), 163–4.

72 On Croce's relations with Ferrarelli, see Giuseppe Brescia, 'Preistoria di Benedetto Croce,' in his *Croce inedito (1881–1952)* (Naples: Società Editirice Napoletana, 1984), 32–42. Ferrarelli himself would later contribute to *Napoli nobilissima* and also join Croce in protesting the destruction of the church of the Croce di Lucca; see 'Per la "Croce di Lucca,"' 97.

73 Croce's writings on Neapolitan history published in the first and second series of the journal are conveniently listed by Silvano Borsari, 'Scritti di storia napoletana di Benedetto Croce,' *Archivio storico per le province napoletane* 73 (1955), 495–500.

74 Benedetto Croce, 'I teatri di Napoli. Secoli XV–XVIII,' ibid. 14 (1889), 556–684; 15 (1890), 126–80, 233–352, 472–564, 724–65; 16 (1891), 3–92, 271–360, 509–91; reprinted in book form with additions (Naples: Pierro, 1891). For his characterization of the book as a 'cronistoria,' see Croce, 'Curriculum vitae,' 15. The book was completely revised and republished as *I teatri di Napoli dal Rinascimento alla fine del secolo decimottavo* (Bari: Laterza, 1947). On the publication history and textual revisions, see Galasso, 'Nota del Curatore,' in Croce, *I teatri di Napoli*, 355–81.

75 By the time a new Presidente was needed in 1916, on the death of Giuseppe De Blasiis (Capasso's successor), Croce was willing to decline the promotion. For informative but uncritical accounts of Croce's involvement with the Società see Ernesto Pontieri, 'Benedetto Croce e la Società napoletana di storia patria,' *Archivio storico per le province napoletane* 73 (1955), 3–20; and Fausto Nicolini, *Benedetto Croce* (Torino: Unione Tipografico-Editrice Torinese 1962), 100–11.

76 Croce's relazione to the general assembly of *soci* on 12 January 1901 is printed in *Archivio storico per le provincie napoletane* 26 (1901), 161–6.

77 Benedetto Croce, 'Il Capasso e la storia regionale,' *Napoli nobilissima* 9 (1900), 42–3 (quotation from 42). For readings of this fascinating and problematic text, see, in addition to the studies cited below, Giovanni Cassandro, 'Bartolommeo Capasso,' *Rivista di studi crociani* 11 (1974), 171–8.

78 Galasso, 'Nota del Curatore,' in Croce, *Storie e leggende napoletane*, 356–7.

79 Angelo Russi, 'Bartolommeo Capasso,' in *La cultura classica a Napoli nell'Ottocento: Secondo contributo* (Naples: Dipartimento di Filologia Classica dell'Università degli Studi di Napoli Federico II, 1991), 201–25; Ajello, 'Benedetto Croce e la storia "ideale,"' 409–14.

80 See Croce's relazione to the general assembly of 12 January 1901, 163. The phrase is introduced with the words 'Così potessimo vedere ancora oggi tra noi l'uomo al quale si rivolge in questo momento il pensiero di noi tutti, Bartolommeo Capasso, che la morte ci ha tolto nel passato anno!'

81 Ibid., 164: 'Or bene: queste accuse sono del tutto erronee quando involgono una condanna della storia regionale a favore o della storia nazionale, o addirittura della storia generale ed universale. Esse si fondano, in tal caso, su una *falsa analogia* tra il procedere della storia e quello delle scienze astratte, naturali, matematiche o filosofiche. Se nelle scienze astratte il particolare è assorbito nel generale, il fatto nella legge ... nella storia invece ... non vale se non ciò che particolarmente si descrive.'

82 Ibid., 166.

83 Ludovico Antonio Muratori, *Della pubblica felicità, oggetto de'buoni prìncipi*, ed. Liliana Bosi di Palma (Turin: Loescher Editore, 1971), 42: 'Dico onesta, perché altrimenti l'erudizione si convertirebbe in veleno. Contuttociò mi sia lecito di dire che si dà qualche minutaglia di secca e sterile erudizione, che può forse servire a qualche ornamento e progresso delle lettere, e nulla poi a qualche utilità della repubblica.'

84 Croce, *An Autobiography*, 45, 46 (trans. modified); *Contributo*, 26, 27: with his return to Naples in 1886, 'quando la mia vita si fece più ordinata, il mio animo più sereno e talvolta quasi soddisfatto, ma ciò accadde perché, lasciata la politicante società romana, acre di passioni, entrai in una società tutta composta di bibliotecari, archivisti, eruditi, curiosi, e altra onesta e buona e mite gente, uomini vecchi o maturi i più, che non avevano l'abito del troppo pensare, e ai quali io mi assuefeci, e quasi mi adeguai, almeno nell'estrinseco.'

85 Croce, *An Autobiography*, 46, 48 (trans. modified); *Contributo*, 27, 28. 'Le speculazioni filosofiche della mia adolescenza erano ricacciate in un cantuccio dell'animo ... Ma, insomma ... io per sei anni, dall'86 al '92, fui tutto versato nell'esterno, cioè nelle ricerche di erudizione).'

86 Croce, *An Autobiography*, 51, 52, 53, 54 (trans. modified); *Contributo*, 30, 31, 33.

5

Croce's Theory of Historical Judgment

RENATA VITI CAVALIERE

In 1951 Croce published *Filosofia, poesia, storia*, an anthology of his writings, in which he made a selection that systematically recasts the enormous amount of theoretical and critical work that he had written since the 1890s.[1] In reviewing the volume, Carlo Antoni, a distinguished interpreter of Croce, was one of the first to call attention to the singular arrangement of the essays collected by the philosopher, representing an ideal progression – without respect for chronology – of his activity as thinker, historian, critic, and polemicist. First and foremost, as if to emphasize their importance, there is a group of essays with the title of 'Logic of Philosophy,' a clear sign of the 'ideal priority assigned to logic.'[2] We should certainly keep in mind Croce's assessment of his own intellectual progress, especially when trying to locate the theoretical core of his philosophy. Nevertheless, Croce has no choice but to follow his real development, in accordance with the progressive examination of the themes. Moreover, for him, thinking is a constant effort to understand the world, and it is valid inasmuch as it is exercised with respect to particular problems.

The young Croce made his appearance on the philosophical stage by entering the debate at the end of the nineteenth century on the 'nature' of history – whether it was art or science – and by opposing the classical positivism of the mid-nineteenth century, denying first of all the validity of its logical premises, of empiricist origin, when applied uncritically to the historical and social disciplines. To him, history seemed closer to art because it was far removed from the rationalistic methods that explain events in terms of causes and laws. In the 1893 essay *La storia ridotta sotto il concetto dell'arte* (History Reduced under the Concept of Art),[3] Croce replaced the empirical – what is perceived by the senses – with the narrative fact that captures historical individualities by way of symbolic intuition. He dismissed the entire dualistic tradition, which had separated sense and intellect, fact and concept, appearance and essence, and considered it not at all suitable to problems of historical knowledge. Through the discovery of a new 'logic of sense experience,' capable of expressing the ineffable individual by means of the narrative-creative act, the 'artistic' nature of history revealed itself in the peculiar character of narrative, which, like art, aims at the particular (although artists of course create their characters, while historians find them in archives). Like art, moreover, narrative 'knows' things within a sphere that is quite different from that of intellectual thought. Croce's investigation of questions of art, which culminated in the publication of the *Estetica* (Aesthetics, 1902), represented a journey towards the renewal of 'logic,' beginning from the intuitive moment of knowledge. Thus as the *Logic* of 1909, which replaces with substantial changes the *Lineamenti di una logica del concetto puro* (Outlines of a Logic of the Pure Concept) of 1904–5,[4] carries with it conclusions reached in aesthetics, so Croce's ongoing reflections on the nature of art are equally indebted to the conclusions that he reached in the logic of historical thought.

We are dealing with a number of interrelated questions to which I can only allude briefly here.[5] Without doubt, Croce saw in the creation of poetic images and in the judgment of taste (after Kant, it could not be otherwise) an entire world free of rules, models, fashions, and fixed criteria. Aesthetics seemed to him a discipline that could hardly be disciplined but rather was open to possibility even during its real production, where one encounters human activity in its extreme singularity, the expression of an immediacy that is synonymous with autonomy, but not of an abstract purity, the bright exterior of an inner finality that poorly tolerates classifications and schematic analyses.

Even though Croce never deviated from these views, he came to think of his ponderous *Aesthetics* as just a sketch, a program that could be fulfilled only in critical practice, and as only the first step towards the fulfilment of the life of the Spirit as a whole, where other moments of judgment, different and yet similar to the aesthetic, would present themselves. This was the case in the *Filosofia della pratica. Economica ed etica* (Philosophy of the Practical. Economic and Ethic) of 1909[6] for the economic and ethical sphere, and in the almost contemporary *Logica come scienza del concetto puro* (Logic as the Science of the Pure Concept) of 1909,[7] for the sphere of knowledge and forms of knowing. After exploring the cognitive moment of the individual in art, it was necessary to examine the question of the universal, until then kept by Croce at a distance because he identified it with the generalizations typical of 'intellectualism.' It was Kant and Hegel (and his countryman Vico) who suggested to Croce the possible pattern of the reciprocal relations between aesthetics and logic. The 'logic of philosophy,' at which Croce arrived as the appropriate form of historical thought, carries within it traces of the anomaly of aesthetic judgment, to which Kant had pointed in the subjective universality of reflection on the beautiful and in the communicability of sentiment, even though they are not founded on a priori concepts of the intellect. Freed from abstractions, the universal had found in Hegel's philosophy the concreteness of 'objective thinking' – that is, the logical and at the same time real form of dialectics, which celebrates the unity of opposites. The universal-concrete is the concept that occurs in history, just as in art beauty is the 'sensible manifestation of the Idea.' It is not surprising then that in the practice of literary criticism Croce attributed a major role to every form of spiritual activity, even while affirming the autonomy of the work of art. Consider, for instance, the stress that Croce placed on the a priori synthesis in *Breviario di estetica* (The Essence of Aesthetic) (1912)[8] and later on the cosmic character of art; and the religious tones of *Aesthetica in nuce* (Aesthetics) (1929),[9] where the universal embodied in the individual work characterizes the presence of the Spirit both as moral conscience and as aspiration to the eternal.

The ideal priority attributed by Croce to logic makes it imperative to clarify in what terms it became the leading principle of his entire philosophy of spirit. None the less, I want to point out from the beginning the close link between logic and aesthetics and the crucial fact that art was for Croce a great reservoir of examples, a kind of paradigmatic blueprint for his work. The narrative theme of the early years endures in the later, more mature works: that is, that history has shifted from the empirical to the imaginative realm. Furthermore, precisely through the works on aesthetics, it was possible for him to bring about a reform of the old concept of the universal. Is it not the case in fact that art represents a concrete representation of forms that never hover over things as evanescent abstractions? That is why art expresses the universal in the mode of the individual, a universal that is not the genus, the species, the number, or the multitude. In this concrete representation, the universal is not lost; it rather inhabits the concrete form and is at home in it. In a 1940 essay entitled *Suggestioni dell'estetica per riforme in altre parti della filosofia* (Suggestions from Aesthetics for Reform in Other Parts of Philosophy),[10] Croce recalled his youthful attempts to 'aestheticize' the discussion of philosophical problems. He showed then an understanding of and almost a sympathy for a plan that he had not carried out literally. That project was neither illusory nor extravagant. Aesthetics, he said, has an exceptional pedagogic function. An identical rhythm of individual and universal belongs to every form of spiritual life. Whether we call it poetic genius, artistic inspiration, scientific intuition, moderation in action, or disposition of the soul towards the good, there is always an original, 'affective,' element, very individual, which is included in the universality of the historical-reconstructive (storico-ricostruttivo) thought. Historical judgment, which is, as we see below, 'story-judgment' (racconto-giudizio), a thought-out narrative of facts – to use expressions that are frequently found in Croce's text – has its place therefore between thought and action, past and future, in support of the ethical dimension of 'my' knowing and as proof of the 'historico-biographical reality' (realtà storico biografica) of everyone's humanity.

The pages of Croce's *Logic* are completely suffused with a vivid sense of the historical concreteness of truth. This complex and well-thought-out work proved to be such an innovation in the cultural climate of the first years of this century that its actual basic objective was more or less overlooked. Croce pointed this out some time later, in 1915, in *Contributo alla critica di me stesso* where he speaks of his conception of truth as history, which eliminates the fear of falling into the scepticism that is the inevitable consequence of truth understood as an extra-historical concept. Croce wrote: 'But the concept of truth as history tempers the pride of the present and opens up hope for the future. It replaces the despairing consciousness that comes from the futile effort to tear the veil away from what is always fleeting and is always concealed, with the consciousness of always possessing what is always enriching.'[11] (Ma il concetto della verità come storia modera l'orgoglio del presente ed apre le speranze dell'avvenire; e sostituisce alla disperata coscienza del vano sforzo di strappare il velo a ciò che sempre sfugge e si cela, la coscienza del sempre possedere ciò che sempre si arricchisce.)

The task of the *Logic* was to provide the instruments for the understanding of the historical world (which, according to Vico, is the only world that can be known). However, it was a question not of searching for a method similar to that of the physical and natural sciences, but of an organic reflection on the judgmental and mnemonic character of human thinking. Croce's proposal was to keep philosophical concepts no longer separate from the particular judgments of history, but it was not a question of simply remembering that there is no thought without real content, or of asserting that there is no fact or experience without the necessary conceptual foundation. His proposal meant to go much deeper, to capture the unity (or identity) of the defining judgment, jealous bastion of pure philosophy, and individual judgment, which is commonly employed in the apprehension of a concrete real world.

For the moment, it is necessary to focus on the consistency of some of the passages in the *Logic*, concentrating our attention on sections 2 and 3 of Part I of the 1909 edition. After distinguishing pure concepts from pseudoconceptual forms – that is, concrete universals (Beautiful, True, Useful, Good) from empirical or abstract concepts (concepts of things or of non-representable figures) – Croce asserts the undemonstrable character of pure concepts, which can only be thought.[12] In fact, the entire life of the Spirit 'moves' through them, without residue, without leaving a series of ulterior specifications and subdivisions. The nature of the concept is, in the last instance, the logical definition itself, which also does not hover in pure and unpolluted air if it needs language. Even empty tautologies find strength and meaning in linguistic expression. Croce moreover calls them 'sublime,' perhaps because there cannot be anything beyond. In the defining judgment, the subject and the predicate are both universals, and therefore the copula 'is' does not have the function of uniting two heterogeneous elements; and yet, Croce added, definitions are always expressed in a well-determined situation, which in some sense required them, and therefore they too are born and flow within the concrete movement of historical life.[13] Individual judgment is without doubt existentializing: it states that something is, according to the perception of its status and character. Paradoxically, Croce does not place beyond time the concept that thinks itself; soon afterward, he emphasizes the presence 'of all possible predicates' (di tutti i predicati possibili) in every act of judging the particular if it is true that judgment would not be expressed without the aid of distinct concepts. To be sure, in individual judgment the subject and predicate are respectively particular and universal, but, as in a definition, in individual judgment is affirmed the act of unity in distinction and therefore the presence of pure concepts.

With these analyses, Croce arrives at the identity of the defining judgment with individual judgment in historical or mnemonic judgment. In this fashion he shows that there is an original interdependence of fact and concept (the concept derives from the actuality of life, one could say, just as any fact is historical because it is thought), which recalls the Kantian a priori logical synthesis at least in the form of an essential relation, which is foundational precisely in the sense that the transcendental has in itself its own legitimacy, without any metaphysical basis. It was a question of removing the established assumption that the true logical form is the definition, while individual judgment is little more than mere representation. Having discovered the unity of the truth of reason and the truth of facts, Croce knew very well that he was going against the logicians' tendency to safeguard the purity of forms and against the historians' obstinate diffidence towards philosophy. He was embarking instead on the unusual road that led to a 'philosophy of judgment,' understood as the 'primitive act' of Spirit, as the logical spirit itself,[14] on which depends the predicability of any world.

Drawing the appropriate conclusions, Croce – in the second part of the *Logic*, dedicated to forms of knowledge – identifies philosophy with history on the basis of the logical doctrine of judgment elaborated earlier, erasing ancient divisions caused by the opposing roles of idealists and materialists. The logical and non-mythological unity of philosophy and historiography (without denying the specificity of either) had no other purpose than that of demonstrating the logical and theoretical consistency of Croce's assertion of the historicity of truth. However, there would have been no point any more in searching for constants and laws in human affairs, where there are so few rules and much judgment and where the model of scientific rationality (from experience to law, and vice versa) seems to progress more or less in a void, decreeing the beneficial checkmate of determinism.

The weightier and wider implications of the doctrine of historical judgment manifest themselves with greater impact in the later developments of Croce's thinking. Special attention should be paid to the writings collected in *Teoria e storia della storiografia* (History, Its Theory and Practice, 1915–17) and in the key work *La storia come pensiero e come azione* (History as the Story of Liberty, 1938).[15] Croce's theoretical commitment in those years becomes steadily more attentive to distinguishing his thought from an obsolete conception of metaphysical and abstract philosophy, incapable of engaging the more difficult road ahead, the one that does not move upward but descends into the labyrinth of history and of the human heart. Giambattista Vico had undertaken a similar journey to the point of thinking the conversion of truth into fact and of the unity of philology and philosophy.

In the events of Italian and European history between the two wars, Croce found dramatic nourishment and encouragement for his conception of the unity of philosophy and history. As a young man, Croce's constant dissatisfaction with every metaphysical history made him declare, 'We ourselves make history, keeping in mind, of course, the objective conditions in which we find ourselves, with our ideals, our efforts, our suffering, and without the possibility of easing the burden onto the shoulders of God or the Idea.' (La storia la facciamo noi stessi, tenendo conto, certo, delle condizioni obiettive nelle quali ci troviamo, ma coi nostri ideali, coi nostri sforzi, con le nostre sofferenze, senza che ci sia consentito scaricare questo fardello sulle spalle di Dio e dell'Idea.)[16]

A similar dissatisfaction when the fascists were in power led him appropriately to use the phrase 'history of liberty' (storia della libertà), a condition that is synonymous with moral conscience and is also the explanatory principle of history and the principle of action.[17] At the same time, the *Logic* itself represented a disavowal of the philosophy of history, of the claim to be able to trace the unitarian design of events and perhaps to point to a precise direction for humanity to take. In his essay on Hegel of 1907, *Ciò che è vivo e ciò che è morto nella filosofia di Hegel* (What Is Living and What Is Dead of the Philosophy of Hegel), Croce had commented inimically on Hegel's dislike for professional historians and for any inappropriate 'philosophizing of history,' which – Croce said – was like a philosopher of art taking poets and artists to task, touching up and fixing up their works philosophically.[18] In the *Logic* the polemic against the philosophy of history also meant to target its ancient opponent, positivism, for wanting to endorse the intrusion of a law of natural necessity in the history of human events. (Perhaps the only acceptable law of natural necessity is the unconstestable one of physical decline, which, however, only in mysterious ways could serve to uphold a theory of linear and indefinite progression.) History for Croce is not nature, but something living, for in the word 'nature' he read the rigidi-fication of life in the fixity of repetition. If we split open a stone, its inside is stone; if we split open a seed, we find not the flower but its potential for development; if we split open the fragments of the past, we find not the causes, only the possibility of undefinable alternatives. Only in the abstract do we claim to have discovered some precedents in the past. It is not the past that explains the present, because it is the present that permits an understanding of the past, and that never entirely.

Another aspect of the problematic context led Croce to the logic of historical judgment. The contents of the *Logic* were thought out together with the themes of *Filosofia della pratica* (Philosophy of the Practical), published a few months earlier.[19] Ample reflection on the practical sphere (economic and ethical) had persuaded Croce of the complexity of the world in which one acts. Not without reason, he conferred on some of its pages strains of realism, even to the point of calling himself the representative of a 'new positivism.' The scenario that he presented was the concrete one of individual volitions made up of factual conditions, mental habits, emotions, desires, and affections, all of which might be subsumed under the dictum that 'the individual is his situation' (l'individuo è la sua situazione). The actions of humans, case by case, instant by instant, construct events or happenings that all together are to be considered the work of God or the Whole. However, the movement of history, seen from the perspective of those who act, provides the awareness that one is never the first cause, and yet one is always a free cause. Liberty is never a real condition (however we try, we can never come up with a situation of total absence of conditioning), but the moral quality of the individual act can intervene in a developing situation and change the outcome, much like the swimmer who in racing an opponent follows and changes his movements according to the current.[19]

Croce's doctrine of historical judgment thus acquires its full meaning in praxis, which is necessarily the complement of theory, as a dialectic of questions and answers, of problems and temporary solutions, similar to the vital rhythm whereby knowledge flows into action and action requires knowledge. In this fashion, Croce brought about a 'peaceful philosophical revolution' (tranquilla rivoluzione filosofica), which he labelled 'methodology of history' (metodologia della storia) – that is, the explanation of cognitive and practical categories with which it is possible to formulate historical judgments.[20] He chose the way of method, but not outside history, in order to avoid the methodological abstractions of his contemporaries. It is not difficult to discern in the new formulation the logical doctrine of historical judgment itself, made mature by its ability to resist the obsolete prejudices of absolute and definitive knowledge, which for a long time had privileged unity over difference, had dealt in rarefied questions that no longer showed any sign of life, and had promoted the worn-out figure of the professional philosopher with his voluminous theoretical treatises, which were almost temples erected to the Eternal.[21]

Croce was always concerned with the question of history,[22] but in the way in which he understood the workings of thought, always in touch with the time in which he lived. He spoke, once again without paradox, of a history that is 'entirely contemporary' (tutta contemporanea), in order to stress the fact that memory of the past originates in a horizon of waiting, which then serves as orientation for action. These theoretical premises were gradually confronted with the history of Europe in the years of greatest change and in the dark times of the victory of totalitarianism. After 1924–5, Croce placed emphasis on ethico-political historiography. On the one hand, the discussion had to do only with a theoretical question of historiography – that is, with the debate between *Kulturgeschichte* and *Statgeschichte*, whether history is only politico-military or can also include ideas. For Croce this was a false problem. History is both one thing and the other, although he felt that in those years greater emphasis should be placed on the ethical progress of humanity, on the victories of civilization over barbarity, of faith over unbelief. The religious tone with which he spoke in 1932 of the theme of liberty, to the point of speaking of opposing religious faiths in the conflict between free and totalitarian world, can be explained by the dramatic events of fascism in Italy.[23] The radical historicism that he professed in *La storia come pensiero e come azione* (1938) revealed itself as quite different from the usual historicist position, which is entirely devoted to things that have already occurred. The title made eloquent reference to practical life and to individual action as the sign of an unavoidable opening towards the future. In this work, the theory of historical judgment has the task of fully acknowledging the value of origin and of origins and at the same time of underlining the preparatory character of thought with respect to action, to which one attributes connotations of novelty, inauguration, and beginning.

None the less, having excluded every extrahistorical permanence, do we face, perhaps inevitably, the abyss of relativism? Are the current hypotheses of 'covering laws' (leggi di copertura) sufficient to defend us from it? In Croce there is a prevailing sense of the incompleteness of the historical journey; the journey is irrevocable as far as what has come before us, but always modifiable for the future. Therefore the connection between logic and ethics is very close. Just as there is no sense in asking whether historical knowledge is inductive or deductive, because it is both in the unity of universal predicate and individual subject, so there is no reason to censor the questionable hypotheses of historical judgment, even when we mean by 'judgment' a sentence of absolution or conviction. At the level of the relation between theory and praxis, in the concreteness of the lives of a people who live their times, the ethical dimension concerns always and only the responsibility of each person, not the morality of events. The ethical imperative is to be reconciled in a certain sense with one's own world and to increase in it the life of the Spirit. There is no other ethical imperative than that of exercising the true and proper fact of thought that is historical judgment placed between the authority of the past and the freedom of the future. To conquer a space for liberty is the individual and common task of humanity.

However, the disturbing presence of the irrational in history and in humanity could not escape Croce. He did not forget later in life to assign an important place to it. He spoke of 'Vitality' (il Vitale) as that original and powerful force that fights with Spirit, not by attacking it from the opposite side, the side of matter, but as an irreducible primitive or instinctual element. To Vitality, Croce attributed the meaning conferred on indeterminism at earlier periods in the historical process. How many times, looking at the past, have we been surprised to see the flower of civilization grow on the naked rock, and how many times too have we hoped for the future – that is, for a change, objectively unpredictable, of direction in a process that is already under way?

In Croce's theory of historical judgment we do not find expressed the historicism that idealizes the past and sometimes justifies its errors. Reality, which is entirely history, as therefore always projected into the moral task of building the future. Otherwise the angel of history, with its shoulders turned to the future and its face to the past, could not avoid being trampled by the storms that hinder its way. To the modern theories of 'no future,' of the non sense of history and of the end of sense, the end of history and humanity, Croce opposes the ethical duty of the *quid agendum?*, or what must I do? He would have agreed only in part with the modern theses of a bracketing of history after the tragedies of this century. He would have derived new stimulus for action from them, as he could not accept the image of a humanity that procedes, as in the parable of the blind in Breughel's painting, ragged and suffering, without eyes and without direction. Anyway, he always shied away from pronouncing facile prophecies of renewal or of future catastrophies. History is made in the freedom of the critical exercise of thought that judges and in the perspective of historico-political action. I would like to conclude this brief exposition with Croce's own words taken from the 'Lessons' (Lezioni) that he gave in his last years at the Institute for Historical Studies, which he founded in Naples's Palazzo Filomarino:

Since truth intertwines with the life of action and action is the unceasing creation of the world, and since at every motion that is created anew, thought has to think it and refer it back to the universal, and shed its own light over it ... particular truths are not fragments of a Truth never quite recognizable in its entirety, but they are the industrious life, the dramatic life, and even the tragic life of this same Truth, which is the life within life ... All statements or judgments are sufficient in their given conditions, and all are rendered insufficient by the new questions raised by new facts, and all have to be integrated, and thus they are not dissipated but are all preserved in our new judgments as facts within facts; a syllable of God can never be erased. (Poiché la verità s'intreccia con la vita dell'azione e l'azione è incessante creazione del mondo, e a ogni moto che si crea nuovo, il pensiero deve pensarlo e riportarlo all'universale, e rivolgervi sopra la luce di esso ... le verità particolari non sono frammenti di una Verità non mai riconoscibile nel suo tutto, ma sono la vita operosa, la vita drammatica, e anche la vita tragica della Verità stessa, che è vita nella vita ... Tutte le affermazioni o giudizi sono sufficienti nelle condizioni date, e tutti sono resi insufficienti dalle nuove domande che i fatti nuovi sollecitano, e tutti sono da integrare e perciò non si dissipano ma si serbano nei nostri nuovi giudizi come i fatti nei fatti; e sillaba di Dio non mai si cancella.)[24]

Croce used to say that in order to understand a philosophical proposition one ought to look for the other proposition against which it was made. The historicist principle whereby one investigates the ideal and cultural context of an author is an erudite, historiographical and philological analysis, always strictly connected with the origin of the historical question that Michel Foucault, under different premises but in ways that perhaps are not too dissimilar, has called 'problematization.' And there is no theoretical problem, however lived in the solitude of speculation, that can avoid entering into dialogue with the ancients and with contemporaries. That is why it is useful to point to those thinkers whom Croce felt were his masters, with whom he especially engaged in lively polemics and questioned the substance of their arguments. This applies above all to Kant and Hegel, and perhaps less to Vico, to whom Croce was deeply attached in the spirit of civil philosophy and in language. The conversion into truth with fact seemed to Croce to be a meaningful precedent of the unity of philosophy and history. Kant's discovery of the transcendental also seemed to him to be an extraordinary door to historical thought, as long as the reflection on art and history can be understood beyond the letter of Kantianism, since for Kant neither of them constitutes knowledge, while for Croce they represent adequate contexts for the practice of that 'ability to judge' (capacità di giudizio), which is the characteristic mode of criticism. Croce accepted Hegel's logic only in its dialectic nucleus, while he rejected any panlogistic project, together with the philosophy of nature and historical metaphysics.

Influenced by considerations of the practical or conventional value of scientific concepts made by theoreticians of science such as Avenarius, Mach, and Poincaré, Croce established, differently from Hegel, a distinction between mathematical and empirical knowledge and philosophy, attributing to them different contexts and functions. Their differences aside, Croce's logic also had affinities with Husserl's anti-psychologism in *Philosophical Investigations* and with Heidegger's early analyses on judgment. From a very different position, Croce thought through the distinction between exactness and truth, which represents what is theoretically interesting in the logico-theoretical investigations of this century taken as a whole and which is still the dividing line between analytic philosophers and followers of Hermeneutics. Suffice it to say that Croce's historical judgment could hardly be related to the concept of truth as *adaequatio intellectus et rei*, while Heidegger's *alètheia* would have been foreign to him because of all the mystical elements that it seems to contain.

In Croce one can find a solid logical apparatus for contemporary debate. One can think, for example, of the debate over practical knowledge, which has a lot in common with the necessity to formulate a theory of historico-political judgment. Sometimes the currents against which Croce wrote polemically have taken on renewed vigour under other names, as it would be possible to verify even nowadays. Therefore it would be possible to re-evaluate the staying power of Croce's thought with relation to these new problematics. His thought, however, should not become for interpreters a definitive system. If it did, this would entail the beginning of its own overcoming and would in fact justify our considering it amply overcome. Croce should be given the honour of discussion that he reserved for his teachers and friends such as Marx and Antonio Labriola, De Sanctis and Gentile, and to positivists and historicists both Italian and foreign. To Hegel, more than to others, he returned constantly throughout his life, without calling himself Hegelian or idealist.[25] In the heart of the *Logic*, in the form of concrete judgment, Croce revived the 'rule' (regola) of the concept that lives solely in relation with the world of human and historical individualities. In Croce, dialectics became the 'alternate breath' (alterno respiro) of thinking between the necessity of what has already been and the freedom of action. The rending opposition of contrasts in which life is steeped 'became settled' (si sistemava), so to speak, in the distinct and not contrasting forms of the spirit.

The result, however, would not be the end of every anxiety and the end of research. Croce never intended the tetralogy of values or of spiritual categories to be rigid figures of unmodifiable essences. The theory of historical judgment is the obvious confirmation. 'Every time,' he wrote, 'we confront a new fact we are as if "in a state of innocence," "without prejudice"' (ogni volta di fronte al fatto nuovo, siamo come in 'uno stato di innocenza,' 'spregiudicato'). And it will not do to apply concepts as realities that we have always possessed and that are ready to use. The onerous task of philosophy is precisely that of 'maintaining and increasing concepts,' because after a judgment is made, concepts emerge rectified and internally modified.[26]

Finally, Croce's theoretical-judging journey was tied to his intense activity as scholar in many fields of culture and thought. He always abided by the duty of having to contribute to the moral progress of his times. He conceived a philosophy of becoming, which, because of the logical assumptions outlined above, is not at all similar to 'a great rolling cart that drags and crushes individuals as it goes,' because reality, he used to say, lies solely in the hearts of individuals.

A philosophy of becoming is perverted into the blind assertion of an inhuman movement when it does not understand becoming as that of each one of us, as the human drama of suffering and love, full of contrasts, catastrophes, and catharses, which the poetry of every age has uniquely sung, having never met anything else of any other quality in the wide expanse of the universe, and in whose terms from time to time can be reduced the antinomies of spirit and nature, humanity and God, world and the beyond, which themselves are also parts and motions of our soul, the only place in which they acquire the dignity of truth. (Una filosofia del divenire si perverte in cieca asserzione di un moto disumano quando non intende il divenire come di ciascuno di noi stessi, come il dramma umano di dolore e di amore, intessuto di contrasti e di catastrofi e di catarsi, che la poesia di tutti i tempi ha unicamente cantato, non essendosi essa incontrata mai con altro di altra qualità nell'ampia distesa dell'universo, e nei cui termini si riconducono di volta in volta le antinomie di spirito e natura, di uomo e Dio, di mondo e oltremondo, che sono anch'esse parti e moti dell'anima nostra, nella quale soltanto acquistano dignità di vero.)[27]

NOTES

1 See Croce, *Filosofia, poesia, storia* (Naples: Ricciardi, 1951; trans. C. Sprigge as *Philosophy, Poetry, History* (London: Oxford University Press, 1966). See also the recent edition of *Filosofia, poesia, storia*, ed. G. Galasso (Milan: Adelphi, 1996).

2 Carlo Antoni's review appeared in *Il mondo* (March 1952) and was reprinted in *Il tempo e le idee*, ed. M. Biscione (Naples: Edizioni scientifiche italiane, 1967), 423–8.

3 The work was first published in the *Atti dell'accademia pontaniana* 23 (1893), 1–29, and later reprinted with many variants in *Primi saggi* (First Essays) (Bari: Laterza, 1918). A critical edition of this text is in B. Croce and P. Villari, *Controversie sulla storia* (Disputes about History) (1891–3), ed. R. Viti Cavaliere (Milan: Unicopli, 1993).

4 *Lineamenti* was first published in *Atti dell'accademia pontaniana* 35 (1905), 1–140. It was later reprinted in *La prima forma della 'Estetica' e della 'Logica.'* (The First Form of the 'Aesthetic' and the 'Logic'). (Messina and Rome: Principato, 1924).

5 See 'Contributo alla critica di me stesso' in *Etica e politica*, 4th ed. (Bari: Laterza, 1956). The essay was translated by R.G. Collingwood as *Benedetto Croce: An Autobiography* (Oxford: Clarendon Press, 1927). See also the recent edition of *Contributo alla critica di me stesso*, ed. G. Galasso (Milan: Adelphi, 1989).

6 *Filosofia della pratica: Economica ed etica*, 8th ed. (Bari: Laterza, 1957). The English translation is by Douglas Ainslie, *Philosophy of the Practical: Economic and Ethic* (New York: Biblo and Tannen, 1967).

7 *Logica come scienza del concetto puro*, 9th ed. (Bari: Laterza, 1963). The translation is by Douglas Ainslie from the 2nd ed. (1909): *Logic as the Science of the Pure Concept* (London: Macmillan, 1917).

8 *The Essence of Aesthetic* was translated by D. Ainslie (London: Heinemann, 1921). It has also been translated by Patrick Romanell as *Guide to Aesthetics* (Indianapolis: Bobbs-Merrill, 1965).

9 'Aesthetica in nuce,' in B. Croce, *Ultimi saggi*, 3rd ed. (Bari: Laterza, 1963). This is the Italian version of the entry 'Aesthetics' written for the *Encyclopaedia Britannica*, 14th ed. (1929), 263–72. It appears in English with the same title in *Philosophy, Poetry, History*, trans. Sprigg, 215–47.

10 The essay was published in *Il carattere della filosofia moderna* (The Character of Modern Philosophy, 1941) and also appears in the critical edition by M. Mastrogregori (Naples: Bibliopolis, 1991).

11 *Contributo alla critica di me stesso*, 63, trans. Massimo Verdicchio.

12 *Logica come scienza del concetto puro*, 75, trans. Massimo Verdicchio.

13 *Logica*, 133.

14 See ibid., 138.

15 *Teoria e storia della storiografia* (1917), 10th ed. (Bari: Laterza, 1973), trans. Douglas Ainslie as *History, Its Theory and Practice* (New York: Russell & Russell, 1960). *La storia come pensiero e come azione* (1938), 7th ed. (Bari: Laterza, 1965),

translated by Sylvia Sprigge as *History as the Story of Liberty* (New York: W.W. Norton, 1941).

16 In *Primi saggi*, 67–8, trans. Massimo Verdicchio.

17 See the first chapters of *Storia d'Europa nel secolo decimonono* (1932) and the famous *Epilogue*, translated by Henry Furst as *History of Europe in the Nineteenth Century* (New York: Harcourt, Brace & World, Harbinger Books, 1963). See also the anthology of political writings, *La religione della libertà* (The Religion of Liberty), ed. G. Cotroneo (Milan: Sugarco, 1986).

18 *Ciò che è vivo e ciò che è morto nella filosofia di Hegel: Studio critico seguito da un saggio di bibliografia hegeliana* (Bari: Laterza, 1907). The essay was reprinted without the bibliography in *Saggio sullo Hegel, seguito da altri scritti di storia della filosofia* (Bari: Laterza, 1913). It was later translated by Douglas Ainslie as *What Is Living and What Is Dead in the Philosophy of Hegel* (New York: Russell & Russell, 1969). A useful anthology of Croce's writings on Hegel is the recent *Dialogo con Hegel*, ed. G. Gembillo (Naples: Edizioni scientifiche italiane, 1995).

19 *Philosophy of the Practical*, 27–8.

20 See *Teoria e storia della storiografia*, ed. G. Galasso (Milano: Adelphi, 1989), 167–81.

21 Ibid.

22 See R. Franchini, *La teoria della storia di Benedetto Croce* (Benedetto Croce's Theory of History 1966), reprint ed. Viti Cavaliere (Naples: Edizioni scientifiche italiane, 1995).

23 See *Storia d'Europa*, chap. 2.

24 Croce's 'Lessons' were published in *Storiografia e idealità morale* (Historiography and Moral Ideality) (Bari: Laterza, 1950). One can now read them in *Dieci conversazioni con gli alunni dell'Istituto Italiano per gli Studi Storici di Napoli* (Ten Conversations with the Students of the Italian Institute for Historical Studies), ed. Gennaro Sasso (Bologna: il Mulino, 1993). See in particular 8–9.

25 See *Indagini su Hegel e schiarimenti filosofici* (Investigations on Hegel and Other Philosophical Essays) (Bari: Laterza, 1951).

26 For all these observations, see Croce, *Discorsi di varia filosofia* (General Discourses on Philosophy), II (Bari: Laterza, 1945).

27 See Croce's *Il carattere della filosofia moderna*, 252, trans. Massimo Verdicchio.

6

Political Doctrine in Croce's *History of the Kingdom of Naples*

DAIN A. TRAFTON

According to Benedetto Croce, all history is contemporary history, by which he means that all serious study of the past is informed by the problems and needs of the writer's own time; the more conscious historians are of their contemporary motives, the more searching and accurate their investigations of the past and the more useful their reconstructions.[1] Of Croce's major historical writings, none illustrates this point more clearly than the *Storia del regno di Napoli* (History of the Kingdom of Naples). First published as a series of essays in Croce's journal *La critica*, then republished as a book in 1925, 1931, and 1944 (each time with minor additions and revisions), the study represents the fruit of Croce's long and somber meditation on both the past travails and the present predicament of his homeland. Above all, Croce saw clearly that the former kingdom, reduced since 1860 to the Mezzogiorno, remained mired in lethargy and corruption while other regions of Italy reaped the benefits promised by the Risorgimento and Unification. To understand and begin to remedy this situation is his book's aim. It employs historical analysis to discredit contemporary attitudes towards the Mezzogiorno's past that frustrate its development in the present and to instruct the region's future leaders in the principles of sound politics.

Two contemporary approaches to the study of history seem to Croce especially harmful: first, the spirit of merely local or regional patriotism represented by Enrico Cenni's *Studi di diritto pubblico*, which Croce subjects to severe criticism in the 'Author's Introduction' (7–42); and second, the positivist view that history can be explained in scientific or naturalistic terms, a view that Croce attacks throughout the book and especially in the conclusion (243–7).[2] In Croce's view, well-meaning but wrong-headed local patriots such as Cenni exaggerate the accomplishments of the old kingdom and thus keep alive the resentment of Neapolitans who are still unreconciled to Italian Unification (40). In response to this reactionary sentimentality, which distracts attention from the necessary task of integrating the Mezzogiorno into the new Italian state, the *History of the Kingdom* offers an account of the past that is 'more rigorous and accurate' (42) (più severo e più adeguato) (41).

As for the positivists, Croce claims that their emphasis on the Mezzogiorno's geographical isolation, the poverty of its soil, the harshness of its climate, and the racial characteristics of its inhabitants implies a kind of fatalism about its future because soil, climate, and so on cannot be changed. In opposition to this fatalism, his work proposes what Croce called an 'ethico-political' view of history, stressing human freedom, creativity, and responsibility: 'Poor lands with great-spirited inhabitants have had a glorious political history' (46) (in terre povere siè svolta vigorosa storia politica quando i loro abitatori hanno dispiegato animo grande) (46); 'poverty may generate daring and vigor on the one hand, or discouragement and lassitude on the other' (246) (la povertà <può> ingenerare vigore e ardimento o per contrario sfiducia e abbattimento) (287); 'the same climate (as Hegel has pointed out) engendered the creative activity of the Greeks and the inanition of the Turks' (246) (il medesimo clima [come diceva Hegel] <può> accogliere indifferente le opere degli Elleni e l'ozio dei Turchi) (287).[3]

By emphasizing human freedom, creativity, and responsibility, Croce claims to provide an account of the Mezzogiorno's past that is not only more accurate than competing accounts but also more useful, because it both teaches and inspires the region's future leaders. And it is to them that the *History of the Kingdom* is primarily addressed. 'Since history is a spiritual action,' he writes in the final paragraph, 'every political and practical problem has a spiritual and moral character. Every problem must be seen in this framework and be solved as best it may; there is no specific, complete remedy. The job is up to educators, by whom I do not mean schoolteachers or schoolteachers alone; we must all strive to be educators, each in his own circle, and educators, in the first place of ourselves' (248). (Come la storia, dunque, è azione spirituale, così ogni problema pratico e politico è problema spirituale e morale; e in questo campo va posto e trattato, e via via, nel modo che si può, risoluto; e qui non hanno luogo specifici di veruna sorta. Qui l'opera è degli educatori, sotto il quale nome non bisgona pensare ai maestri di scuola e agli altri pedagoghi, o non a essi soli, ma a tutti, in quanto tutti siamo e dobbiamo e possiamo essere effettivi educatori, ciascuno nella propria cerchia e ciascuno in prima verso se stesso) (289).

The task of these educators is to perpetuate the tradition of past 'teachers and thinkers' (248) (uomini di dottrina e di pensiero) (290) who laid the foundations for the nation's progress. Like their predecessors, the new educators must free minds – starting with their own – from regionalism and positivism and all other limiting ideas in order to promote a spirit of freedom, creativity, and responsibility that makes a people great. Moreover, although 'there is no specific, complete remedy' – a position consistent with Croce's emphasis on the uniqueness and unpredictability of each historic moment – the *History of the Kingdom* provides a general understanding of the principles of politics designed to guide educators and reformers of the Mezzogiorno.

These principles come to light initially in the central section of the 'Author's Introduction,' where Croce interrupts his critique of Cenni in order to look back to a pre-Norman south that, he claims, offers a more effective 'stimulus to patriotic pride' (ricordi eccitanti a patriottica compiacenza) and more stirring 'images of patriotic virtue' (23) (immagini di patriottica virtù) (19) than can be found in the history of the kingdom itself. Focusing on three cities – Benevento, Amalfi, and Naples – Croce emphasizes the political virtues that they shared. Primary among these was a public-spiritedness based on self-confidence and self-assertiveness, on the inhabitants' pride in themselves and in their ancestors. Of Benevento, Croce writes that in spite of internal strife 'the national feeling of the *gens Langobardorum* ... endured in all its pride for centuries' (24) (la coscienza di questa *gens Langobardorum* ... si serbò vigorosa per secoli, cinta d'orgoglio) (20). In Amalfi, moreover, as in the other 'minor Venices' of the south, 'there flourished a very real political life, a spirit of conquest and defence, civic pride and patriotism' (25–6) (si svolse vita propriamente politica, fiammeggiarono ardimenti di difesa e offesa, zelo civile, amor di patria) (22). And if the duchy of Naples 'was so long defended by its sons it was because they loved it so well, as is witnessed by the chronicles of its bishops and the eulogy at the beginning of the *Vita Athanasii*, which voices admiration and glorification of its great age and nobility, its superb location, its powerfully fortified walls, the religious zeal of its citizens, and the abundance of every conceivable resource, which made it unnecessary for Neapolitans to seek their fortune in far places' (27–8). (Cosí a lungo fu difesa dai suoi figli perché da essi molto amata come attestano le cronache dei suoi vescovi e quel caldo elogio con cui s'apre la *Vita*

Athanasii, nel quale si cingono di ammirazione e di gloria la sua antichità e nobiltà, il suo sito stupendo, le sue mura munitissime, la relgione dei suoi cittadini, l'abbondanza che godevano d'ogni cosa, onde non erano costretti ad andare in giro pel mondo [24]).

More particularly, and more usefully, given the educational intentions of the book, Croce's discussion shows that the public spirit that made Benevento, Amalfi, and Naples great expressed itself pre-eminently in four kinds of activity: in military endeavours, including wars of conquest; in commercial enterprise and competition; in works of religious zeal and piety; and in the promotion of high culture – learning, literature, and the arts. The Langobards were warriors first and foremost, but Croce also stresses their piety and their patronage of learning. When they came into southern Italy they brought with them memories of Wotan, their warrior god, which they 'later transfused into the equally warlike cult of the Archangel Michael' (24) (trafuso poi nel culto del non meno guerriero arcangelo Michele) (22), and their princes supported chroniclers to record their history and their traditions (24). Commerce is absent from Croce's account of the Langobards, but it is central to his praise of ancient Amalfi, one of the great maritime cities of the early Middle Ages, where commercial activity went hand in hand with 'a spirit of conquest,' religion, and art. Croce calls attention to the city's role in the Crusades and to its artistic patronage, which produced such masterpieces as the bronze doors of the cathedral as well as those presented to Saint Michael's on Monte Gargano and Saint Paul's in Rome (25). And as for the Neapolitans, Croce claims, they were 'constantly in arms' (26) (sempre in armi) (22); they applied themselves energetically to trade – even to the slave trade, selling Lombard prisoners whom they took in battle; they were full of ostentatious piety, relying confidently on the authority of their patron saints, 'good friends of the Lord Jesus' (27–8) (grandi amici del nostro signor Gesù (24); and they developed schools and libraries that made the city a centre of culture as well (28).

At times, Croce's glowing descriptions of these pre-Norman cities seem to exhibit some of the simplistic enthusiasm for which he takes the patriotic Cenni to task: 'O venerable bell towers of Santa Maria Maggiore and Santa Maria a Piazza,' Croce writes, 'O ancient Stephania; O Monastery of San Marcellino, seat of the dukes' magistracy! What joy I have had in strolling among you and gazing upon you, in the knowledge that you were gazed upon by a Sergius, an Athanasius, a Stephanus, a Caesar ...!' (28–9). (O antica Stefania; o monastero di San Marcellino, dove era il pretorio dei duchi: quante volte me piace ag-

girarmi tra voi e contemplarvi, ricordando che tra voi vissero e vi con-
templarono i Sergi e gli Atanasî gli Stefani e i Cesarî ...!) (25).

If such a passage suggests a degree of kinship between Croce and
Cenni, however, it must be understood in the light of Croce's remark
elsewhere in the 'Author's Introduction' that a people cannot live without 'a history or a legend' (41) (una storia o una leggenda) (41) that
inspires it with confidence to meet the challenges of the present and the
future. Sometimes, when the recent past is too problematic – as in the
history of the kingdom, for example – people must look to remote periods or even other places for the edifying history or legend that they
need.[4] Looking to a remote period for an inspiring history or legend is
precisely what Croce is doing in his eulogies of Benevento, Amalfi, and
Naples. The account that he gives – essentially history, but with something of the colouring of legend – is calculated to indicate to the people
of the depressed Mezzogiorno that no disadvantages of climate, geography, or race need prevent their building a better future. The peoples
who inhabit southern Italy once flourished; Croce's enthusiastic tone
emphasizes this encouraging fact. And they can thrive again, provided
that they understand and apply to contemporary circumstances the
vision of politics that underlies Croce's account of the region's pre-
Norman past. Indeed, the *History of the Kingdom* as a whole represents
an elaboration of this vision of politics and the inspiring message that
accompanies it.[5]

Croce presents the kingdom's history in four sections: the Angevin
and Aragonese monarchies (1268–1504); the Spanish viceroyalty (1504–
1713); the period from the expulsion of the viceroys through the creation
of the Bourbon monarchy down to the French Revolution (1713–1789);
and the Bourbon kingdom, from the French Revolution to the kingdom's absorption into a unified Italy (1789–1860). Although the work
itself makes us aware that this division is to some extent arbitrary, that
history never moves in the simple, neat steps that such a scheme
implies, the structure enables readers to understand Neapolitan history
in a way that Croce believes is both true to the past and useful for the
future. As he explains in the preface, his aim is not to tell the whole
story, but only to bring out key apects of it that have not been properly
understood (5–6).

The first section reveals how a failure of military virtue compromised
the other qualities of the Angevin and Aragonese kings. They were in
many ways public-spirited and effective rulers: they promoted trade

(48, 80–1) and culture (81–3), and, in spite of their unhealthy depend-
ence on the papacy, they sought to reform religion through an influence
that was 'pedagogical and educational' (75–6) (allevatrice ed educatrice)
(80). Some of them, moreover, acquired a reputation for military
strength (49), but this came mainly from their successes abroad. At
home, they failed to make themselves masters of their own great
vassals, the unruly barons, who defied them in spite of numerous con-
cessions and regularly reduced the kingdom to turmoil (54–75). Croce
cites Machiavelli's judgment of these turbulent barons as the principal
obstacle to political health in the kingdom. To develop 'a real political
life,' such as the Lombards, the Amalfitani, and the Neapolitans for-
merly enjoyed, the Angevin and Aragonese kings would have had to
begin by destroying the great nobility, and this they never did (60).[6]

As for the barons themselves, they lacked every political virtue except
the capacity for war, and this virtue by itself, detached from public-
spiritedness and uncontrolled by the kings, proved mainly destructive
(58). Concerned only with protecting their limited individual interests,
the barons were so politically inept as a class that they never even
thought of transforming the kingdom into an aristocratic republic or
some other political order that they might have dominated; 'not one of
them' – and this is Croce's most damning and most Machiavellian comment on the barons – 'no matter how important he was on account of the
vast possessions that he had put together at certain periods of the kingdom's history, dreamed of making himself into a native king in opposition to the foreign dynasties' (66) (neppure alcuno mai di essi, per
grande che fosse, per immensi possedimenti che avesse raccolti nelle sue
mani in certi momenti di quella storia, aspirò a farsi re indigeno contro le
dinastie forestiere) (70). Those who are unwilling to be ruled, Croce
implies, must accept the responsibility of ruling, and because the barons
failed to understand this fundamental point, their military virtue constituted a plague rather than a source of strength for the nation.

The properly political cultivation of military virtue figures as a prominent theme in the second section of the *History of the Kingdom* – 'The
Viceroyalty and the Lack of a National Political Life.' Rejecting the prev-
alent view that Spanish rule had been a disaster for the kingdom, Croce
argues that outside arms were necessary at the beginning of the sixteenth century to curb the anarchy of the barons and protect the kingdom from the Venetians, the Turks, and others. But the achievement of
the viceroys went beyond the mere exercise of repressive power. In fact,

they accomplished the truly political – the educational – goal of transforming the barons' feistiness into a kind of patriotism. Under Spanish leadership, Croce writes, 'the barons developed a new sentiment, which by their example and authority spread to the other classes: the individualism of the past gave way to loyalty' (100) (un nuovo sentimento si venne formando presso i baroni e, sul loro esempio e sulla loro autorità, allargando a tutte le altre classi, invece di quello individualistico che aveva dominato in passato: il sentimento della fedeltà) (109). The barons rallied to defend the kingdom at home and to serve the king of Spain with distinction abroad. Moreover, the common people, whom the barons trained and led, became famous for their virtue, exciting the commendation of outstanding military leaders such as Wallenstein (109). Thus, under the educative discipline of Spanish rule, derived 'from firm political direction' (110) (dal fermo indirizzo politico) (120), the unruly barons were educated and became educators themselves, not only in military matters but in broader, political ways, working by 'example and authority' to promote the common good.

In other ways, too, Spanish rule promoted opportunities for the public-spiritedness on which a healthy political community is built. By taming the barons, for example, the viceroys liberated the commercial energies of the middle class, not only in the capital (116–19), but also in the provinces, where 'the vassals who turned into freeholders and direct subjects of the state, the peasants who shook off the last shackles of medieval servitude, the "honourable citizens" – the doctors of law and medicine – who defended their native lands provided one of the more edifying aspects of the kingdom' (123). (Quei vassalli che si convertivano in liberi proprietarî e in sudditi diretti dello stato, quei contadini che scotevano gli ultimi segni della servitù medievale, quei 'cittadini onorati,' dottori in legge e medici, che si facevano difensori delle loro terre native, davano, tra gli abitanti del Regno, lo spettacolo più degno) (135). The viceroys' religious policy, moreover, aimed at the reform of religion by moderating the powers of an unproductive and irresponsible clergy (137–8). And under their patronage, Naples as well as cities such as Cosenza, Aquila, and Bari became centres of learning, literature, and art (140–1).

In the last analysis, however, the viceroys did not provide the kind of leadership that could have given the kingdom a true political life. Although they exhibited a genuine grasp of political reality, directing their attention to all the areas of politics that Croce identifies as fundamental, their position in Naples was fatally compromised by the fact that they were primarily agents of a foreign power. Their public-spiritedness was inevitably focused on Spanish rather than Neapolitan interests. As a result, the barons and their soldiers fought and died admirably not for their own nation but for a foreign king, whose interests were not always consistent with theirs (110). Similarly, commercial development under the viceroys was frustrated by policies that subordinated it to the interests of the Spanish crown through state monopolies, high tariffs, and other devices of governmental control (133). Finally, the culture of the period, impressive though it was, bloomed as a kind of hothouse flower, detached from healthy contact with the life of the nation as a whole. Art and poetry tended towards elaborate and sensual display, while mere erudition became the ideal of learning (141). In Croce's view, it is especially revealing that the most original thinkers of the period – Bruno, Campanella, Telesio – were more appreciated in other countries than they were in their own, where they formed no schools and where their ideas led to no practical improvements (141). As long as southern Italy was ruled as the possession of foreign monarchs, there could be little hope for a vigorous national life.

According to Croce, it was only after the restoration of the kingdom as an independent state in 1734 that the work of earlier intellectuals could once again bear political fruit. The story of these intellectuals and of the advances in national life for which they prepared the way constitutes Croce's theme in the third part of the *History of the Kingdom*. He concentrates on the activities of men such as Carl'Antonio Broggia, Antonio Genovesi, Pietro Giannone, and Bartolomeo Intieri, philosophers, scholars, and public servants imbued with the spirit of Cartesian rationalism, who brought the Enlightenment to Naples and made the city a centre not simply of erudition but of serious thought capable of transforming the national culture. According to Croce, these were the men who prepared the kingdom for a better future and for unification with Italy. In a sense, they made the kingdom into a modern nation: 'For a nation is not a geographical expression, but rather a spiritual entity, a will, a conscience, and none of these took shape in southern Italy before the movement of which Giannone was one of the first and most important promoters and Genovesi the most communicative educator and master' (163–4). (Perché una nazione non è una cosa fisica, ma una personalità morale, una coscienza, e questa volontà e coscienza non si formarono davvero nell'Italia meridionale se non nel moto spirituale del quale il

Giannone fu tra i primi e principali autori, e il Genovesi il piú diretto e pratico educatore e maestro) (185).

By contrast, Vico, whom Croce judges to have been in many ways a deeper and profounder thinker than any of his contemporaries, failed to grasp the political needs of his time and therefore played no direct role in its major developments. For Croce, Vico exemplifies the paradox of the philosophical mind whose very superiority becomes a practical defect, rendering it excessively critical and aloof so that the thinker misses the opportunity to function as an educator (158).

Central to the educational effort of the Neapolitan Cartesians was the spread of a new religion. If they shaped the spirit of their times, 'it was because they were inspired by the faith that we have seen was lacking in the Naples of the preceding centuries and which was now born or reborn as the religion of Reason' (158). (perché riscaldava i loro petti quella fede e quella relgione della quale abbiamo avvertita la deficienza nella vita napoletana dei secoli precedenti, e che nel nuovo secolo era nata o rinata come fede e religione della Ragione) (179). Croce insists that Enlightenment rationalism should be considered as much a religion as, for example, the religion of the Quakers (158), and he judges the religion of Reason to have been healthier in its effects than the Christianity controlled from Rome with which the rulers of the kingdom had contended since the days of the Angevins. In fact, the new religion appears to have been as beneficial as the older forms of Christianity that inspired the Lombards, the Amalfitani, and the Neapolitans; it gave the new educators of the kingdom courage and energy to accomplish their many notable reforms – especially of the church (171–2, 181–2), of the kingdom's economy, including the institution of feudalism (172–6, 182–4), and of the armed forces (177–8, 185–6).

Although the third section of the *History* is almost entirely an account of 'national progress' (187) (progresso nazionale) (14), the beginning of the fourth section makes it clear that in fact the story is more complicated and less simply positive. Giannone, Genovesi, and their followers reformed institutions, but they did not succeed in transforming the national spirit. The nation as a whole remained untouched by the the new religion of Reason that inspired its leaders, and as a result many of the reforms of the eighteenth century proved superficial and short-lived (192). Indifferent to the new ideals were not only the urban lower classes and the peasants, but also most of the middle class – the artisans and small business men – as well as the aristocracy, with its crowd of dependants (192–5). And even though the eighteenth-century Bourbon kings were in many ways receptive to the new religion, they failed to grasp one of its – and Croce's – main teachings: the importance of military strength to a healthy national life. Croce stresses the admiration felt by the reformers for the kingdom of Sardinia, which they held up as an example, 'not only for its sound financial structures ... but also and above all for its military setup' (187) (non solo per gli ottimi ordinamenti finanziarî ... ma sopratutto per l'ordinamento militare) (213). To such advice, however, the Neapolitan kings remained deaf, foolishly complacent about their security even as they grew more and more distrustful of the expansionist designs of their northern rivals. 'The fact is,' writes Croce, 'that the kings of Naples frankly declared that they had no unfulfilled wishes and aimed at no aggrandizement. "We have no claims; we are lacking in ambition," Charles of Bourbon wrote in 1756 to his ambassador in London. This very lack of ambition, that is, of any aim to expand, boded ill for the future fate of the kingdom of Naples' (187). (Veroè che fin d'allora i re di Napoli presero a dichiarare, e con sincerità di sentimento, che essi non avevano nulla da desiderare e non miravano ad alcun ampliamento ['non pretendiamo niente, manchiamo d'ambizione,' faceva scrivere ne 1756 Carlo di Borbone al suo ambasciatore a Londra]; e questa mancanza di ambizione, cioè di spirito d'espansione, non dava buon indizio per le sorti del regno di Napoli nell'avvenire) (214). Like Machiavelli, Croce considers ambition to expand a sign of a nation's political health, and expansion requires the cultivation of military virtue.

Failure to persuade the rest of the nation to embrace their new religion doomed the political program of those in the kingdom who considered themselves the heirs of Descartes. And according to Croce this failure resulted from an over-confidence common to intellectuals at the time. The reformers were idealists, and they thought that the nation's backwardness would disappear almost miraculously once the enlightened ideas for which they themselves were so enthusiastic began to spread. Naïvely, they under-estimated the stubborn roots of the nation's poverty and the recalcitrance and demoralization of the middle and lower classes, who failed to grasp what they had to gain from reform (194). Restoring real political life to a nation is a more complex and difficult task than intellectuals in their ivory towers may imagine. This is one of the practical lessons that the third and fourth sections of the *History* are designed to impress on reformers of Croce's own day.

The work's fourth section – 'The Age of Revolutions and the End of the kingdom of Naples' – extends the main lines of analysis established in part III, charting the transformation of the eighteenth-century reformers first into Jacobins (198–204) and then into reluctant absolutists (210–15) and analysing the rise of a new religion to replace the religion of reason in the Risorgimento. This new faith, arising out of the broad cultural movement of Romanticism (218–20), manifested itself in two distinct but related forms: 'a noble Catholicism, restored and reconciled with the idea of progress' (220) (un cattolicesimo di nobile sembianza, restaurato e conciliato con l'idea del progresso) (254); and 'a philosophical Idealism which extolled Reason, not the Reason that in the eighteenth century interrupted and straightened the course of historical events, but a different kind of Reason, immanent and operative in every period of history' (220) (un idealismo filosofico, celebrante l'Idea o la Ragione, non più la Ragione che nel secolo decimottavo sopravveniva a interrompere e a raddrizzare il corso della storia, ma un'altra Ragione, immanente e operosa in ogni tempo della storia) (254).

According to Croce, who is describing here the origins of a moment in history in which he felt himself, albeit with some qualifications, to be participating, the new culture of Romanticism and its concomitant religious spirit were profoundly revolutionary because they gave to the eighteenth-century project of unifying Italy an urgency that it had never had. The Romantics conceived of Unification not simply as a political expedient to promote liberal reform, but rather as 'a divine mission' (221) (un dettato divino, col carattere di una missione) (255), necessary to the advance of historical Reason. To work for Italian Unification during the Risorgimento was to strive for nothing less than the fulfilment of history.

Not surprisingly, the new religion had the power to transform educators and thinkers into men of action – especially military action, whose importance Croce stresses once again. On the one hand, he celebrates the idealists who defended the Neapolitan Republic of 1799 to the bitter end of its short life: although untrained in arms, they 'fought like professional soldiers' (202) (combattevano da soldati) (231). On the other hand, he condemns the short-sightedness of Ferdinand II's policy, which, like that of his great-grandfather Charles of Bourbon, sought to avoid foreign entanglements and therefore supported 'no more of an army than was necessary to the maintenance of domestic order and no navy other than that sufficient to protect its shores from the inroads of corsairs or pirates' (227) (non altro esercito che quanto bastasse per l'ordine interno e non altra marina che quella che proteggesse le coste dai corsari) (263).

Indeed, as this comment on Ferdinand II suggests, Croce's principal criticism of the Romantic reformers is that they too, like the leaders of the Enlightenment, failed to engage the energies of the nation as a whole in their project. Although superstitious and uncultivated, Ferdinand II was in some respects an able ruler, actually quite interested in military and commercial affairs (226–7). Able, too, were many of the conservative aristocrats who served him and the other Bourbon rulers of the period (223). Moreover, the common people, the *sanfedisti*, who rallied around the throne under Cardinal Ruffo in 1799, and the Neapolitan *lazzaroni*, who considered Ferdinand I practically one of themselves, possessed a number of fundamental virtues on which reform of the whole nation could have been based: a genuine religious sense (207) and, as one of their adversaries, Eleonora Fonseca, recognized, 'energy ... strength of character ... power, misguided power, but still power ... a good omen for the future' (206) (energia ... vigor di carattere ... forza mal applicata sí, ma forza ... buoni auspicî per l'avvenire) (236). Because the Romantics were unable to win such people over to their cause, they failed, and as a result the Unification of Italy, on which Croce believes depended the progress of every part of Italy, especially the Mezzogiorno, had to be imposed on Naples from outside by the kingdom of Sardinia.

In the concluding pages of Croce's analysis, the kingdom of Sardinia emerges as the embodiment of the four crucial political virtues that pre-Norman Benevento, Amalfi, and Naples represent in the introduction. With 'its sound financial structures,' its healthy military establishment, and its role as the place of refuge for leaders of the new culture and religion of Romanticism who had been exiled from Naples and other parts of Italy (229), Sardinia stands out as 'the only Italian power constantly at work to broaden its territory, increase its population, and make its weight felt by other nations' (235) (la sola potenza italiana sempre all'opera per ampliare i confini dello stato, e crescere nella grandezza dei possesi e nel numero dei sudditi, e pesare con maggiore autorità verso gli altri stati) (272). Sardinia constituted the nucleus from which the currents of political vitality known as the Risorgimento spread to other parts of Italy and finally brought about Unification of the peninsula. Thus Croce frames his history of the kingdom of Naples with models of political health that are, strictly speaking, outside that history but that emphasize the ethical and political aims of the work. The early sections on pre-Norman Benevento, Amalfi, and ducal Naples constitute an inspiring history or legend of the kind that is necessary to enable a people to flourish, while the kingdom of Sardinia provides a similar inspiration from the traditions of a place that was once remote but is now, through Unification, available to be appropriated as their own by Neapolitans.

Commerce, culture, religion, and war – these are activities with which the political educators whom Croce identifies as his primary audience must concern themselves – the activities that southern Italians must once again cultivate with all their talents and energies. About this, the *History of the Kingdom* is quite specific, as it is in expressing confidence that the political talents and energies that are needed can be found in the Mezzogiorno as readily as in any other country. At various times in the kingdom's history, all the ingredients of political vitality have manifested themselves separately and in fragmented, partial combinations. The task now, Croce wants his readers to see, is to revive, within the context of a unified Italy and with proper attention to the needs of the historical moment, the full and happy conjunction of these ingredients that made Benevento, Amalfi, and Naples flourish in pre-Norman times. Such a revival, which alone can produce what Croce calls a 'real political life,' including the spirit of conquest and defence, civic pride and patriotism, commercial expansion, and an efflorescence of culture and religious zeal, is the goal that the complex mixture of scholarship and political doctrine in the *History of the Kingdom* aims to promote.

NOTES

1 On this idea, which in one way or another informs most of Croce's historical writings as well as his theories about history, see his *History: Its Theory and Practice*, trans. Douglas Ainslie (New York: Russell & Russell, 1960) 11–26, 108–16; and his *History as the Story of Liberty*, trans. Sylvia Sprigge (New York: Norton, 1941) 15–22, 43–4, 149–50, 310–11. On the development of Croce's theory and practice of history, see A. Robert Caponigri, *History and Liberty: The Historical Writings of Benedetto Croce* (London: Routledge & Kegan Paul, 1955); Federico Chabod, *Lezioni di metodo storico* (Bari: Laterza, 1969), 179–253; and David D. Roberts, *Benedetto Croce and the Uses of Historicism* (Berkeley: University of California Press, 1987).
2 Page references are to Benedetto Croce, *History of the Kingdom of Naples*, ed. H. Stuart Hughes, trans. Frances Frenaye (Chicago: University of Chicago Press, 1970). The English versions are Frenaye's unless otherwise noted. The stan-

dard Italian edition is Benedetto Croce, *Storia del regno di napoli* (Bari: Laterza, 1944); page references after Italian quotations refer to this edition.

3 On Croce's concept of 'ethico-political' history as an alternative to positivism and other historiographical theories, see his *Politics and Morals*, trans. Salvatore J. Castiglione (London: Allen & Unwin, 1946), 67–77; and *History as the Story of Liberty*, 59, 161–2, 178, 223–6. Cf. Caponigri, *History*, 3–53; Chabod, *Lezioni*, 213–33; Roberts, *Croce*, 272–81; Hughes's introduction to the *History of the Kingdom* xv–xxiii, and his *Consciousness and Society: The Reorientation of Social Thought – 1890–1930* (New York: Knopf, 1961), 213–29.

4 Frenaye translates 'una storia o una leggenda' simply as 'myth,' thus obliterating an ambiguity that is both interesting in itself and essential to Croce's historiography. See Massimo Verdicchio's discussion of 'history' and 'legend' in the second chapter of this volume.

5 Misled perhaps by Croce's remarks about the lack of continuity in the kingdom's history (233), modern scholars have failed to understand the kind of coherence based on political doctrine that informs Croce's account of that history. As a result, admirers of the work have contented themselves with appreciations of the most general kind, while detractors have tended to quarrel with details or launch very generalized attacks on Croce's 'idealism' and his theory of ethico-political history. Thus Chabod praises the work as the most organic and coherent of Croce's histories (229), but his brief and general discussion hardly supports his judgment. Roberts stresses the fact that Croce throught of historical writing as a way of preparing contemporary action but gives little attention to the concrete ways in which the *History of the Kingdom* embodies that idea. All Croce's histories, he concludes, 'were calls to action, but only in the most general sense did they illuminate present problems toward which such action might be directed' (286). Cf. Giuseppe Galasso, *Mezzogiorno medievale e moderno* (Torino: Einaudi, 1965), 24–9 and Hughes, Introduction, xvii–xix and xxii. For an example of a detractor, whose criticisms betray his failure to read the book with sufficient care, see Raffaele Ajello, 'Benedetto Croce e la storia "ideale" nel Regno di Napoli,' *Archivio storico per le province napoletane* 110 (1992): 351–440.

6 *Discorsi*, I, 55.

7

Croce and Mosca: Pluralistic Elitism and Philosophical Science

MAURICE A. FINOCCHIARO

The aim of this paper is to improve our understanding of Croce by means of a critical comparison of his thought with that of Gaetano Mosca (1858–1941). Since Mosca was one of the founders of the discipline of political science in its present form, as well as Italy's best-known political scientist of his generation, this exploration involves questions about politics and about science. In fact, these two thinkers are each sufficiently well known that the mere association of their names usually brings to mind two things. The first is that they were on the same side of the political spectrum; that is, they were both exponents of liberalism.[1] The second is that they were on opposite sides of the epistemological spectrum, Mosca being supposedly an exponent of positivism and scientism,[2] and Croce supposedly the originator of the 'idealist reaction against science' and the culprit for the sorry state of scientific culture in twentieth-century Italy.[3] My analysis reveals that Croce's political liberalism has a Moschian character – that is, that it is best interpreted in terms of Mosca's 'pluralistic elitism.' My comparison also shows that Croce's epistemological anti-positivism and instrumentalism are not necessarily 'anti-science' and that his system of thought contains the resources for a positive (though of course *not* positivist) appreciation of scientific practice.

I base my account on an analysis of Croce's 1923 review of Mosca's second edition of *Elementi di scienza politica* (The Ruling Class)[4] and an analysis of Croce's *Elementi di politica*,[5] as well as my interpretation of Mosca's *Elementi*. For about twenty-five years after the Second World War Croce's review was reprinted as a foreword to the only available edition of Mosca's book; its importance has also been explicitly claimed by at least one scholar.[6] Since Croce's review is very favourable, this leads to an examination of the common points of the two thinkers' political philosophies; and Croce's major statement of his political philosophy is to be found precisely in the 'elements of politics' just mentioned.

Moreover, in the review Croce cannot hide the fact that Mosca seems to be some kind of positivist, which he has to explain away. The way in which he does so is interesting and important and raises questions about the relationship between the science of politics and the philosophical theory of knowledge. The critical examination of this aspect of the review leads to an exploration of the meaning and import of Croce's anti-positivism, his philosophy of science, and his view of the theory–practice nexus.

I offer first a brief account of the historical background to these Crocean writings. Part of this background consists of the vicissitudes of Italian political history in the early 1920s. A less mundane element of this background consist of the conceptual details of Mosca's political theory.

Historical Background

In June 1920, Giovanni Giolitti was given the task of forming a new government in Italy, in the hope that such an experienced and astute statesman might be able to lead the country out of its turmoil and anarchy. Despite the victory in the world war, the country had experienced not only great suffering but a deep social upheaval, because of the large numbers of people directly involved in the war effort, the threat of a socialist or Bolshevik revolution, and the incipient fascist reaction. Rumours soon spread to the effect that Croce would be the new government's minister of public instruction, and indeed Giolitti soon invited him to go to Rome for a personal conference. Croce's first reaction was one of worry and bewilderment, since he had no political and administrative experience. However, his wife advised him that 'if this is the duty to which you are called, you must accept it' (se questo è il dovere a cui sei chiamato, devi accettarlo).[7] Then Giolitti pleaded: 'I know I am asking you to make a sacrifice by taking you away from your studies. But Italy is in such trouble that we must all make an effort (and I do not know whether we will be successful)' (so che le chiedo un sacrificio distogliendola dai suoi studi. Ma l'Italia è in tale travaglio che tutti dobbiamo sforzarci [e non so se vi riusciremo] a salvarla).[8] Croce's sense of patriotism was too great for him to be able to refuse such a plea.

Thus began a period in Croce's life during which for the first time he was directly involved in practical politics. To be sure, he had been a senator for about a decade, as a result of a royal appointment for life on account of scholarly merits; but such service did not require much political involvement, and he had not become too involved. Moreover, his work as government minister lasted only about a year, since elections in 1921 led Giolitti to resign. However, for about five years circumstances forced Croce to continue his political activity in other ways.

For example, after the march on Rome in the autumn of 1922, when the fascists gained control of the government, they began courting Croce for various positions. Although he initially supported the fascist government, he never went so far as to want to join it. However, his friend Giovanni Gentile did become minister of public instruction in the initial coalition. Gentile then proposed a reform of the Italian educational system equivalent in its essentials to the one which Croce had formulated when he occupied that position but which he had not had the opportunity to get passed. Croce supported Gentile, and his backing was instrumental in the proposal's being enacted.

As time went on, however, and the government became more and more authoritarian and illiberal, Croce's attitude became less and less favourable and then turned into opposition. In 1924–5, together with Mosca, he was one of the organizers of the Liberal party,[9] although this effort came to nothing because soon thereafter all organized opposition to Fascism was outlawed. In 1925 Gentile, who had become more and more favourable to fascism, wrote a 'Manifesto of Fascist Intellectuals,' and in response Croce wrote a 'Manifesto of Anti-Fascist Intellectuals,' which was circulated and signed by many, including Mosca. This action may be regarded as bringing to a close Croce's first period of practical political involvement, for soon thereafter his house was attacked and seriously damaged by fascist thugs, and from then on his opposition to Fascism became purely intellectual. That is, the fascists consolidated their power to such an extent that any practical political opposition became impossible.[10]

It ought to come as no surprise that Croce's most sustained thinking and writing in political theory stem from the same period. Thus in 1923 he read Mosca's *Elementi di scienza politica*, which was probably the best-known and most important work on the subject published in Italy in the previous half century. The book had just been published in a second edition consisting of two volumes, the first equivalent to the text of the first edition (published in 1896), while the second volume represented additional material, doubling the length of the book. There is no evidence that Croce had ever read the book before, whereas now he read it and promptly published a long review of it in the November 1923 issue of his own magazine *La critica*.

In 1924, Croce published a series of essays, which were collected into a volume in 1925 as *Elementi di politica*.[11] These were later incorporated into *Etica e politica* (1931), which remains the bibliographical location of these essay in the corpus of his writings. These 'elements of politics' thus constitute about one-half of the only book in the eighty or so volumes of Croce's writings dealing explicitly, theoretically, and systematically with political questions.

Neither before nor after the period in question do we find a comparable effort on Croce's part to articulate a political philosophy. Of course, afterward he must have felt that he had no need to do so because he had already accomplished the major task, so that it was enough for him to apply his basic principles and make appropriate minor revisions and reformulations. This is in fact what happened between 1943 and 1947, his second and last period of intense political activity, as he helped to rebuild the country's political institutions after Italy's formal surrender to the Allies during the Second World War.[12] In contrast, before 1920 he had barely touched the subject. For example, his *Filosofia della pratica: Economia ed etica* of 1909 contains little on politics, and its emphasis is on ethics and economics. In that work, the second category of practice, besides ethics, was the useful as the economical. In the elements of politics of 1925, the useful remains the second category of the practical, but subdivided into the political and the economic.[13] Thus the 'elements of politics' represent Croce's major theoretical effort in political philosophy.[14]

Thus there is a chronological, titular, and practical-political convergence between Mosca's *Elementi di scienza politica* and Croce's *Elementi di politica*: Croce wrote his views soon after having read and studied Mosca's theory; and Croce gave his own reflections a title reminiscent of Mosca's, and the two men were at the time political allies – old liberals, strongly opposed to socialist or Bolshevik solutions and critical supporters of fascism, hopeful that the violent and authoritarian streak of the latter could be soon tamed.[15] Was there a theoretical, conceptual, and intellectual similarity between their doctrines? If so, to what extent? To this exploration we now turn.

Intellectual Background

The character of Croce's political philosophy and its relationship to

Mosca's political theory can best be explored against the backdrop of Mosca's doctrines.[16] Mosca's most fundamental claim is that in every society political power is not equally distributed but rather concentrated in the hands of one or more elites, which rule over the masses in various ways. Mosca himself seldom uses the term 'elite' and only occasionally 'mass'; he speaks rather of the governing and governed classes, or the class of leaders and the class of followers, or the political class and the people; however, he is not always consistent in his choice of terminology, and there is no universal terminological convention in the literature. At any rate, he believes this principle to be the foundation for the scientific study of politics, and so we may call it the fundamental elitist principle. He also regards it as a descriptive, analytical, and explanatory principle, rather than a normative or evaluative one. He does not subscribe to the ideal of a value-free social science, for as we see below, he advances various normative principles, but the elitist principle is not one of them. He thinks that the principle is in part an empirical generalization true in every society that has reached even a rudimentary level of political development. However, he also regards it as a methodological principle – it suggests fruitful lines of research and recommends as crucial the study in a given society of the distinction and the interaction between elites and masses.

Mosca's theoretical system consists also of several principles describing ways in which elites and masses may interact. One of the most important of these involves the notions of democracy and aristocracy. Mosca defines democracy as a relationship between elites and masses such that elites are open to renewal of their membership through the influx of individuals from the masses; aristocracy is the opposite of democracy: elites are closed, and there is no mobility from the masses to the elites, which perpetuate themselves by heredity. What we have here is Mosca's own distinctive theory of democracy, which defines democracy in terms of open elites. This theory does contradict others' definitions in terms of such things as majority rule and universal suffrage; however, it does not necessarily deny these institutions, and their connection with democracy as defined by Mosca is a question to be resolved by further inquiry. That is, Mosca does claim that it is wrong (or at least unfruitful) to equate democracy with majority rule and universal suffrage, but this is not to say that these institutions are themselves wrong or have no role in democracy; their role is an open question from the viewpoint of his definition of democracy. Besides the formulation and clarification of these definitions, the analytical part of Mosca's theory of democracy consists of an examination of the advantages and disadvantages of both democracy and aristocracy and of the interpretation of various historical and empirical facts by means of these concepts.

The democracy–aristocracy spectrum is not the only tool for analysing the relationship between elites and masses. Another one is provided by Mosca's contrasting notions liberty–autocracy. Political liberty exists when authority flows from the bottom up, from the masses to the elites, while in autocracy authority flows from the top down, from elites to masses. Republics would be examples of liberal systems in this sense, and absolute monarchies examples of autocracies.

Mosca notes that other thinkers (especially Plato) define what they call 'democracy' in terms of such an upward flow of authority, but he prefers to define it in terms of open elites and to call the upward flow of authority 'liberal.' He does this in part because he thinks it best to adopt Guicciardini's definition of political liberty: namely, that a people is free when it governs itself, when its rulers derive their authority from the people themselves. It follows from this that one must, when comparing Mosca's theory of democracy to that of other thinkers, consider both of his pairs of fundamental terms: democracy–aristocracy and liberty–autocracy. Because both pairs are crucial in his general political theory, it is possible to have an autocratic democracy as well as a liberal aristocracy; the Catholic church would be an example of the former, while the Republic of Venice would be an example of the latter. Above all, his 'elitism' ought not to be equated with aristocracy or autocracy, nor his notion of liberty with democracy.

In regard to Mosca's normative principles, one of the most basic is the ideal of mixed government. That is, he believes that the best form of government is one which tries to incorporate and combine in a judicious fashion the various opposite principles (such as democracy and aristocracy), as well as the distinct dimensions (such as democracy and liberty). Accordingly, he believes that to carry too far the requirement of any one particular principle (such as democracy) or set of principles (such as democracy and liberty) to the complete exclusion of their opposites is a recipe for disaster. In fact, his most fundamental normative principles are moderation and pluralism, and his ideal of mixed government may be regarded as a special case of moderate pluralism applied to forms of government. Mosca himself does not use the terms 'moderation' or 'pluralism' and instead speaks of *difesa giuridica*; while the reasons for his terminological choice escape me, there can be little doubt about the conceptual content of this phrase.

Another special case of his moderate pluralism is what he calls the separation of powers, which in turn has two subcases, the separation of politics and economics and the separation of church and state. For Mosca, not to separate politics and economics means essentially that the same group that holds political power also holds economic power; and not to separate church and state means that the same group that controls political institutions also runs religious institutions dealing with the holy and the supernatural. In both cases there would be a monopoly of power, unchecked and unbalanced by other forces, which would lead to excesses and abuses and to unspeakable injustices, suffering, and oppression. Conversely, to uphold the separation of such basic structural elements of the social system means that no one force or group has too much power vis-à-vis others, which makes it clear that such separations are special cases of moderate pluralism.

Further, Mosea advances a normative principle of checks and balances, which he adopts from Montesquieu, and which is a special case of moderate pluralism with respect to branches or functions of government (legislative, executive, and judicial). Finally, he is inclined to believe that membership in the ruling class should be based on individual personal merit – not, for example, on birth or inherited privilege. However, he is also careful to point out that carrying this concept too far would entail the unacceptable abolition of both private property and the nuclear family; it would soon run into the insurmountable obstacles of fortune and luck; it would produce so much competition and anxiety as not to be worth the effort from either a personal or a social point of view; it would create irreconcilable conflicts because personal merit has some irreducibly subjective elements (both from the side of the evaluee and from the side of the evaluator) and because there are irreducibly distinct kinds of personal merit (for example, moral goodness, intellectual power, and political wisdom, which in turn can themselves be broken down into distinct subspecies). Despite these and other prudential considerations, meritocracy remained for Mosca a basic value, and so his discussion of meritocracy may be seen an yet another instance of moderate pluralism, applied to the distinction between merit and birth as bases for entrance into an elite.

Thus Mosca's political theory has an analytical component, consisting of democratic elitism, and a normative component, moderate pluralism. There is also a third element, a methodological one, which may be labelled realism. This is an approach to the study of political phenomena that can be traced back in part to Machiavelli, although Mosca did not like to elaborate the fact that he shared this approach with him but instead tended to be negatively critical and stress the Florentine's limitations. The realistic approach consists partly of an emphasis on realities vis-à-vis ideals; that is, there is a willingness, and indeed a demand, to justify normative ideals on the basis of historical and empirical facts, and otherwise to criticize them as utopian. For example, once one admits the empirical ubiquity and historical universality of the elite-mass distinction, a realist feels entitled to reject as misconceived any egalitarian vision of society. The realistic approach also emphasizes realities vis-à-vis appearances – that is, there is the willingness and requirement to determine whether an apparent empirical fact is really a fact; for example, once universal suffrage has become a reality of democratic life in modern societies, a realist tries to determine whether this is really a sign of rule by the people or merely a method of selecting elites. Finally, the realistic approach is 'anti-formalistic' in the sense that it believes that social conditions are more important than legal formalisms; for example, while realists need not reject as useless the checks and balances among branches of government advocated by Montesquieu and embedded in the American constitution, they stress that it is more important to have checks and balances among various economic, intellectual, and social groups.

Croce's Anti-Positivism

Against the background of these general principles, let us now turn to Croce's views, beginning with his famous essay, which was originally a review of the 1923 edition of Mosca's *Elements* and later served as a foreword to several postwar editions of the same book. Croce's review is very favourable, but he also calls attention to a difference between himself and Mosca that we must address at the outset to put into perspective the 'Moschian' reading of Croce that this paper proposes. Moreover, as I suggested above, Croce's understanding of this difference is enlightening from the point of view of his own thinking. Croce states (ix): 'Mosca accepts philosophical presuppositions and holds an epistemology that are certainly not those I profess. For example, he believes in the "method of the natural sciences," which should be introduced into the "moral sciences."' (Il Mosca accetta presupposti filosofici e si attiene a una gnoseologia che non sono di certo quelli che io professo. Crede, per esempio, al 'metodo delle scienze naturali' da introdurre nelle 'scienze morali.')[17] Now, this is an accurate interpretation of Mosca as far as it goes. That is, Mosca did believe that political science was a 'moral science' that could benefit by adopting some aspects of the natural scientific method. One of these was the idea that a science must be based on some theoretical principle that is universally true and subject to no exceptions. He felt that he had found such a principle in elitism and was thus in the position of being able to found a scientific discipline.

Mosca also believed that in the natural sciences theoretical principles are supported by observational evidence that is both considerable in quantity and wide-ranging in variety. Applied to political science, this meant that one must practise what is sometimes called the historical comparative method – one must use evidence from many historical periods and from many societies, cultures, and civilizations. He felt that earlier political theories had been based on or tested by evidence that was too limited in either time or space but that recently various branches of history as well as such disciplines as anthropology and sociology had collected such a wealth of information that it was possible for political theorizing to advance to a qualitatively higher level.

However, while Croce's interpretation of Mosca as a believer in the method of the natural sciences is correct, he does not describe Mosca as a positivist, although many others have, and in fact Mosca is usually regarded as one.[18] Croce's restraint in avoiding the term 'positivism' indicates that he may have been aware that the interpretation of Mosca as a positivist was misleading. To explain why Mosca should not be described simply as a positivist will help us understand the relation between his thought and Croce's.

We may begin by agreeing that positivism does include the above-mentioned thesis that the method of the natural sciences should be extended into the social sciences. However, there are several other theses that are clearly a part of positivism. One is the idea that normative principles and value judgments have no place in scientific inquiry; in short, that science is 'value-free.' Now, we have seen above that Mosca does not preach or practice a value-free political science; examples of normative principles crucial to his theoretical system are the ideal of mixed government, the separation of politics and economics, the separation of church and state, the principle of checks and balances, and the ideal of meritocracy.

Another typical positivist doctrine involves the ideal of prediction, claiming that an important aim of scientific inquiry is the prediction of events and that this is another way in which the social sciences should try to model themselves on the natural sciences. However, Mosca was not at all prone to make predictions and was very much aware of the problematic nature of this activity in his own discipline. He even formulated an interesting principle of asymmetry between negative and positive predictions in the social sciences: while it is impossible to predict what will happen in the future, especially if remote, one can easily predict what will never happen.[19] I am not sure that such a thesis is acceptable, or that Mosca's supporting argument is valid, but they both illustrate his non-positivistic sensitivity to this issue.

How much of this Croce had thought through is not clear. His review, however, finds fault with Mosca's belief in extending the method of natural science into social science. Croce objects (ix) that Mosca 'does not notice that during the past century the opposite has happened, and the historical method or method of the moral sciences, evolution, the doctrine of the struggle for existence, and dialectics have been introduced into the natural sciences with striking consequences.' (non si avvede che da un secolo in qua è accaduto l'opposto, e nelle scienze naturali è stato introdotto, con cospicui effetti, il metodo storico o delle scienze morali, l'evoluzione e la dottrina della lotta vitale e la dialettica.)

Moreover, Croce had a low opinion of the natural scientific method *per se*. His *Logic* of 1909 defined 'science' as a practical activity consisting of concepts that are not descriptions of reality but convenient instruments for summarizing such factual descriptions; the concepts of natural science he labelled 'pseudo-concepts,' and science has no genuine cognitive value and significance, but only a mnemonic and instrumental function. Further, he explicitly applied that general account to political science in one of the essays in the 'elements of politics' of 1925.[20] Finally, it is a historical fact that Croce and his followers paid little attention to the natural sciences.

However, this typical logical criticism is absent in Croce's review. Instead, he adds (ix): 'But my readers know that I abhor philosophical pedantry; therefore, just as I am not pleased with a good idealist epistemology when it accompanies a foolish thought about particular problems, so I am readily indulgent towards a naturalistic epistemology when it accompanies serious critical research on the problems that the scholar is studying. If Mosca affirms and demonstrates truths, it is evident that he is practising philosophy, indeed good philosophy.' (Ma i miei lettori sanno che io aborro la pedanteria filosofica; e perciò, come non mi letifica una buona gnoseologia idealistica quando accompagna uno sciocco pensiero sui problemi particolari, così indulgo volentieri a una discutibile gnoseologia naturalistica quando accompagna una seria ricerca critica dei problemi che lo studioso si propone.) This is a crucial point, which, to my knowledge, Croce applied only on one other occasion in regard to the work of a scientist. In regard to Galileo Galilei, Croce was willing to concede that his work did not contain just pseudo-conceptual mnemonic devices, but genuine philosophical truths.[21] But Croce does not explain how this is possible. My own reconstruction involves two points. First, Croce seems to have used vis-à-vis Mosca (and Galileo) a more supple and refined critical method than he generally applied to thinkers whom he identified as scientists – a method closer to the one that he used in his literary criticism and his philosophy of history. Second, Mosca's theory of governments can be shown to have a formal structure analogous to Croce's own theory of mental activity (*filosofia dello spirito*). Let me explain.

Croce defined art and poetry in terms of intuitive activity or linguistic expression, which in turn is the individualizing aspect of theoretical cognitive activity. Now, he was genuinely interested in the actual works of art, poetry, and literature that we find in history; thus in applying the theory of art in his aesthetics to the history of literature, he conceived his key task to be that of distinguishing what was really poetical and what was not really poetical in a given literary work. He did *not* uncritically equate poetry with meter and rhyme and then dismiss prose works as lacking artistic value. Instead, his analyses often found in so-called prose works a considerable amount of what he meant by poetry (for example, Shakespeare and Corneille); and conversely he often discovered that so-called verse lacked what he called poetry (as was often the case even for parts of Dante's *Divine Comedy*).[22]

Similarly his philosophy of history distinguished between a genuine historiography and a chronicle, on the basis of the problem-orientation of the thinking involved rather than on the basis of external features such as amount of documentation and the like. The consequence was that even the work of great scholars such as Ranke and Burckhardt was not completely or primarily historical; or conversely, a chronicler could be engaged in a genuinely historical effort.[23]

If Croce had followed a similar procedure in regard to science, then he would have uncovered many more cases of scientific works that contain considerable amounts of what he would call philosophical truth. The cases of Galileo and Mosca would not have been isolated exceptions to his rule that science has no cognitive import.

However, this account is still too general, and thus we come to my second point. How and why, according to Croce, can a scientist think philosophical truth (which is the analogue of how a prose writer can be a poet, and how a chronicler can be a historian)? The case of Mosca pro- vides a very instructive example. It involves his contribution to the clas- sification of governments and his critique of the traditional methods of doing so. This was the problem with which he grappled at the begin- ning of his career, and the original advantage of the fundamental elitist principle was that of criticizing the traditional classification.[24]

In his 'elements of politics,' Croce does mention the traditional defini- tion of monarchy, aristocracy, and democracy and does point out that they represent merely empirical distinctions without philosophical rig- our (180–1 and 197–8). He does not elaborate and makes no reference to Mosca. However, for someone acquainted with Mosca's critique, the 'Moschian' flavour of the point is unmistakable.

In its original conception, Mosca meant his principle of elitism to be a better way of classifying governments than the two classic ones of Aristotle and Montesquieu. Aristotle[25] had classified governments into monarchical, aristocratic, and democratic, according to whether the supreme power is held by one person, a small group, or the majority. Montesquieu,[26] in contrast, classified them into despotic, monarchical, and republican: despotic if there exists a hereditary ruler with absolute power, monarchical if the hereditary ruler has limited power, and republican if the ruler or rulers are not hereditary but elected by some or all of the citizens.

Mosca's main objection to these classifications is that they are insuffi- ciently realistic. For example, by Aristotle's own definition, the class of democracies known to him was an empty one because even in Pericles's Athens most of its inhabitants were slaves or foreigners who had no rights of citizenship, and so it was really an aristocracy rather than a democracy. Similarly, by Montesquieu's definition, at the end of the nineteenth century Belgium and Britain were (constitutional) monar- chies, while France and the United States were republics; and yet Bel- gium and France were more similar than either Belgium and Britain or France and the United States;[27] in other words, Montesquieu's account allows for significant intra-class differences and significant inter-class similarities, and so it is based on superficial criteria, which do not grasp the underlying reality.

This criticism is interesting and important, but purely destructive. It was not enough for Mosca to say that all governments conform to his fundamental elitist principle. This principle does tell us what they all have in common, but Mosca also needed to delineate how they differ and what are the deeper features that distinguish them. This is one function of the previously made distinctions between democracy and aristocracy and between liberal and autocratic systems.

Now, to grasp the reason for Croce's attraction to Mosca's theory of government, the following additional points should be noted about his four fundamental concepts. First, each distinction applies to all governments. Second, each involves a gradual, non-discrete criterion; that is, all four basic concepts involve matters of degree, rather than being an all-or-none affair. Third, each involves an opposition between two contrary directions of a spectrum. Fourth, each pair is such that both opposite members are always present simultaneously to some extent; neither is totally absent; when one side prevails over the other, the other is not totally absent; that is, each point along either spectrum is conceived as the result of the two co-existing tendencies. Fifth, although there is an opposition between the members of each pair, there is only a difference (but no opposition) between one pair and another; thus the two distinctions criss-cross each other to generate four theoretical types: liberal democracies, liberal aristocracies, autocratic democracies, and autocratic aristocracies. Sixth, the relationship of these theoretical types to empirical and historical reality is that actual, past or existing, governments approximate the theoretical types to a greater or lesser extent, so there is no pretence of finding perfect illustrations of these types. Seventh, historically and empirically speaking, there is always an interaction between the two opposites within each spectrum – such interactions are the moving forces of political history. Eighth, there may be contingent correlations between members of different pairs – for example, between democracy and liberalism and between autocracy and aristocracy – even though logically and conceptually this is not necessary.

Such a conceptual framework is very similar to Croce's own system of four 'distincts': intuitive, aesthetic, or expressive theoretical activity; conceptual, philosophical, or ratiocinative theoretical activity; moral or universalistic practical activity; and useful or individualistic practical activity. My own exposition here is of course more explicit than one finds in Mosca and than Croce's own account of Mosca. Thus to some extent my account here may involve a certain amount of 'Crocean' reading of Mosca. Nevertheless, there seems to be a significant analogy between this aspect of Mosca's political theory and Croce's own theoretical philosophy (his filosofia dello spirito). So it is not surprising that Croce would see 'philosophical' truth in Mosca's political 'science.'

In this regard, it is significant that in his review Croce at one point

(xii) claims that Mosca's theory of forms of government is reminiscent of Vico – 'a writer whom Mosca does not seem to have studied, but if he had he would have certainly been able to strengthen his thesis' (scrittore che il Mosca non pare abbia studiato e certamente, se l'avesse fatto, ne avrebbe tratto sussidi alla sua tesi). Indeed, this corresponds to another famous judgment on Mosca published by Piero Gobetti a few months before Croce's review; Gobetti described Mosca as 'a Vichian who has not read Vico' (un vichiano che non ha letto Vico).[28] These possible connections with Vico of course require more analysis and evaluation. Here I take them as merely emblematic. However, I would claim that a major element of the deciphering of this emblem is the analysis that I have just given of Mosca's theory of the forms of government. That is, Mosca's account of the meaning, interrelations, and historical-empirical import of democracy, aristocracy, liberal government, and autocracy is strikingly similar (though of course not identical) to Croce's own account of the meaning, interrelationships, and historical-empirical import of art, philosophy, utility, and morality. In turn, this similarity should be explored further, for example by analysing in a more theoretical manner the method involved in such a manner of thinking.[29]

Croce's Endorsements of Mosca

The point just elaborated began with an apparent difference in epistemological theory between the two thinkers and ended with a striking similarity in their actual manner of thinking in their respective domains – in their epistemological practice. This point may explain Croce's statement that Mosca actually thinks like a philosopher, whatever self-reflective pronouncements to the contrary he may express. However, there are more explicit and more substantive endorsements of Mosca in Croce's review.

First, Croce begins by apparently endorsing Mosca's fundamental elitist principle. After stating it in his own words, Croce claims (viii) that 'this concept is extremely important for the interpretation of political history' (l'importanza di questo concetto è somma per l'interpretazione della storia politica). From the point of view of the elite–mass distinction (ix), the challenge of interpreting political history 'becomes manageable for the intellect, acumen, diligence, and the mental impartiality of the historian, and can yield tasty fruit' (diventa tale che potrà provarvisi l'ingegno, l'acume, la diligenza, l'equilibrio mentale dello storico, e dare frutti sapidi). Croce contrasts such an approach to others such as those of a socialist and a democrat, meaning the latter in the sense of majority rule by the people. To these he objects (ix) that 'democratic historian, socialist historian, and the like are equivalent by definition to unhistorical historians, at least in the initial aim' (storico democratico, storico socialista e simili equivalgono per definizione a storici antistorici, almeno nel proposito iniziale). This is only the first of many barbs directed at the populist theory of democracy stemming from Rousseau, or what might be called simply egalitarianism; but of this more below.

Second, another statement of endorsement by Croce is that Mosca's fundamental principle (x) 'is the compass for political education in our time, as it is at all times' (è la bussola per l'educazione politica ai nostri tempi, come in tutti i tempi). Croce's point is that the principle is also politically useful and relevant in so far as it suggests that one should concentrate one's efforts on the proper education of an elite or ruling class.

Third, another endorsement involves a specific interpretation of the problem of forming a properly educated class of leaders. Such a problem is ultimately a moral and religious problem, in the general sense of religion, according to which Catholicism or traditional Christianity is only one particular instance.

Fourth, Croce thinks that traditional Christianity is no longer the most viable religion (in his sense of the word). He also thinks that the same may be said (x–xi) 'of the substitution of Christian religion with the three empty words "liberty, equality, fraternity," which constitute the idiotic religion of freemasonry' (della sostituzione della religione cristiana con le tre vuote parole 'libertà, eguaglianza, fraternità,' che formano l'idiota religione massonica). Here we have another expression of anti-egalitarianism, but, more important, he agrees with Mosca that at the time patriotism was the most viable religion. Croce, however, stresses that the patriotism about which they are talking must be sharply distinguished from nationalism. He does not elaborate on this point, but what he probably has in mind is that some aspects of fascism should be rejected as 'nationalistic,' whereas the key idea of the Risorgimento should be endorsed as a triumph of patriotism. From another point of view, it would be consistent with the rest of the interpretation being elaborated here to say that Croce would regard nationalism as patriotism carried too far. At any rate, this agreement represents a fourth endorsement of Mosca.

Fifth, Croce endorses Mosca's peculiar theory of democracy. He stresses that Mosca's theory is opposed not to democracy, but rather to a particular alternative theory of democracy. It does not oppose various actually existing democratic tendencies; rather it tries to understand them, by giving due attention to opposite ('aristocratic') tendencies and by making democracy and aristocracy correlative notions. As hinted at above, this clarification is very important and, I believe, essentially correct.

Sixth, Croce offers a final endorsement of Mosca (xiii): 'Far from being at war against the liberal state, he is thus a resolute defender of this institution, which is the most mature form of European political life' (non che partire in guerra contro lo Stato liberale, egli è dunque risoluto difensore di questa che è la forma più matura della vita politica europea). Moreover (xiii), for Mosca 'everything considered, the liberal state is not the democratic state, but its constitutive principle is sound" (tutto considerato, lo stato liberale non è lo stato democratico, e il suo principio informatore è sano). This last statement looks like an acceptance of Mosca's distinction between democracy and liberal government discussed above. However, the liberalism meant by Mosca in that context is, as we have seen, a theoretical and eternally present form that is the opposite of autocracy. It is not 'the constitutive principle' of 'the most mature form of European political life.' Unfortunately, Croce does not explain in this context what this constitutive principle is. Therefore, while it is clear that he is here endorsing some kind of liberalism, and that in so doing he is agreeing with Mosca, it is unclear exactly what meaning he is attaching to this notion. However, in a number of essays of his 'elements of politics,' Croce does elaborate his conception of liberalism. After all, this was perhaps the central concept of his political philosophy.

Croce's Liberalism

An examination of the relevant essays reveals that by liberalism Croce means primarily two things – pluralism and anti-egalitarianism. These elements correspond to what I have called Mosca's pluralism and elitism respectively. To see this, let us begin by noting that the term 'liberalism,' together with its cognates 'liberal' and 'liberty,' has many meanings. A system is liberal when authority flows from the bottom up, from the masses to the elites. This is the technical meaning that the term has in Mosca's theory of the forms of government; and, as we saw above, his conceptual framework is such that this liberalism is opposite to autocracy and distinct from (but not opposite to) democracy. This is a specific and restricted meaning, and it makes no sense to accept it without accepting the rest of the conceptual framework. However, we saw above that Croce is favourably inclined towards this conceptual system.

Then there is liberalism in the sense of an institutional arrangement of the economic system such that the government minimizes its interference in economic decisions. This is something that Croce labelled *liberismo* and was at pains to distinguish from liberalism in the ethico-political sense. Liberismo corresponds to the doctrine of the laissez faire, and we might translate it simply as economic liberalism. In his 'Elementi di politica' (Elements of politics), Croce includes a whole essay entitled 'Liberismo e liberalismo' (263–7). In it he states that he is favourably disposed towards economic liberalism, but he makes a number of qualifications. First, the normative principle of economic liberalism is an approximate maxim and cannot be given a precise formulation, which would specify exactly where the government cannot intervene, where it can, and how far it can. Second, the justification of economic liberalism lies in ethico-political liberalism; that is, Croce finds economic liberalism attractive primarily for ethico-political reasons. In short, liberismo or laissez faire is not an absolute, either in what it prescribes or in its normative force.

Note the connection with Mosca. It is obvious that Croce's liberismo corresponds to Mosca's principle of the separation of politics and economics. It is equally true that for Mosca this separation was not an ultimate or irreducible principle, but rather a consequence of the principle that no single force, institution, or class should hold absolute or excessive power.

In regard to the primary meaning of liberalism, Croce's 'Elementi di politica' contains an even longer essay, 'The Liberal Conception as a Conception of Life' (La concezione liberale come concezione della vita). He summarizes (236) this conception as follows (emphasis added):

In effect, it reflects all the philosophy and religion of the modern age, which are centred on the idea of dialectics or development; by means of the *diversity and opposition of spiritual forces*, this idea constantly expands life, renders it more noble, and gives it its only and entire meaning. From this theoretical foundation originates the liberal practical disposition to trust and favour a *variety of tendencies* and offer them an open field so that they can compete among themselves, be tested, and cooperate by *agreeing to disagree* ... [in contrast to] the opposite practical disposition, called authoritarian, which mistrusts spontaneous and *mutually conflicting forces*, tries to prevent or eliminate *conflicts*, prescribes the ways to follow and to behave, and pre-establishes the rules to which one must conform. (In effetto, in essa si respecchia tutta la filosofia e la religione dell'età moderna, incentrata nell'idea della dialettica ossia dello svolgimento, che, mercè la diversità o l'opposizione delle forze spirituali, accresce e nobilita di continuo la vita e le conferisce il suo unico e intero significato. Su questo fondamento teoretico nasce la disposizione pratica liberale di fiducia e favore verso la varietà delle tendenze, alle quali si vuole piuttosto offrire un campo aperto perchè gareggino e si provino tra loro e cooperino in concorde discordia ... [in contrasto con] l'opposta disposizione pratica, che si chiama autoritaria, e che diffida delle forze spontanee e tra loro contrastanti, cerca di prevenire o troncare i contrasti, prescrive le vie da seguire e i modi da tenere, e prestabilisce gli ordinamenti ai quali conformarsi.)

The italicized words are clues to the fact that an essential part of Croce's liberalism is what I have been calling pluralism. This may be usefully compared to Mosca's formulation of the principle of moderate pluralism – 'the absolute preponderance of a single political force, the predominance of any over-simplified concept in the organization of a state, the strictly logical application of any single principle in all public law are the essential elements in any type of despotism, whether it be a despotism based upon divine right or a despotism based ostensibly on popular sovereignty.' (La preponderanza assoluta di una sola forza politica, il predominio di un concetto semplicista nell'organizzazione dello Stato, l'applicazione severamente logica d'un solo principio ispiratore di tutto il diritto pubblico, sono gli elementi necessari per qualunque genere di dispotismo; tanto per quello fondato sul diritto divino, che per l'altro che presume di avere la sua base nella sovranità popolare.)[30]

Another essential element of Croce's 'liberalism' is, as I stated above, anti-egalitarianism. To see this, let us begin by noting that anti-egalitarianism is a crucial part of Croce's political philosophy. In fact, the issue receives prominence in the first section ('The Political Sense' Il senso politico) of the first essay (entitled 'Politica "in nuce"') of his 'Elementi di politica.' That section ends with a criticism of egalitarianism (181–3) in the form of a reductio ad absurdum, which begins by assuming that egalitarianism is correct and on the basis of this assumption derives the consequence that egalitarianism is incorrect. Croce argues that if egalitarianism is correct, individual equality would be the foundation of the state; but if individuals were equal, then no one would be in a position of asking for anything or giving anything to anyone else; in that case, no state or government would be needed; thus, the appropriate situation for a collection of equal individuals would be one of complete individual autonomy or 'autarky" (*autarchia*); but this situation is simply a denial of the state or government (as we know it); thus political egalitarianism implies the absence of politics.

In this argument, at one point Croce states that if individuals were equal there would be no 'diversity' (182). This statement links his anti-egalitarianism to his liberal pluralism. The connection is that egalitarianism advocates a uniformity or conformism that is antithetical to the pluralism at the heart of liberalism – a point that Croce makes more explicitly in the essay on 'The Liberal Conception as a Conception of Life' in the context of a criticism of communism and Marxist socialism. Croce's objection (238) is that Marxism

has as its proper foundation the idea of 'equality'; that is, not equality understood as an awareness of our common humanity, which is at the bottom of liberalism itself and of every true ethics; but rather equality construed mathematically and mechanically ... Precisely because of such a substantial negation of struggle and history, because of the authoritarianism to which it is compelled to resort and which it sometimes calls 'dictatorship' (to make it look hopefully temporary), and because of its inevitable inclination to suffocate the variety of tendencies, the spontaneous developments, and the formation of personality, socialism meets the hostility of the liberal conception, and they become engaged in a conflict which takes the already mentioned religious character. (ha a proprio fondamento l'idea di 'eguaglianza,' cioè non punto l'eguaglianza intesa come coscienza di comune umanità, la quale è nel fondo dello stesso liberalismo e di ogni vera etica, ma l'eguaglianza matematicamente e meccanicamente costruita ... Appunto per siffatta sostanziale negazione della lotta e della storia, per l'autoritarismo al quale è costretto ad appigliarsi e che talvolta chiama 'dittatura' (volendo farlo sperare provvisorio), per l'inevitabile inclinazione a soffocare la varietà delle tendenze, gli spontanei svolgimenti e la formazione della personalità, il socialismo incontra l'ostilità della concezione liberale, e tra loro vengono a un conflitto, che anch'esso prende il già avvertito carattere religioso.)

Another of Croce's liberal arguments against political egalitarianism is that it is utopian in presupposing an unrealistic, unhistorical, and empirically untrue view of human nature. This appears in a chapter on 'History and Utopia' in *History as the Story of Liberty*. The crucial consideration there is the following:

Social participation should not be understood as the diffusion of an idea which, spreading equally to all sides, receives an equal response from all sides ... The liberal method cannot convert all men into politicians, against their nature and against the very nature of things; nature does not allow that everyone should be that, as it does not allow that all should be poets, philosophers, and heroes; it needs variety, diversity, and opposition, the negative as well as the positive, in order to weave the cloth of reality. (La partecipazione sociale non è da intendere quasi la risonanza di un'idea che, spargendosi egualmente in ogni parte, ottenga da ogni parte eguale risposta ... Nè può il metodo liberale convertire tutti gli uomini in politici contro la loro natura e contro la natura stessa delle cose, che non consente che tutti siano poeti e filosofi ed eroi, e ha bisogno del vario e del diverso e dell'opposto, del positivo e del negativo, per tessere la tela della realtà.)[31]

Once again, the connection between liberal pluralism and liberal anti-egalitarianism is clear.

Anti-egalitarianism was also an essential element of Mosca's political theory. His fundamental elitist principle may in fact be construed simply as a principled denial of egalitarianism. For example, this is explicit in his 'Elementi,' where, immediately after formulating the elitist principle, he adds: 'We almost could not imagine the real existence of a world differently organized, in which everyone equally and without a hierarchy was subject to a single person, or where all equally would manage political affairs' (Non sapremmo quasi nella realtà immaginare un mondo organizzato diversamente, nel quale tutti egualmente e senza alcuna gerarchia fossero sottoposti ad un solo o tutti egualmente dirigessero le cose politiche.)[32]

Finally, there is in Croce another passage (239) that is both an explicit statement of the connection between liberalism, pluralism, and egalitarianism and an explicit expression of 'Moschian' ideas. It thus can serve as a concluding remark to summarize both the content of Croce's and of Mosca's political philosophies and the nature of their connection: 'For liberalism, which was born and remains intrinsically anti-egalitarian, liberty is the means to bring about and promote (to use Gladstone's aphorism) not democracy but aristocracy; the latter is truly vigorous and serious when it is not a closed aristocracy but an open one, firm indeed in rejecting the popular masses but always ready to accept whoever lifts himself to it.' (Pel liberalismo, che è nato e intrisicamente rimane antiegualitario, la libertà, secondo un motto del Gladstone, è la via per produrre e promuovere, non la democrazia ma l'aristocrazia, la quale è veramente vigorosa e seria quando non è aristocrazia chiusa ma aperta, ferma bensì a respingere il volgo, ma pronta sempre ad accogliere chi a lei s'innalza.)

Epilogue

Historical conditions in Italy in the early 1920s induced Croce to make a major effort at political theorizing and to write the 'Elementi di politica,' which makes up half of his *Etica e politica* (Ethics and Politics). The intellectual background to his political philosophy consists primarily (though, of course, not exclusively[33]) of the political theory expounded in the second edition of Mosca's *Elements of Political Science* (1923). This work provided the occasion for Croce's thinking, as his review indicates. Mosca's treatise provided Croce with some key concepts and theoretical principles, as a comparative analysis of their views shows. The two main principles of Mosca's political theory are elitism and moderate pluralism. Elitism means simply that one takes the most fundamental political distinction to be that between elites and masses, and then one examines all political phenomena and problems in terms of the relationship and interaction between elites and masses. And moderate pluralism means the principled avoidance of any one-sidedness and all extremes.

Croce's anti-positivism presented a stumbling block to his appreciation and appropriation of Mosca's political science. However, he overcame it by distinguishing between concrete scientific achievement and abstract epistemological reflection; this distinction enabled him to endorse the former while rejecting the latter. At a more implicit level, Croce was attracted not only to the substantive content of Mosca's political theory, but also to the formal structure of his system. For example, Mosca's critique of the traditional classifications of governments seems to presuppose the theory of pseudo-concepts in Croce's *Logic*; and the constructive theory of types of government is formally analogous to Croce's own general theory of mental activity, usually known by the label of filosofia dello spirito. Although Mosca's criticism goes back to the first edition of the *Elements* (1896), which antedates Croce's *Logic* (1906/1909), Mosca's constructive theory emerged between the first and second edition of the 'Elements,' and so it is possible that it was at least partially and indirectly influenced by Croce's theory of mental activity.

Croce's endorsements of Mosca in the review of the *Elements* involve at least five points. One of these concerns the factual historical truth of the fundamental elitist principle. Another involves the pedagogical value and function of this principle for the education of political leaders. A third refers to the nature and function of traditional religion and its relationship to political and moral education. Fourth, Croce agrees with Mosca on the value of patriotism and the distinction between patriotism and nationalism. Finally, Croce expresses a general endorsement of Mosca's liberalism.

Croce's liberalism is elaborated in his 'Elementi di politica.' It contains two main principles – pluralism and anti-egalitarianism. These may be seen to be equivalent to the two most fundamental principles in Mosca's political theory. In fact, while the latter's elitism is not anti-democratic, or anti-meritocratic, or autocratic, it does amount to a principled denial of egalitarianism.

These conclusions have, primarily, historical import, in the sense of the history of thought and the history of ideas. They suggest that Croce and Mosca, as thinkers, are much closer than ordinarily supposed. The two main areas of convergence are political theory and epistemological practice. In political theory, besides a set of shared views, one could also hazard a direction of influence from Mosca to Croce. In epistemological practice, the direction of influence is likely to be the other way. If the essence of Mosca's political theory is reduced to an attempt to combine democracy and elitism that may be labelled 'pluralistic elitism,' then we can say that Croce was essentially a pluralistic elitist. And epistmeologically speaking, I suggest neither that Mosca was a simple-minded positivist nor that Croce was a dogmatic anti-positivist, but rather that they both in effect combined science and philosophy into a position that may be called judicious realism.

These conclusions and these suggestions in turn suggest further historical inquiries. For example, in regard to Croce per se, one could examine his later period of political involvement to test whether his views and his actions conform to the pluralistic elitism attributed to him here. Another possible investigation would be to determine whether the judiciously realistic epistemology that I am attributing to Croce manifests itself in other ways than those mentioned here.

In regard to the Croce–Mosca relationship, the investigation above has made me curious about whether there is any record of views that Mosca may have expressed about Croce. Moreover, the conceptual and formal similarities between Croce's theory of mental activity (filosofia dello spirito) and Mosca's theory of governments are so striking that one should search for concrete historical connections between them, to determine whether or not either influenced the other in that regard or whether both were influenced by some third source.

Expanding our historical horizon somewhat, it would be important to explore whether Croce's and Mosca's pluralistic elitism is part of a tradition that includes other important figures.[34] Here, one obvious possibility would be to examine the thought of someone who is regarded as something of a twin brother of Mosca, so much so that the two of them are frequently mentioned in the same breath – Vilfredo Pareto. There is of course no question that Pareto adhered to the fundamental elitist principle; I am less sure, however, in regard to his commitment to democracy, although his notion of the 'circulation of elites' is reminiscent of Mosca's concept of democracy in terms of open elites. At any rate, Pareto's place in the tradition of pluralistic elitism may be more intimately tied to the concept of pluralism than to Mosca's technical definition of democracy; and in turn his pluralism may have to be teased out of his theory of equilibrium rather than out of any explicitly 'pluralist' terminology.

A more surprising but equally fruitful inquiry would involve the thought of Antonio Gramsci. Although I am aware that Gramsci is usually regarded as a patron saint of the left (just as Mosca is for the right, and perhaps Croce for the centre), it is possible to reconstruct some important elements of Gramsci's *Prison Notebooks* as conforming to the pluralistic-elitist paradigm.[35]

A more obvious but largely unknown instance of democratic elitism is found in James Madison. The key elements here would be his concern with the avoidance of tyranny and his definition of tyranny as the excessive accumulation of power. Putting the two together, we get a principle that is almost identical to Mosca's principle of moderate pluralism quoted above. One question would be to see whether Mosca was influenced by Madison. A more important task would be to reconstruct Madison's political theory to see how it could enrich the tradition of pluralistic elitism.[36]

These suggestions and inquiries provide examples of the further implications that my conclusions may be taken to have in the area of the history of ideas. However, the pluralistic elitism and epistemological realism attributed to Croce (and to Mosca) have such an inherent believability that my interpretive conclusions acquire theoretical and practical relevance as well.

In regard to the 'epistemological realism' that I have attributed to them, there is obviously a considerable amount of theoretical elucidation that needs to be done. To begin with, I have argued that Mosca held one epistemological thesis that might be termed positivist (the extension of the method of natural science to social science), but not others (the predicitivist requirement and the principle of value-freedom). We have also seen Croce claiming that while Mosca's philosophical epistemology is wrong, his political science is correct. Finally, I have claimed that although Croce's theory of science is instrumentalist, his interpretation of Mosca's political science is not – i.e., he attributes cognitive worth to it. Now I believe that ultimately the best way to describe these three attitudes (of Mosca, Croce, and myself) is in terms of an attitude that aims to avoid one-sidedness and extremes. This in turn is a kind of moderate pluralism in the realm of epistemology and methodology, and it thus suggests that a deeper unity may underlie the two sets of issues discussed in this paper.

However, independently of such higher unity, this epistemological realism (i.e., judicious avoidance of methodological one-sidedness and extremes) could be explored theoretically and applied practically further by examining more systematically and exhaustively whether it characterizes the rest of Mosca's and of Croce's work. One could also consider to what extent it may be found in important examples of scientific practice, either contemporary or past, and involving either the natural or the social sciences.[37]

Let us now turn to some of the theoretical and practical implications of pluralistic elitism. For example, the centrality of pluralism in a modern democracy is an idea that finds resonance in contemporary democratic theory, especially in the work of Robert Dahl, which is one of the most important contributions to this field. Dahl has provided considerable theoretical and empirical support for the idea that democracy finds the best empirical approximation in modern, dynamic, pluralistic societies and that 'what is crucial about an MDP [modern, dynamic, pluralistic] society is that on the one hand it inhibits the concentration of power in any single unified set of actors, and on the other hand it disperses power among a number of relatively independent actors.'[38]

Or consider the ideal of 'an aristocracy open to the popular masses and ready to accept all who lift themselves up to it,' expressed in Croce's last quotation above. Here one cannot help but be struck by the fact that this ideal has recently been elaborated anew by a leading political theorist, Bernard R. Barber, in a work titled *An Aristocracy for Everyone*[39]; and it is difficult to believe that the correspondence will turn out to be merely semantic.

Finally, let us turn in a more practical direction. It seems obvious to me that this Crocean and Moschian political philosophy has implications for such practical political issues as affirmative action and term limits. For example, although term limits have been criticized by some as undemocratic in so far as they would prevent the people from re-electing a candidate past the stipulated maximum period of service, this criticism presupposes a populistic definition of democracy. However, if, following Mosca, one defines democracy in terms of open elites, then one could argue that term limits enhance democracy by increasing the degree of openness of the ruling elites.[40]

NOTES

1 See, for example, Richard Bellamy, *Liberalism and Modern Society: A Historical Argument* (University Park: Pennsylvania State University Press, 1992); Norberto Bobbio, 'Croce e il liberalismo,' in his *Politica e cultura* (Turin: Einaudi, 1955); A. Robert Caponigri, *History and Liberty: The Historical Writings of Benedetto Croce* (London: Routledge and Kegan Paul, 1955); Mario Delle Piane, *Gaetano Mosca: Classe politica e liberalismo* (Naples: Edizioni scientifiche italiane, 1952); Antonio Gramsci, *Quaderni del carcere*, critical edition by Valentino Gerratana and the Gramsci Institute, 4 vols. consecutively paginated (Turin: Einaudi, 1975), 1007, 1229–32, and 1293, and *Lettere dal carcere*, ed. S. Caprioglio and E. Fubini (Turin: Einaudi, 1965), 220–1.

2 See, for example, Richard Bellamy, *Modern Italian Social Theory* (Stanford, Calif.: Stanford University Press, 1987); Norberto Bobbio, *Saggi sulla scienza politica in Italia* (Bari: Laterza, 1969); V. de Caprariis, 'Profilo di Gaetano Mosca,' *Il Mulino* 3 (1954), 343–64; Gramsci, *Quaderni del carcere*, 956; and Giorgio Sola, 'Una rilettura critica dei pricipali testi di Gaetano Mosca,' in *La dottrina della classe politica ed i suoi sviluppi internazionali*, ed. E.A. Albertoni, Archivio internazionale Gaetano Mosca per lo studio della classe politica, serie italiana, vol. I (Palermo: Società Siciliana per la Storia Patria, 1982), 169.

3 See, for example, Antonio Aliotta, *La reazione idealistica contro la scienza* (Palermo: Casa Editrice 'Optima,' 1912), trans. Agnes McCaskill as *The Idealistic Reaction against Science* (London: Macmillan, 1914); and Maria Luisa Dalla Chiara, 'Preface' to *Italian Studies in the Philosophy of Science*, ed. by M.L. Dalla Chiara (Dordrecht, Netherlands: D. Reidel Publishing Company, 1981), ix.

4 The review was first published in B. Croce, Review of Mosca's *Elementi di scienza politica*, *La critica* 21 no. 6 (Nov. 1923), 374–8; it is now also available in

B. Croce, *Nuove pagine sparse* (Bari: Laterza, 1966), II, 220–7; and in B. Croce, 'Premessa,' to G. Mosca, *Elementi di scienza politica*, 4th ed. (Bari: Laterza, 1947); 5th ed. (Bari: Laterza, 1953), vii–xv. The first edition of the book under review is G. Mosca, *Elementi di scienza politica* (Turin: Bocca, 1896); the second has the same title and publisher and bears the imprint date of 1923; it is now available in a critical edition: *Scritti politici*, II, ed. Giorgio Sola (Turin: UTET, 1982). The English translation of Mosca's book bears the curious title of *The Ruling Class*, trans. H.D. Kahn, ed. with intro. by A. Livingston (New York: McGraw-Hill, 1939); a later reprint (Westport, Conn.: Greenwood Press, 1980) is now out of print.

5 B. Croce, 'Elementi di politica,' in *Etica e politica*, first economical ed. (Bari: Laterza, 1967), 171–297.

6 Paolo Frascani, 'Croce e Gaetano Mosca: Significato di una recensione,' *Rivista di studi crociani* 4 (1967), 470–5.

7 B. Croce, *Nuove pagine sparse*, I, 64. Here and elsewhere, all translations are my own unless otherwise noted.

8 Ibid.

9 B. Croce, *Scritti e discorsi politici* (Bari: Laterza, 1963), II, 300.

10 My account here is largely based on B. Croce, 'Ricordi politici,' in *Nuove pagine sparse*, I, 63–106; and B. Croce, 'Note autobiografiche,' in *Etica e politica*, 357–73.

11 This is stated by Croce himself in the preface to his *Etica e politica*, 5.

12 These activities are recorded in B. Croce, *Scritti e discorsi politici*.

13 Or at least this is my interpretation. Croce makes it look as if 'political action is not only useful action, but these two concepts are coextensive, and one will never be able to adduce a characteristic which would distinguish the first within the orbit of the second' (l'azione politica non solo è azione utile, ma questi due concetti sono coestensivi, nè si sarà mai in grado di addurre alcun carattere che distingua la prima nell'orbita della seconda); *Etica e politica*, 173. However, I believe that this is belied by Croce's own argument – for example, by his distinction between economical-political and ethical-political history, which is the central subject of one of these essays (225–34).

14 Here I am concurring with a conclusion advanced by other scholars – for example, Norberto Bobbio, 'Croce e il liberalismo.'

15 I mentioned above that at the end of the period they cooperated in the organization of the Liberal party and the signing of the manifesto of anti-fascist intellectuals. Moreover, as senators for life, they were two of a very small group of members of parliament who did not endorse one of the first concrete signs of fascist authoritarianism – namely the bill against freemasonry; see G. Mosca, 'Senate Speech, 18 November 1925,' *Atti Parlamentari*, Senato

del Regno, Legislatura XXVII, Sessione I, Discussioni (Rome: Tipografia del Senato, 1925), IV, 3660–2; see also B. Croce, 'Speech to the Senate, 20 November 1925,' now in B. Croce, *Discorsi parlamentari* (Rome: Bardi, 1966), 164–6; and cf. my 'Gramsci, Mosca, e la Massoneria,' *Teoria politica* (Turin) 9 no. 2 (1993), 135–61.

16 This account is along the lines provided in my forthcoming *Beyond Right and Left: Democratic Elitism in Mosca and Gramsci* (New Haven, Conn.: Yale University Press, 1999). Other valuable accounts are found in Bellamy, *Modern Italian Social Theory*; Bobbio, *Saggi sulla scienza politica in Italia*; James H. Meisel, *The Myth of the Ruling Class: Gaetano Mosca and the Elite* (Ann Arbor: University of Michigan Press, 1958); G. Sola, 'Elements for a Critical Reappraisal of the Works of Gaetano Mosca,' in E.A. Albertoni, ed., *Studies on the Political Thought of Gaetano Mosca* (Milan: Giuffre, 1982), 91–112, and 'Introduzione,' to Mosca, *Scritti politici*, ed. Sola, I, 9–79.

17 Croce, 'Premessa,' to G. Mosca, *Elementi di scienza politica* (Bari: Laterza, 1947), ix. Subsequent references to this review appear in parenthesis in the text.

18 See, for example, Bellamy, *Modern Italian Social Theory*; Bobbio, *Saggi sulla scienza politica in Italia*; de Caprariis, 'Profilo di Gaetano Mosca'; Gramsci, *Quaderni del carcere*, 956; and Sola, 'Una rilettura critica dei pricipali testi di Gaetano Mosca,' 169.

19 Mosca, *Scritti politici*, II, 875–6; and *Ruling Class*, 283–4.

20 Croce, 'La scienza empirica della politica,' *Etica e politica*, 196–203. Subsequent references to this book appear in parenthesis in the text.

21 B. Croce, *Storia dell'età barocca in Italia* (Bari: Laterza, 1929), 60–4, especially 62.

22 See B. Croce, *Ariosto, Shakespeare e Corneille* (1920), 4th ed. (Bari: Laterza, 1950), trans. D. Ainslie (New York: Holt, 1920); and *La poesia di Dante* (1920), 11th ed. (Bari: Laterza, 1966).

23 See B. Croce, *Teoria e storia della storiografia* (1917), 9th ed. (Bari: Laterza, 1966), especially chap. 1; *Theory and History of Historiography*, trans. D. Ainslie (London: George G. Harrap & Co., 1921); *La storia come pensiero e come azione* (1938), economical ed. (Bari: Laterza, 1966), especially 73–100; and *History as the Story of Liberty*, trans. S. Sprigge, first pub. New York: Norton, 1941 (Chicago: Henry Regnery Company, 1970).

24 See, for example, G. Mosca, *Sulla teorica dei governi e sul governo parlamentare. Studi storici e sociali* (Turin: Loescher, 1884), now in *Scritti politici*, ed. Sola, I, 183–542.

25 *Politics*, III, 7, 1279a–b.

26 *Spirit of Laws*, books II and III.

27 Mosca, *Scritti politici*, II, 610; Mosca, *Ruling Class*, 52.

28 Piero Gobetti, 'Un conservatore galantuomo,' *La rivoluzione liberale* 3 no. 18 (29 April 1924), 71, reprinted in Gobetti, *Scritti politici*, ed. P. Spriano (Turin: Einaudi, 1960), 655.

29 My hunch is that this manner of thinking is largely 'dialectical,' in the sense of dialectic elaborated in my *Gramsci and the History of Dialectical Thought* (Cambridge: Cambridge University Press, 1988); my meaning, however, is not to be confused with other meanings of this problematic and much abused concept.

30 Mosca, *Ruling Class*, 134; Mosca, *Scritti politici*, II, 689.

31 Croce, *La storia come pensiero e come azione*, economical ed., 236–8; for a criticism of this passage, see Meisel, *The Myth of the Ruling Class*, 353–6.

32 Mosca, *Scritti politici*, II, 609, my translation; cf. *Ruling Class*, 50.

33 Other sources are (obviously) Machiavelli and Vico and (more controversially) Marx.

34 One useful, though unsatisfactory contribution in this direction is P. Bachrach, *The Theory of Democratic Elitism: A Critique* (Boston: Little, Brown and Company, 1967), reprint, Lanham: University Press, of America, 1980.

35 See my forthcoming *Beyond Right and Left: Democratic Elitism in Mosca and Gramsci*.

36 Cf. J. Madison et al., *The Federalist Papers*, ed. C. Rossiter (New York: Penguin 1961), No. 47, p. 301; and Robert A. Dahl, *A Preface to Democratic Theory* (Chicago: University of Chicago Press, 1956), 4–33.

37 See, for example, my 'Empiricism, Judgment, and Argument: Toward an Informal Logic of Science,' *Argumentation* 2 (1988), 313–35; and my 'Methodological Judgment and Critical Reasoning in Galileo's *Dialogue*,' in *PSA 1994: Proceedings of the 1994 Biennial Meeting of the Philosophy of Science Association*, ed. D. Hull et al., 2 vols. (East Lansing, Mich.: Philosophy of Science Association, 1995), II, 248–57.

38 Robert A. Dahl, *Democracy and Its Critics* (New Haven, Conn.: Yale University Press, 1989, 252). Here I am referring to Dahl's theory of democracy, not his interpretation of Mosca; Dahl seems unaware of Mosca's pluralism and instead interprets him in terms of an anti-democratic theory of minority domination (265–79).

39 B.R. Barber, *An Aristocracy of Everyone: The Politics of Education and the Future of America* (New York: Ballantine Books, 1992).

40 I thank Dain Trafton of Rockford College for many useful comments on this paper, which resulted in several improvements.

8

Croce and Collingwood: Philosophy and History

MYRA MOSS

Collingwood on Croce's Theory of History

When historians of philosophy have attempted to ascertain the influences of Croce's thinking on Collingwood's idea of history, they usually have noted some of the similarities between the concepts that these thinkers held in common.[1] More important, many historians have assumed that Collingwood's interpretations of Croce's philosophy are correct. The purpose of my essay is to evaluate Collingwood's interpretations and to reconsider some major differences between the two thinkers' conceptions of philosophy and history. In conclusion, I will discuss what remains vital in Croce's theory of history.

Commentators have written that Collingwood's early essays offer their reader an anti-Crocean position. After 1936, Collingwood implicitly withdrew most of his early criticisms.[2] He then converted to a kind of 'radical historicism' that supposedly reflected Croce's philosophy.[3] In 1921, he wrote to Croce that his criticisms seemed more serious than they really were: for the most part he agreed with Croce's theory of history; and his positive influence could be seen throughout Collingwood's work.[4]

What were Collingwood's early criticisms? How did he propose to correct the errors that he found in Croce's philosophy? In 'Croce's Philosophy of History'[5] (1921), Collingwood argued that Croce's *Teoria e storia della storiografia* (1917), translated from its second edition as *History: Its Theory and Practice* (1921), reveals a debate between Croce as naturalist and as idealist. By 'naturalist,' Collingwood meant dualist, realist, empiricist, one who holds to formal distinctions, and by 'idealist,' one who engages in 'warfare upon transcendence and naturalism in all their forms' and who makes 'an effort to sweep away dualisms and to reunite distinctions in a concrete or immanent unity.' According to Collingwood, 'A great part of Croce's written work consists in a debate between these two, one building up dualisms and the other dismantling them; sometimes failing to dismantle them.'[6] As a consequence of Croce's dualistic thought, his conception of acts of the human spirit required that they fall under either one or the other of two mutually exclusive heads – theoretical and practical, thought and rational will. In sum, Collingwood's criticisms of Croce's so-called dualisms – as, for example, life versus death, thought versus science – amounted to confused variants of his major criticism of Croce's separation of theory from praxis.

Ironically, what Collingwood erroneously saw as Croce's separation of theory from praxis he himself would acknowledge later in his *Autobiography*[7] as a mote in his own eye – that is, as among the most important problems, along with the rapprochement between philosophy and history, of his own entire academic career, as well as of his personal life. His resolution of these dilemmas was incomplete in 1919, and he would modify his conceptions of philosophy and history.

In 'Croce's Philosophy of History,' however, Collingwood failed to understand that the relations in Croce between thought and rational will are phenomenological. The two expressions of will – the economic and the ethical – do not exclude but rather include the intuitional and conceptual expressions of thought. Will is not blind, since it necessitates thought for its expression. The a priori synthesizing activity of rational will transforms individual judgment of thought into a plan for action that is directed towards an immediate (economic) or a long-term (ethical) goal.

Croce's activities of thinking and willing, moreover, are not themselves sense objects – that is, subject-matter for an empirical science – as Collingwood would have it.[8] Nor is the distinction between them an empirical one, since it is not sensed: it is recognized instead by reflective introspection. Croce described his philosophy thus as a speculative and not as an empirical psychology.[9]

According to Collingwood, Croce also advocated a naturalistic concept of annals or chronicles,[10] since the judgments in chronicles were not the true theoretical ones that form the core of historical narrative. As expressions of rational will, chronological records are composed of what Croce called empirical and abstract pseudo-concepts. Such pseudo-concepts and the pseudo-judgments formed from them are neither true nor false, but they could prove useful or not useful for historical inquiry. Considered as arbitrary classifications, pseudo-judgments can be evaluated in terms of utility and need. Thus to say, as Croce did, that chronicles are devoid of truth is not to say that they are devoid of thought or meaning, as Collingwood maintained, since instrumental or empirical judgments amount to useful classifications of data created for mnemonic purposes.

Supposedly, according to Collingwood, along with accepting the idealistic theory that 'thought thinks itself,' Croce also unconsciously maintained 'the realistic or transcendent theory that the will wills not itself but the existence of a lifeless object other than itself, something unspiritual held in existence by an act of the will.'[11] Moreover, whenever Croce appealed to the concept of will, he was laying aside his idealism and falling back into a transcendent naturalism. Yet, contrary to Collingwood, consistently after the publication of Croce's *Estetica come scienza dell'espressione e linguistica generale* (1902), translated as *The Aesthetic as the Science of Expression and of the Linguistic in General*,[12] which Croce himself admitted contains a residue of naturalism, Croce denied the existence of *res* as *res* or the thing-in-itself, assumed by naturalistic philosophies.

After 1902, Croce maintained a phenomenology of the human spirit. He described his philosophical position as post-Berkeleian absolute or new idealism. Although later he preferred the label 'absolute historicism,' his epistemology did not fundamentally change.[13] By 'idealism' and 'absolute historicism,' he meant that the existence of an object depends on its expression by consciousness. He denied the existence of anything that bears no relation to mind. In other words, he denied absolute existence or existence as a non-object for rational consciousness. To restate his view in positive terms: whatever exists must be conceived in relation to consciousness. Mind is foundational to reality in the sense that the synthetic a priori logical act is the source of the categories, and the synthetic a priori aesthetic act provides the representations of historical judgment. The world exists solely as a manifestation of human spirit, and nature is understood only in so far as it bears the stamp of spirit (*lo spirito*). Croce's epistemology affirms objects and qualities in their possible and actual relations to consciousness only and denies any object or quality that claims ontological status independent of such relations. For him there occurs no ontological alienation between subject and object, between consciousness and nature, considered as fundamentally other than spirit.

Collingwood concluded his essay by considering Croce's conception of philosophy in its relation to history. Here the critic interpreted *Teoria e storia della storiografia* of 1917 as maintaining two fundamentally different views, without any attempt to reconcile them: first, philosophy and history are identical; and second, philosophy is a component part of history. Subsequently in an appendix Croce supposedly adopted the second, naturalistic position in which 'philosophy is immanent in history while history is transcendent with reference to philosophy.'[14] Collingwood interpreted the evolution of Croce's conception of philosophy in its relation to history as amounting to an abandonment of philosophy for history – an interpretation at best ironic, since Croce held that neither discipline could exist in abstraction from the other. So to abandon either philosophy or history would have required his putting aside the reality of both disciplines: a position that Croce never advocated.

What was Croce's own response to Collingwood's long list of complaints? A detailed reply to Collingwood's early criticisms and more generally to his views on history and philosophy occurs in an essay written in 1945, after his colleague's death, entitled 'In commemorazione di un amico inglese, compagno di pensiero e di fede'[15] (in commemoration of an English friend, companion in thought and faith). Here Croce noted that in the *Hibbert Journal* Collingwood's criticisms were the same as the critique offered by the actual idealists, Giovanni Gentile and Guido de Ruggiero. This statement is perceptive, because we know that when de Ruggiero travelled to England, he communicated his negative evaluation of Croce's philosophy to Collingwood. He warned Collingwood against Croce's so-called backward philosophizing, which was naturalistic and empirical. For this reason, Collingwood had concluded his essay with a greeting to Croce's two successors de Ruggiero and his teacher and companion, Gentile. But these were persons whom Croce considered not as successors but as predecessors, last representatives of the old and worn-out Hegelian panlogism that had lost freshness, vigour, and richness.[16]

From Croce's perspective, he and Collingwood held certain major concepts in common: most important was the concept of philosophy as the methodological moment of historiography. They held further that the interpretations of philosophers should make explicit the questions to which they respond. They also agreed on the specific treatment of problems in the history of philosophy, on the degeneration of every sort of history that was based on mere testimonies, and on the contemporaneous nature of every history – the life of the past in the present.[17]

By 1928, Collingwood had developed the idea that new history, which is to inform its readers about the present, is related to practical life and can teach humans how to control their situations. History consists of narratives of purposive activity.[18] In 1930, Collingwood's 'The Philosophy of History' made explicit his agreement with Croce's view that the subject-matter of historical narrative is formed of individual judgments (not generalizations or laws) about particular objects.[19] Here, in a summary of intellectual thought about the nature of history, Collingwood cited Croce's 1893 essay that likens history to art rather than to science. Further developments of Croce's concept of history occurred in *Logica come scienza del concetto puro* (1909), translated as *Logic as the Science of the Pure Concept* (1917), and in *Teoria e storia della storiografia* (1917), which by 1930 Collingwood described as 'by far the most important work of our time on the subject.' Collingwood concluded 'The Philosophy of History' with an outline of his own philosophy of history that amounts to a summary of the main tenets in Croce's theory of history.[20]

Collingwood's last major publication that evaluates Croce's conceptions of philosophy and history is entitled *The Idea of History*.[21] This work consists of his ideas on history, most taken from thirty-two lectures delivered in 1936 that were collected and, as we now know, heavily edited by T.M. Knox after the author's death. Although Collingwood had intended that eventually the lectures would form two books, his illness prevented him from completing his plan. *The Idea of History* also includes a fragment of a major manuscript, written early in 1939 and entitled *The Principles of History*, which was never published.[22]

Despite the composite nature of *The Idea of History*, its contents, including the essays in the 'Epilegomena,' share a central aim: to conduct a philosophical inquiry into the nature of history, regarded as a special form of knowledge, with a special type of object. The business of history, for Collingwood, is to apprehend the past, to learn what really happened, whereas the task of philosophy is to make explicit the character of knowledge about the past. Philosophical inquiry moreover cannot separate its study of the way the past is known from the study of what is known.

The majority of Collingwood's references to Croce's philosophy appear in the fourth part, entitled 'Scientific History,' under the subheading 'Italy.' Here again he seems to have erroneously imputed to the Italian philosopher a posited separation between theory and praxis, history and science, such that praxis can exist independently of thought: 'For him, natural science is not knowledge at all, but action ... The concepts of science ... are arbitrary constructions: there is not one of them that need be thought.'[23] According to Croce, however, the constructions of will – the pseudo-concepts of the inductive and deductive sciences – are rational. They depend on and include thought as transformed into plans for action. Nor does Croce consider nature as real only if viewed as part of history and as unreal if held as part of science.[24] Although Croce sees the pseudo-concept 'existence' as an arbitrary one, used for purposes of classification in the natural sciences, it does presuppose historical existence. Thus the 'is' of empirical statements is related to the pure concept 'existence' in the same phenomenological respect that will depends on thought. In the case of the empirical concept, 'existence' is implied moreover by the class that the concept signifies. In short, the objects of the natural sciences imply the reality of artificial constructions of will. In a passage taken from *Teoria e storia della storiografia* quoted by Collingwood, Croce suggested that the methods of understanding used by human history and natural history are analogous, even if in natural history empathy at times proves useless; and only classification and the inevitable distortion of process, when captured by slides and photographs, remain. Croce held thus, within the framework of his epistemological idealism and his denial of metaphysics, that the subject-matter of the human and natural sciences consists of expressions of the human spirit.[25]

Moreover, like Croce, Collingwood argued that the historian must enter imaginatively into the mind of the historical figure. Before 1936, there may have been only two places wherein Collingwood refers to the idea of rethinking. This concept occurs in 'Croce's Philosophy of History,' and it appears also in 'Oswald Spengler and the Theory of Historical Cycles' (1927).[26] Subsequently the notion of rethinking or re-entering is present, for example, in 'Human Nature and Human History' (1936), which distinguishes between the 'outside' and the 'inside' of an event.[27] The former consists of bodies and their movements, whereas the latter comprises thought. According to Collingwood, for a historian the cause of an event does not exist in the relations between external bodies but lies instead in the thought of its agent. The historian discovers such mental objects by re-enacting them in his or her mind. It follows that all history amounts to the re-enactment of past thoughts in the historian's mind. All such imaginative construction is also critical, because the thought that re-enacts the past evaluates it during the act of construction. What is the subject-matter of special interest to the historian? He or she investigates the social customs that humans create by thought. Societal mores serve as a framework, within which appetites find satisfaction in ways sanctioned by convention and morality.

Both philosophers also maintained that historical knowledge requires the a priori activity of mind. As we have seen for Croce, mind was foundational to reality in the sense that the synthetic a priori activity of imagination – intuition – provides the subjects of historical judgment; and the synthetic a priori logical act is the source of the categories of historical interpretation. In 'The Historical Imagination' (1936),[28] Collingwood described the constructive activity of imagination as a priori, because it is the *sine qua non* for historical knowledge. The historian asks further whether his or her picture of the past is coherent and continuous, which amounts, for both Collingwood and Croce, to asking whether a history is true.

With these assertions, Collingwood argued against attempts by some late-nineteenth- and twentieth-century philosophers to show that history is a science – that is, to demonstrate that its subject-matter consists of what Collingwood called the 'outside' of events, along with their causal relations. In short, these philosophers treated history as closed to mind. Twentieth-century illustrations include Carl Hempel's discussions of the covering law model[29] and what today is called 'quantitative history.'[30]

The problems involved in implementing a scientific approach to historical narrative, as for instance those of generalization, retrodiction, and verification, have been widely discussed. Yet even if we agree that what Collingwood described as the 'inside' of an event – the imaginative re-enacting of past purposive thought – forms the subject-matter of investigation, then difficulties still remain. The methodological problems in establishing motive for action are well-known and must increase greatly when we try to determine motive as expressed within a culture very different from our own, even if, as Collingwood urged, we rely on evidence for our determination. Nevertheless, Collingwood's conception of history, along with its method and subject-matter, as *sui generis* is appealing and fundamentally Crocean. Unfortunately, his deteriorating health and death prevented him from fully developing his ideas.

In his preface to *The Idea of History*, Knox proposed that the similarities between the views of the two resulted from their parallel development, not from any influence from one to the other.[31] How are we to

understand 'parallel'? Not in the sense of 'chronologically simultane-
ous.' For by 1909, in the second edition of his *Logic*, Croce had worked
out his conception of individual judgment, which formed the corner-
stone of his theory of history; and by 1916 he had published in *La critica*
his essay 'Filosofia e metodologia' (Philosophy and Methodology),
where he maintained that philosophy remains distinguishable from history by its methodological function.[32]

In what sense then were the developments of Croce and Collingwood
parallel? According to Knox and other critics, Collingwood's *Essay
on Philosophical Method* (1932) and his 1936 lectures on philosophy
and history distinguished between the two disciplines. Collingwood's
standpoint, however, changed radically between 1936 and 1938, and,
supposedly like Croce, he came to hold that philosophy, considered as a
separate discipline, became liquidated by being converted into history.[33]
Yet despite Knox's claims to the contrary, for Croce the methodological
task of philosophy distinguished philosophy from history. Indeed, in a
letter written to de Ruggiero in 1937, Collingwood himself seemed to
recognize the differences in their views: 'Philosophy in history is not, as
Croce has said, simply its methodology. The absorption is mutual: the
product is not philosophy based on history nor history based on philosophy, it is both these things at once ... It is as if one took Croce's *Storiografia*, and turned it inside out: greatly expanding Part II, and absorbing all
the subject-matter of Part I into its interstices. I find this method *effective*
in practice. People who are rendered suspicious of contradictions by
Croce's method of presentation, where his own central idea is stated *first*,
become quite tame and intelligent if the very same idea is led up to by
showing how it developed out of a determinate situation. Like Hegel,
they are annoyed by having the Absolute fired at them out of a pistol!'[34]
If Collingwood rejected Croce's conception of philosophy as the methodological moment of historiography, what was his later position regarding
philosophy in its relation to history? A good case can be made that
Collingwood believes that every metaphysics is historically conditioned
and forms the subject-matter for the historian of philosophy[35] and that
the subject-matter for philosophical investigation consists of the conditions that make historical knowledge possible.[36]

Philosophy as the Methodological Moment of Historiography

Despite Collingwood's claim to the contrary, Croce's conception of the
relations between philosophy and history, along with his theory of the

categories of historical interpretation, are still viable. What were the historical determinates of his views? Early in his career Croce was influenced by Giambattista Vico's notion that knowledge of the past falls within the province of philosophy. Croce later maintained that, logically speaking, neither discipline is subordinate to the other. His theoretical change follows from the view that definition and individual judgment presuppose each other, much as pure concept becomes expressed via historical representation. In short, philosophy cannot be resolved simply into history, and philosophy of history is based on what Croce described as a category mistake. Furthermore, neither history nor philosophy occurs without the other. Historical narrative requires categorial interpretation but philosophical categories and concepts necessarily present themselves in historical contexts, providing thereby a framework within which events and subjects are to be interpreted.

The philosopher is to investigate the intuitional, logical, economic, and ethical functions of the human spirit. Mind is to become cognizant of its own functions and structures. Croce's description of philosophical method and task, however, does not imply some version of traditional metaphysics. As we have seen above, he called his method speculative and thereby wished to distinguish it especially from forms of empiricism. Croce's fundamental philosophical tenets do not amount to empirical claims, since his introspective method purported to discover categories and concepts not derived a posteriori and by induction. The goal of critical reflection is instead to make explicit the a priori categories that direct historical interpretation. This is what Croce meant when he described philosophy as the methodological moment of historical narrative.

Autocritical thought establishes its principles and categories for understanding events and objects. When a person *reflects* on these principles and categories he or she acts as a *philosopher*-historian. Such principles and categories are not abstract. They are evaluated as filled with historical content; and so when one *applies* these principles and categories with their concrete content, he or she is acting as a *historian*-philosopher. The distinction between the two activities of philosophy and history remains just that – a distinction, not a separation; and the presence of either discipline may be emphasized as the context demands.

Along with Croce's conception of the function of philosophy as methodological, his theory of the categories of historical interpretation remains vital. The categories evolved out of the reciprocal relations between Clio and philosophy that pervaded his long career – one that lasted from 1886 to 1952. A brief look at the development of his theory of categories can aid us in further understanding his conception of philosophy in its relation to history.

During the years between 1886 and 1892, immediately following Croce's departure from the University of Rome, he became aware of a need for categories[37] of interpretation in historical narrative. At that time Croce was absorbed with studies on the kingdom of Naples and the diplomatic relations between Italy and Spain. But he soon wearied of 'lifeless and disconnected facts at the expense of much toil and with no constructive result.'[38] And while attempting to solve specific difficulties of hermeneutical research, he turned to the general topics of history and knowledge. With their explication in mind, he studied Italian and German books on the philosophy and method of history. Out of the various perplexities that beset him while pursuing these inquiries emerged in 1893 his first philosophical work, *La storia ridotta sotto il concetto generale dell'arte*[39] (History Subsumed under the General Concept of Art), which temporarily organized his ideas in terms of two categories – art[40] and philosophy. Each of these categories of historical interpretation represents an activity of human consciousness – intuitional or aesthetic, which is the fundamental and particular cognitive expression on which all knowledge depends; and conceptual or logical,[41] which includes intuition but also transforms it in the universality of its conceptual representation. As yet, however, Croce had not distinguished clearly between the theoretical disciplines that issue from reason, such as aesthetics, philosophy, and history, and the practical sciences that depend on will, such as empirical and abstract sciences.

Immediately after the publication of *La storia ridotta*, there followed a period (1893–4) of intense historical investigation of the relations between Spain and Italy. Eventually Croce's research was broken off, this time by Antonio Labriola's invitation to read the first of his essays on Marx's conception of historical materialism. Croce's subsequent work with Marx's philosophy resulted in his adoption of a third category of historical interpretation – the economic – in addition to the aesthetic and philosophical ones.[42] This category represents human practical activity and thus the striving of will to achieve immediate goals. We saw above that its manifestations include what Croce named 'pseudo-concepts,' which amount to empirical and abstract class names, whose denotation and connotation are limited by need and interest.

Among such classifications are divisions of history into ancient, feudal, Renaissance, and modern, or into classical and Romantic.

The only major category of historical interpretation that follows on the economic is the category of ethical value. It represents the fourth fundamental activity of the human spirit and comprises volition of a relatively universal goal. Moral or ethical will extends beyond the fulfilment of immediate economic needs. It expresses itself as the quest for greater degrees of political liberty. Croce's writings on history completed during the fascist regime, such as *La storia come pensiero e come azione*[43] (1937), translated as *History as the Story of Liberty* (1941), clearly illustrate the importance that he attached to this concept, which was reinforced by restrictions on his own personal and political freedom. Even social justice, for Croce, plays a role subordinate to political freedom.[44]

Collingwood also proposed that the new history is related to praxis, in the sense that history consists of narrative that describe purposive activity. Nevertheless, he never developed his idea of history into the Crocean conception of the moral aim of history. Perhaps the reason for his failure to conceive of the moral function of historical narrative lies in his incomplete conception of the organic unity of the human spirit. The issue that stimulated Collingwood throughout his life, but that he was unable to answer fully – the conditions for unity, order, and stability in the modern world – is neither vain nor empty. For Croce, the work of the modern world would depend entirely on the elaboration of a new faith: given the disappearance of religion since the Middle Ages, the unity of self would be the problem of our times.[45] Although written in 1924, this view, when considered from the perspective of the 1990s, has proved prophetic, especially if understood in terms of the failures of humanistic psychology and of Marxist ideology to unify the self and thus to unify our world.

With his description of ethical will, Croce's inventory of the four fundamental activities of consciousness, their interrelations, and their representations is complete. The phenomenological links between diverse expressions of consciousness form, metaphorically speaking, a circle. Intuitions nevertheless remain relatively autonomous, and pure concepts or categories include them in the concrete universality of their conceptual representations. Rational volition of immediate goals originates from conceptual knowledge, just as will of universal ends arises out of the satisfaction of immediate desires and needs. Ethical volition in turn

stimulates new intuitions, which, however, do not explicitly include ethical volition in their expressions. The phenomenological interconnections between intuition, concept, will of an immediate goal, and will of a
universal end are mirrored by the relations that hold among the four
fundamental categories of historical interpretation – aesthetic, philosophical, economic, and ethical. By this time, Croce had delineated most
of the concepts that are deducible from these categories. Aesthetic terms
include beauty, lyricality, aesthetic universality; philosophic terms, concrete universal, truth, and judgment; economic terms, utilitarian or
instrumental value; and ethical terms, moral good and liberty.

The historian is to respond to specific questions, and his response
becomes limited by the category – aesthetic, philosophical, economic, or
ethical – that he or she chooses to treat. As we could surmise, much of
historical narrative also makes use of conceptual fictions or pseudo-
concepts and pseudo-judgments formed from them for purposes of classification and quantification. Errors of category arise when the historian
asserts that pseudo-judgments correctly and not merely usefully
describe events and objects and that narrative is formed exclusively of
them. Since Croce's categorial theory of error also remains vital in his
theory of history, let us take a close look at it.

Croce's Categorial Theory of Error

A categorial theory is unusual in a philosophy such as Croce's, since
usually idealist systems espouse some form of coherence conception for
determining true and false judgment.[46] What was the historical anteced-
ent for Croce's view? Early in his career, he was influenced by Vico's
notion of error 'as an improper combination of ideas.'[47] Categorial mistakes consist of improperly substituting intuition or pseudo-concept for
a category in judgment. They stem also from disrupting the organic
unity between subject and predicate. Attempts to attribute logical or
moral value to art and to deduce history from a priori concepts are
included among Croce's examples of categorial mistakes. A limited
number of improper combinations of intuition and concept can be
deduced from the phenomenological relations among the four kinds of
human expression – intuitional, logical, economic, and ethical. Nevertheless, one of Croce's major philosophical tasks was to refute the errors
that derive from these sources.

Categorial mistakes do not derive simply from purely theoretical acts.
They moreover require volitional activity, since they express the false

affirmation (will) that any combination of representation and category that serves human short-term needs (practical goals) is true. Such affirmations always include something of the contingent and arbitrary in them. Categorial mistakes include prejudices of country, class, and profession, along with deceptions based on wishes to satisfy vanity and ambition. In sum, according to Croce, categorial error is neither exclusively a theoretical expression nor simply a volitional act but includes both thought and will.

Collingwood also evaluated Croce's categorial theory of error, which, alas, he confused with Croce's privation conception of truth.[48] And his critique distorts Croce's privation theory of value to mean that the statement 'nothing is merely bad' implies that 'everything is wholly good, and not bad in any sense at all,'[49] even though Croce held no such view. According to Croce's privation concept, error, if understood in a purely theoretical sense, does not occur as such, but truth does exist to various degrees. In other words, although a purely theoretical judgment may be completely true, or more or less true, it cannot be completely false. According to Croce's categorial theory, however, in the sphere of praxis positive error does occur, when a judgment expresses confusion and misrepresentation among the functions of the human spirit and is affirmed as true. I would argue that Croce's categorial theory, far from being absurd, as Collingwood judged, remains vital, even though it has been rarely held, and never in the developed form in which Croce expressed it.

Let us take a look at several types of categorial error that Croce listed. A priori approaches to history that occur in philosophies of history, for instance, improperly combine subject and predicate for practical purposes. Events and objects are designed to agree with a preconceived theory of the general nature of history. The historian then attempts to deduce events a priori and not in accordance with concrete occurrences. In this case narrative is written without confirmation by documentation, and the past is understood in terms of false analogies. Croce offered examples of such erroneous judgments: 'The Middle Ages are the negation of ancient civilization'; 'The modern epoch is the synthesis of these two opposites'; 'Greece was thought and Rome action.'[50]

Croce also applied his categorial theory to what he called 'poetical history.' This incorrect interpretation of events derives from an attempt to rectify the 'barren' discoveries of philological treatises. Sentiment (intuition) overwhelms critical thought. Aesthetic coherence becomes substituted for logical consistency. Examples occur in historical biography, where the author's feelings dominate, or in the history of a country in which the historian justifies events in accordance with political ideals.[51]

Universal history provides another example of categorial error in historical narrative. Like other pseudo-histories, this variant includes an unrealizable claim – to 'form a picture of all the things that have happened to the human race, from its origins upon the earth to the present moment.'[52] The historian could never satisfy such a requirement. Universal narrative amounts to either chronicle, which Croce named 'dead history,' or poetry. In the case of chronicle, statements consist of representation and pseudo-concept. A true judgment is not expressed. In poetry, no true concept occurs. Merely poetic expression exists.

What then did authentic historical inquiry involve for Croce? The subject of an investigation of the past is the individual object or event, and the categories that direct historical narrative represent what is concretely universal. Interpretive categories – economic, political, aesthetic, psychological, ethical, religious, and so forth – remain distinct from one another. To evaluate an economic interpretation of events with aesthetic or ethical concepts would amount to categorial error, and to interpret history of art in terms of economic and political concepts would be equally unsuitable. Accordingly, the historian should avoid miscombining categories, or accounting for multifarious experience by appealing to one category only (sometimes described as 'reductionism'). History does amount to histories, and the application of Croce's categorial conception does provide solutions to important problems raised by philosophies of history.

NOTES

1 Some of the material presented here was published in Giuseppe Cantillo and Renata Viti Cavaliere, eds., *La tradizione critica della filosofia: Studi in memoria di Raffaello Franchini* (Naples: Loffredo, 1994). I include it in this revised and expanded essay by permission of the publisher, Loffredo, and the A. Aliotta Department of Philosophy of the Federico II, University of Naples. My thanks to Dain R. Trafton, Jack D'Amico, and Massimo Verdicchio for their careful reading and helpful evaluation of this essay.

2 See Alan Donagan, *The Later Philosophy of R.G. Collingwood* (Chicago: University of Chicago Press, 1985), 131.

3 See R.G. Collingwood, *The Idea of History* (New York: Oxford University Press, 1956), x–xi; and Lionel Rubinoff, *Collingwood and the Reform of Meta-*

physics (Toronto: University of Toronto Press, 1970), 16–21, for a critique of Knox's interpretation.

4 For the letters (1912–39) by R.G. Collingwood to Benedetto Croce, see 'Lettere di Robin George Collingwood a Benedetto Croce (1912–1939),' edited and introduced by Amedeo Vigorelli in *Rivista di storia della filosofia* 4 (1991), 545–63. Also see Donagan, *Later Philosophy*, 314.

5 R.G. Collingwood, 'Croce's Philosophy of History,' *Hibbert Journal* 19 (1920–1): 263–78.

6 Ibid., 267.

7 R.G. Collingwood, *An Autobiography* (London: Oxford University Press, 1959), 149ff. The accuracy of this autobiography has been challenged by the author's friend and editor, T.M. Knox. See Collingwood, *Idea of History*, v–xxiv.

8 Collingwood, 'Croce's Philosophy of History,' 266–7.

9 See M.E. Moss, *Benedetto Croce Reconsidered: Truth and Error in Theories of Art, Literature, and History* (Hanover, NH: The University Press of New England, 1987), 22.

10 Ibid., 266–9.

11 Ibid., 268.

12 The most recent English translation of Benedetto Croce's *Estetica*, Part I, is by Colin Lyas. See Benedetto Croce, *The Aesthetic as the Science of Expression and of the Linguistic in General*, trans. Colin Lyas (Cambridge: Cambridge University Press, 1992). For an English translation of parts I and II, see Benedetto Croce, *Aesthetic as Science of Expression and General Linguistic*, trans. Douglas Ainslie (New York: Noonday Press, 1956).

13 See for example, Benedetto Croce, 'Lo storicismo,' *Quaderni della 'Critica'* 13 (March 1949), 83. Also see Moss, *Benedetto Croce Reconsidered*, chap. 5.

14 Collingwood, 'Croce's Philosophy of History,' 277.

15 Benedetto Croce, 'In commemorazione di un amico inglese, compagno di pensiero e di fede, R.G. Collingwood,' in *Nuove pagine sparse* I (Naples: Riccardo Ricciardi, 1949), 25–39.

16 Cf. Rik Peters, 'Croce, Gentile, and Collingwood on the Relation between History and Philosophy,' in David Boucher, Tariq Modood, and James Connelly, eds., *Philosophy, History, and Civilization* (Cardiff, Wales: University of Wales Press, 1993).

17 Croce, 'In commemorazione,' 34.

18 Ibid., 107–9.

19 In his lectures of 1929 on the philosophy of history, Collingwood asserted that history is not formed simply of the aesthetic intuitions with which Croce had identified history in his first essay. History is not intuition but judgment.

See W.J. van der Dussen, *History as a Science: The Philosophy of R.G. Colling-wood* (The Hague: Martinus Nijhoff, 1981), 33, 306–7.

20 R.G. Collingwood, 'The Philosophy of History,' in W. Debbins, ed., *Essays in the Philosophy of History by R.G. Collingwood* (Austin: University of Texas Press, 1965), 135.

21 In 1993, Jan van der Dussen published a revised and expanded edition of *The Idea of History*, with lectures 1926–8. See R.G. Collingwood, *The Idea of History*, rev. and intro. Jan van der Dussen (Oxford: Oxford University Press, 1993). In his introduction, van der Dussen critically evaluates the Knox edition. Unless otherwise indicated, however, for purposes of discussing Knox's interpretation, all references to *The Idea of History* will be to the Knox edition.

22 For a discussion of Collingwood's unpublished manuscripts, see W.J. van der Dussen, *History as a Science*, 161.

23 Collingwood, *Idea of History*, 197.

24 Ibid., 198.

25 See ibid., 200, for Collingwood's critique of Croce's position.

26 R.G. Collingwood, 'Oswald Spengler and the Theory of Historical Cycles,' in W. Debbins, ed., *Essays in the Philosophy of History by R.G. Collingwood* (Austin: University of Texas Press, 1965), 57–90.

27 Collingwood, *Idea of History*, 205–31. Also see 'History as Re-enactment of Past Experience,' ibid., 282–302.

28 Ibid., 231–49.

29 See Carl Hempel, 'The Function of General Laws in History,' *Journal of Philosophy* 39 (1942), 35–48.

30 See Robert Swierenga, ed., *Quantification in American History: Theory and Research* (New York: Atheneum, 1970); Roderick Floud, *An Introduction to Quantitative Methods for Historians* (Princeton, NJ: Princeton University Press, 1973); and Theodore K. Rabb and Robert I. Rotberg, eds., *The New History: The 1980s and Beyond* (Princeton, NJ: Princeton University Press, 1982). Thanks to Charles A. Lofgren, professor of history and government, Claremont McKenna College, Claremont, Calif., for supplying these references. Also see Robert William Fogel, *Without Consent* (New York: Norton, 1994); Hal Barron, *Who Stayed Behind: Rural Society in 19th Century England* (Cambridge: Cambridge University Press, 1984); and Robert R. Dykstra, 'Field Notes Overdosing on Dodge City,' *Western Historical Quarterly* 27 (winter 1996), 505–14. Thanks to Andrew F. Rolle, professor emeritus of history, Huntington Library, California, for providing these references.

31 Collingwood, *Idea of History*, viii.

32 Subsequently, 'Filosofia e metodologia' would be incorporated in *Teoria e storia della storiografia* (Bari: Laterza, 1917).

33 Rubinoff, *Collingwood*, 16ff.
34 van der Dussen, *History as a Science*, 60.
35 R.G. Collingwood, *An Essay on Metaphysics* (Oxford: Clarendon Press, 1958), 49ff.
36 See Collingwood, *Idea of History*, 3–7.
37 Croce used the terms 'category,' 'concrete-universal,' 'pure concept,' and 'directive concept' interchangeably; I follow his practice. For an evaluation of Croce's understanding of the pure concept, see M.E. Moss, 'The Crocean Concept of the Pure Concept,' in *Idealistic Studies* 17 (1987), 39–52.
38 Benedetto Croce, *An Autobiography*, trans. R.G. Collingwood (Oxford: Oxford University Press, 1927), 52.
39 Benedetto Croce, 'La storia ridotta sotto il concetto generale dell'arte,' *Atti dell'Accademia Pontaniana* 23 (1893), 32ff, republished in Croce, *Primi saggi* (Bari: Gius. Laterza & Figli, 1919), 1–46.
40 For discussions of Croce's category of art, see M.E. Moss, 'Croce's Theory of Intuition Reconsidered,' *La rivista di studi crociani* 59–60 (July–Dec, 1978), 292–306.
41 For discussions of Croce and Hegel on the concrete-universal, see Raffaello Franchini, *Croce interprete di Hegel: E altri saggi filosofici* (Naples: Giannini, 1964), and *La teoria della storia di Benedetto Croce* (Naples: Morano, 1965).
42 See Benedetto Croce *Materialismo storico ed economia marxistica: saggi critica* (Milan: Sandron, 1900). Some of the essays in this book were translated into English in Croce's *Historical Materialism and the Economics of Karl Marx*, trans. C.M. Meredith, intro. by A.D. Lindsay (London: Latimer Ltd., 1914).
43 Benedetto Croce, *La storia come pensiero e come azione*, 7th ed. (Bari: Gius. Laterza & Figli, 1965). The 3rd edition without 'final considerations' or the appendix and philological notes was translated by S. Sprigge as *History as the Story of Liberty* (New York: Meridian Books, 1955). Subsequently the section entitled 'La storia come pensiero e come azione,' in *La storia*, 1–50, was retranslated by C. Sprigge in Benedetto Croce, *Philosophy, Poetry, History* (London: Oxford University Press, 1966), 546–88.
44 See Gilbert Murray, Manlio Brosio, and Guido Calogero, *Benedetto Croce* (London: Westerham Press, 1953), 34–5.
45 Croce, *Ultimi saggi*, 347–8. Also see Croce's letter to the American Historical Association on the present state of historiography, in *American Historical Review* 39 (Jan. 1934), 229–31, where he discusses the confusion of spiritual order, present in modern times.
46 For a discussion of Croce's coherence theory, see Myra Moss Milburn, 'Benedetto Croce's Coherence Theory of Truth: A Critical Evaluation,' *Filosofia*, 19

(1968), 107–16. Also see Benedetto Croce, *Logic as the Science of the Pure Concept*, trans. D. Ainslie (London: Macmillan, 1917), 391ff.

47 Raffaello Piccoli, *Benedetto Croce: An Introduction to His Philosophy* (New York: Harcourt, Brace & Co., 1922), 117–18. Also see Croce, *Logic*, 397.

48 Collingwood, 'Croce's Philosophy of History,' 272ff.

49 Ibid., 273.

50 Croce, *Logic*, 425–6.

51 Croce, *History: Its Theory and Practice*, trans. Douglas Ainslie (New York: Russell and Russell, 1960), 35. Also see Croce, *Logic*, 291, 406–7.

52 Croce, *History: Its Theory and Practice*, 56.

9

Croce on Vico

GIUSEPPE MAZZOTTA

By the time Benedetto Croce published his monograph on Giambattista Vico, *La filosofia di Giambattista Vico* (Bari, 1911), his reputation as possibly Italy's foremost thinker of his generation was well established. Years earlier he had founded *La critica* (1903), a journal of cultural criticism that programmatically aimed both at inserting Italian thought within the coordinates of European discourse and at subjecting the major events of European intellectual life to severe scrutiny. The enterprise brought Croce international recognition. The high journalism that he practised was an extension of and the laboratory for a number of philosophical works that he had been publishing since the beginning of the century and that he intended as discrete building blocks of a full-blown philosophical system. Some of the essays dealt with questions of logic, economics, and ethics.

At the heart of Croce's project, however, was the epoch-making *Estetica come scienza dell'espressione e linguistica generale* (1902). The treatise gives a hint that the overall design of Croce's thought emerges sharply defined from early on, and esthetics, which for him is an intuitive 'science,' remains the fulcrum around which he constantly rethinks the most disparate questions. The reasons for the centrality of the 'science' of aesthetics in Croce's mind are plain. His immediate objective is to challenge radically the nineteenth-century conception of natural science by attacking the dogmas of empiricism and naturalism as well as the objectifying attitude that modern scientific method entails. Within the calcified framework and the guidelines laid out by positivism there are no possibilities, so Croce believes, for a new or authentically historical way of thinking. In an attempt to retrieve the creative sources of life, which are crystallized by poetry and history and which come forth as the philosophy of freedom, Croce elaborates a theory of art and aesthetics. Art is viewed as an activity essentially free from practical interest, as a primary and disinterested mode of knowing distinct from all other forms of knowing and making. Because of the special status granted to the original status of aesthetics, art turns into the inevitable path that Croce's thought steadily pursues.

The emphasis on aesthetics as a mode of knowledge signals that it is not really a philosophy of art that Croce produces. He is interested less in a philosophy of art – in a general conception about the material processes of making – than he is in a theory of knowledge. At the centre of this theory lies the category of aesthetic intuition, which he understands as a primary imaginative experience preceding all scientific conceptualizations and differing from logical, economic, and ethical acts. These terms (aesthetic, logic, economic, and ethics) are Croce's own designations for the four activities of the spirit, each autonomous from the others, and all sharing in the endless circularity of Spirit.

On the basis of this construction of Croce's body of reflections, there is cause to dwell on the deeper reasons for Croce's turn to Vico. The turn was by no means sudden. In his *Contributo alla critica di me stesso* (1915), which is an intellectual autobiography modelled on Vico's own *Autobiography*, Croce recounts his search for a historical method that led him to reading the *New Science*.[1] In his early research on the cultural life of Naples, Croce had frequently relied on Vico's own erudition, and his interest in Vico's work never wavered. The essay of 1893, 'La storia ridotta sotto il concetto generale dell'arte' (History Subsumed under the General Concept of Art), which argues that the real is the product of Spirit and is itself absolute Spirit, and which marks the foundation of Croce's neo-idealism, echoes Vico's sense of the primordial bond between poetry and history. One could even suggest that Croce's definition of aesthetics as a 'science of expression' unequivocally recalls and discloses his indebtedness to Vico's *New Science*. Like Vico, Croce abandons the traditional Cartesian understanding of science as a system of true propositions and makes it rather an aesthetic, human activity, in the sense that poetry expresses the historical way of being in the world.

One can easily grasp the several points at which Croce throughout his work agrees with and depends on the thought of his forerunner. The epitome of such a pattern is defined by one conspicuous element: in his extensive polemic with the positivist sciences Croce's procedure largely retrieves Vico's sharp critique of both Cartesian foundationalism and of technology at the dawn of modernity. But listing the areas in which Croce's particular conceptual formulations depend on Vico's teaching would be tedious and too mechanical an exercise, radically at odds with Croce's sense of what constitutes original thinking: the creative rethinking of tradition. Vico's place in Croce's thought goes well beyond occasional conceptual borrowings. Rather, Vico is a steady point of reference for Croce, and his work on Vico, as I would like to argue below, encapsulates nothing less than Croce's whole sense of philosophy. By exploring the specific outline of *La filosofia di Giambattista Vico* I also suggest, however, the ways in which Croce's reading of Vico bypasses the most radical aspects of Vico's own thought.

Because Vico was a living memory and even a felt presence in the intellectual circles of Croce's Naples, Croce's monograph on him in a way belongs to his well-known cultivation of local history. But it is quickly apparent to the reader that, more than an innocent compilation of erudite curiosities, it bears the mark of inevitability. Behind Croce's decision to devote to Vico's philosophy a massive study, there lay a number of personal and political reasons, some of which he shared with his then collaborator and friend Giovanni Gentile. Vico was the *altvater* of Italian philosophical speculation, so Croce says in the 'Preface' to his volume.[2] The metaphor about Vico's paternal authority suggests that Croce's turn to him symbolizes a natural shift towards the vital source of his thought, literally to his own philosophical progenitor, whose legacy had long been ignored or dismissed in Europe. What gives the turn poignancy as well as the stance of a moral vindication is the fact that Vico's legacy was fiercely contested by the oddest assortment of his Italian heirs. At stake in the interpretation of Vico's philosophical work, then, is the sense of the Italian philosophical tradition as well as the direction it was bound to take in Europe in our times.

Croce's dedication of *La filosofia di Giambattista Vico* to the historian of philosophy W. Wildeband, who discusses Vico's thought in the fifth edition of his *History of Modern Philosophy* (Leipzig, 1911), and the critical success of the monograph (quickly translated into several European languages), give some evidence of Croce's desire to introduce Vico into the circuit of European intellectual debates. However, Croce's impulse in wanting to impose his own reading of Vico over and above rival critical interpretations was not – and really could not have been – destined to be unanimously endorsed. He knew that to succeed in this area he had to counter a number of legitimate and powerful claims about the substance of Vico's thought. But what exactly is the essence of Vico's legacy for Croce, and who are the other claimants to that legacy?

Catholic readers of a neo-Thomistic bent, mainly those who were to operate around the influential journal *Civiltà cattolica*, sought to canonize Vico's thought by making him a theorist of Providential history and placing his ideas within the parameters of the *philosophia perennis*. This theological interpretation of Vico, which is grounded in the genuine concerns of his texts, was opposed over the whole arc of the nineteenth century by readers of the *New Science*, such as Cuoco, De Sanctis, Genovesi, and Spaventa. They variously saw in Vico's work, though not in his life, which was in fact marked by unmistakable piety, the avatar of secular modernity and the forerunner of the liberal revolution – the Risorgimento that Italy came finally to experience in the second half of that century. Croce's interpretation of Vico stands in a direct line of continuity with the liberal tradition.

It is clear from this simplified overview of Vico's symbolic value in Italian intellectual debates towards the end of the nineteenth century that there is certainly no fatuity in Croce's vindication of Vico as the *altvater* of Italian philosophy. The implications of this metaphor, however, have not been fully exploited. The suggestion of a philosophical family tie in the metaphor (significantly given in German) conveys, first of all, his belief in a palpable dynastic continuity between Vico and himself, and the continuity in turn is a way for Croce to legitimize himself as a philosopher rooted in a noble tradition. The metaphor is also a way of giving legitimacy and specificity to the whole Italian philosophical speculation.

The charge against Croce's own cousin, the Hegelian philosopher Bertrando Spaventa, was that he 'germanized' thought.[3] The criticism implied that Spaventa, who held the chair of philosophy at the University of Naples in post-Unification Italy, focused his teaching on German philosophy as if it were the authentic expression of the problematics of modern self-consciousness. Such an understanding of philosophy was taken to entail the neglect of the philosophers of the Renaissance – Bruno, Campanella, Ficino, Telesio, and Vico. In the nineteenth-century climate of recent political Unification and uncertain national identity, such a charge, which was levelled by Francesco Fiorentino, amounted to investing Spaventa's philosophical activity with subversive powers or, at least, with the power of weakening the newly found Italian national sense. Within this political-intellectual context, thinking comes to be seen as having specific national and geographical traits. It is thus likely that Croce may have felt compelled to cast both himself and contemporary Italian thought as something other than pale reflections of Hegel. From this standpoint, the retrieval of Vico's philosophy comes to signify the resurrection of a national, indeed of a familiar speculative tradition (a matrix that paradoxically is cast as the point of origin of German philosophy itself). The territorialization and nationalization of philosophy find expression just at the time when the political phase of the Italian Risorgimento is on the wane.

To be sure, Croce is too much of a cosmopolitan, ironic thinker ever to lapse into intellectual jingoism. Francesco Fiorentino, proud of his Calabrian roots and lured by the golden promises of the Risorgimento, posits a continuous, specifically Italian philosophy that mythically stretches from the pre-Socratics and Pythagoreans, through the Renaissance and Vico, up to the present. Unlike Fiorentino, who eventually, to his credit, modifies his views of Spaventa, Croce (and in this he agrees with Gentile) never goes to such extremes.[4] To echo Gentile's words, the Eleatics, though born in southern Italy, are Greeks. They belong completely to the spiritual configuration of the classical world, and no amount of political manipulation of that tradition can legitimately alter the record.

At stake in the argument about the nationality or extra-territoriality of philosophy, clearly enough, is the radical question of the relationship between politics and philosophy. For all their agreement on a modern – as opposed to mythical – idea of Italian philosophy, Croce and Gentile disagree sharply about the manner of conceiving the politicization of philosophy. In the wake of Vincenzo Gioberti's musings on ethics and politics and his claims about the 'primacy' of the Italians, Gentile articulates the thought of the necessary unity of both theoretical and practical activities.[5] For his part, Croce resists the identification of politics and philosophy. It cannot come as a surprise therefore that the intellectual collaboration between the two will stumble against this crux just about ten years later. Retrospectively, their divergent readings of Vico's own version of the relationship between politics and philosophy adumbrate their radical differences about the place that philosophy occupies within the domain of history. Both Croce and Gentile hold to the general 'Vichian' principle that philosophy and the history of philosophy are not separable and that philosophy is immanent in and is at one with political life. Vico's *New Science* provides an original philosophy of history as the sphere of humanity's making and existence purports to be a 'rational civil theology of divine Providence,' is predicated on the assumption that we know only what we make, and hinges on the interrelations between history and consciousness – and it provides the blueprint for the subsequent reflections by the two Italian neo-idealists.

Gentile reads Vico within the larger context of the unfolding history of Italian philosophy from its medieval and Renaissance origins. He starts working on his project in 1904, but only in 1912–15, after Croce's publication of his volume on Vico, does he write his *Studi vichiani*. The essays in this volume trace with extraordinary rigour the parabola or 'phases' of Vico's philosophical maturation from Neoplatonic (Piconian) positions to the retrieval of the political-rhetorical substance of Italian civic humanism. In this reading, the *New Science* comes through as a rewriting of Machiavelli's political theories, and Vico as nothing less than a Machiavelli *moralisé*.

It can hardly be denied that Croce is fundamentally, like Gentile, a political philosopher. His 'religion of liberty' – which he upholds against totalitarian ideologies and which he erects as the central moral purpose of philosophy – interprets the Italian Risorgimento as the expression of a secular-minded liberalism that derives directly from Renaissance humanism. None the less, it is clear that politics and philosophy are not for him of the same intellectual order as they are for Gentile. In Croce's universe of sharply drawn distinctions and autonomous, fragmentary categories of the mind, there can be no overlapping of activities and modes: aesthetics is separate from politics, ethics from economics. The unity of these categories or fragments – which is the unity of Spirit – can be imposed only by an act of will.

It is plain that these two philosophical conceptions are radically at odds with each other. Gentile criticizes Croce for lacking a sense of a unified whole in which the parts are all vitally involved, and the critique no doubt goes to the heart of Croce's enterprise. Croce, however, with no less intellectual sharpness, attacks Gentile for creating totalitarian systems of identities wherein all distinctions are abrogated. His totalitarian or 'pantheistic' sense of the whole, which renders thought and action self-identical modes, makes impossible, so Croce argues, the exercise of judgment.[6] And just as Gentile reads Vico's philosophy as an evolving and all-embracing system, Croce's monograph on Vico, which seeks to account for the whole of Vico – his ideas about philosophy, history, poetry, religion, ethics, and law – is dotted with the sense of the necessity of logically distinct spheres of knowledge. In effect, Vico's thought, which hinges on the relation between fragments and totality and seeks to reconstitute a modern sense of the whole out of the broken pieces of

experience, simultaneously comprehends the two interpretive possibilities voiced by Gentile and Croce. But what is Croce's specific and creative misreading of Vico?

La filosofia di Giambattista Vico begins by correctly projecting Vico as
opposed to Descartes.[7] In a way, Vico comes forth as an oblique intellectual self-portrait of Croce himself, as a thinker who shuns the abstractions of theories, who delves into the concreteness of experience, and
who grasps the historicity of the order of knowledge. With extraordinary precision Croce highlights the core of Vico's critique, which
consists in his perception of Descartes's confusion, implicit in the formulation of cogito, ergo sum, of self-consciousness with certain knowledge.
In opposition to Cartesian foundationalism, moreover, Vico retrieves the
human sciences as the legitimate domain of knowledge. On the basis of
a principle of delimitation of philosophy's sphere, whereby only God
has full knowledge of the cosmos, Vico is cast as the innovative thinker
whose philosophy has abandoned metaphysics and who has founded
the first sustained philosophy of history. These introductory generalities
lead Croce to consider both the most vital and the most problematical
aspects of Vico's thought: on the one hand, imagination and poetry, and,
on the other hand, religion.

Croce presents Vico as the inventor of a modern science of aesthetics
(50). The acknowledgment of Vico's originality as an aesthetetician is
countered by Croce's clear sense that his own speculations have gone far
beyond Vico's insights. The claim dramatizes a genuine predicament in
Croce's epistemology, which is betrayed by the rhetoric of La filosofia di
Giambattista Vico. Written, as is Croce's customary style, with the confidence of a man who has attained a global, transcendent understanding
of himself and his world, the text exposes Croce himself as essentially a
mind or a consciousness that has achieved a purified and objective
standpoint. One can say that Croce has paradoxically taken a Cartesian
stance, even as he lucidly stages Vico's critique of Cartesian epistemology. This Cartesian standpoint both enables Croce to chart the history of
aesthetics and allows him to bring Vico's thought into the life of his own
self-consciousness. His reading of Vico thus presupposes the collapse of
the historical distance between them. At the same time, however, Croce
must establish a distance in degrees of consciousness between his transcendent perspective and the historical limitations of Vico's insights.
The predicament suggests that Croce holds an ironic view of history and
time: as a modern, he can claim to know what the ancients, such as Vico,
could not have known. This ironic view, which accounts for Croce's

understanding of the provisional, historical quality of all knowledge, his own included, runs against the grain of Vico's sense of the irreducible otherness of the past. It follows that as Croce perceives limitations in Vico's thought about poetry and religion, he radically misunderstands Vico's project.

Vico's originality is said to lie in his decisive departure from the pedagogical-allegorical theories of poetry practised in the Middle Ages (63ff). He is also credited with discarding the functionalist poetics of the Renaissance, when, according to Croce, poetry is conceived as mere ornamentation or function of philosophy and theology (74ff). By moving beyond these traditional views (as well as the Aristotelian view of poetry as diversion), Vico accomplishes what Croce, deploying a rhetoric of religious awe, calls a true 'miracle' (miracolo). The term, which is unusual in the lexicon of the sober-minded Croce, designates Vico's fresh discovery, seemingly out of nowhere, of the profoundly creative dimension of poetry. Thereby, Croce says by following closely Vico's text, Vico dismantles traditional paradigms of aesthetics, from Plato and Aristotle to the present, and invests poetry with a new epistemological role. At the very moment, however, that Vico's ideas are said to foreshadow Croce's own speculations on aesthetics, Croce privileges the present and himself at the expense of the past. By arguing, as he does, that Vico's ideas about poetry are self-contradictory, Croce in fact turns into a Descartes who dismisses Vico's powerful sense of the *otherness* of the past.

Vico's various statements about poetry, scattered throughout the *New Science*, include the opinion that poetry is rooted in children's imitation; the assertion of its power to make the impossible credible; and the belief that it is born from poverty of expression and aims at teaching virtue to the masses. These diverse views are dismissed by Croce as mutually exclusive errors impinging on the purity of the poetic intuition, possibly as residues of Vico's own chaotic readings, and as signs of a philosophical mind that is not fully conscious of the contradictions lodged in the folds of its own discourse.

What seems to be Vico's argumentative confusion or lack of rigour turns out to be a radical formulation that violates and transcends Croce's delimitation of pure aesthetic concerns. Read from within Vico's own intellectual world, his alleged contradictions about the primacy of the imagination in the act of knowing and about poetry's didactic aims, which Croce abhors, are crucial elements in the reorganization of the unity of knowledge that he envisions out of the fragments of the modern world. One might even say that Vico's fabric of thought is radically anti-Crocean just as it is anti-Cartesian. Whereas Descartes posits a universe of discontinuity between the rigour of philosophy and the fablings of poetry, Vico elides the boundaries between poetry and philosophy. And whereas Croce believes in the distinct domain of pure poetry, Vico shows that poetry is not a self-enclosed lyrical experience. As the *New Science* has it, poetry shapes all the sciences and is indeed the foundation of all knowledge. Accordingly, the *New Science* speaks of 'poetic history,' 'poetic astronomy,' 'poetic geography,' and so on. Retrospectively one thing is clear: Gentile fully grasps the unifying impulse of Vico's mind. By contrast, Croce reduces Vico to the role of a thinker of fragments, who unavoidably thinks against himself. This reduction conspicuously figures in Croce's treatment of religion in the *New Science*.

Vico scholars have historically argued about the religious or secular substance of Vico's thought. The issue, far from being otiose, involves Vico's modernity and the meaning of modernity. For his part, Gentile views Vico's theology in terms of the classical distinction between the order of grace and the order of nature. The premise of Gentile's thought lies in his subscribing to the radical Aristotelian idea of the double truth – that of the philosophers and that of the theologians. For medieval philosophers, such as Averroes, the doctrine of double truth entails the rupture between reason and faith. By contrast, Gentile twists this doctrine to highlight the ultimately essential identity between the two routes carved by theology and philosophy, grace and nature. Thus he concludes his studies on Vico by stating that 'grace came to be identified for him, however darkly, with nature itself' (e la grazia veniva quindi per lui ad identificarsi, per quanto oscuramente, con la stessa natura).[8] By the identification of theology with religion, Gentile aims at putting Vico in the line of political speculation of the founders of modernity, such as Bacon, Galileo, and Spinoza.

Croce also casts Vico with the founders of modernity, but he rejects Gentile's interpretation of Vico's theology as philosophy. He is sceptical about (although he ultimately endorses) the common suspicion that Vico may have deliberately shrouded his essentially secular beliefs behind the mask of dissimulation or nicodemism. In his belief that modernity and secularism coincide, Croce presents Vico as a secular thinker and thereby discards the theological vocabulary of the *New Science*. The most radical aspect of Vico's thought, so holds Croce, lies in his theory of history, in the notion of humanity as the maker of history. This tenet stumbles against Vico's repeated statements that Providence acts in history over and against human projects and even rescues humanity from its destructive impulses. As a way out of this apparent conceptual contradiction, Croce attributes a merely nominal value to Vico's Providence, making it somewhat akin to Hegel's 'cunning' of reason or Croce's own understanding of Spirit.

It is clear that Croce's secular reading of Vico is rooted in a pre-Vico, humanistic (Piconian or Cartesian) sense of humanity as the centre of consciousness, around which entities of the past revolve and are relived as one's own experience. And it is equally clear that, in writing the most comprehensive account to date of Vico's thought and in making Vico come truly alive within the landscape of modern philosophical debates, Croce brings into view a Vico whose concerns adumbrate Croce's own.

One could easily show that, from this point of view, Croce misses Vico's sense of philology as the domain of unabridgeable difference between self and others. He misses the scandalous quality of Vico's thought, whereby he subverts the self-centred complacencies of the present, though he endorses Vico's notion that philosophy is coextensive with politics. And he misses the radical critique of modernity, of its founders, and of its politics that Vico unleashes in the *New Science*. In effect, with a rigour that edges towards visionariness, Vico takes to task modern science (which he believes was inaugurated by Machiavelli, Galileo, Bruno, Bacon, Descartes, Hobbes, and Spinoza), and modern science for him embraces the modern world of politics, ethics, and technology. In his construction of modernity, values are determined by an ethos of power and utilitarianism and express themselves as divisive ideologies and fragmentary, ironic perspectives.

It is more than likely that Vico thought of himself as a 'sage' who rethinks the presuppositions of philosophy, posits the centrality of poetry as the model for thinking about politics, and sees philosophical knowledge as the discipline showing the way to the forgotten sources of human history. Croce deliberately swerves away from what to him appears to be the somewhat unclear path of Vico's new all-encompassing, poetic–philosophical project. From Vico's viewpoint, Croce's ironic humanism appears akin to the modern scientific mentality whose sovereingty he steadily questions but ends up enthroning.

For his part, Croce never loses sight of modernity as the focus of his own speculations, and there are signs that the times may be ripe today for a political re-evaluation of his thought. There are ongoing efforts by the philosopher C.G. Ryn (and the journal *Humanitas*) to revive Croce's political–ethical theories and to show their kinship with the conservative neo-humanism of Irving Babbitt and, beyond that, of Leo Strauss.[9] These efforts signal growing awareness about Croce's centrality to the moral and political debates of the present.

NOTES

1 Benedetto Croce, *Contributo alla critica di me stesso* (Bari, 1926), 26. The text is available in English as *An Autobiography*, trans. R.G. Collingwood (Oxford, 1927), 53.
2 The metaphor reappears in Croce's *Autobiography*: 'philosophy as the science of spirit certainly recognizes in Hegel not so much its father (for clearly it can have no father except its own author) as its great forerunner; and in Vico another, more remote and no less venerable' (100–1). The Italian text in the *Contributo alla critica di me stesso* reads as follows: 'la *Filosofia come scienza dello spirito* riconosce, se non proprio come suo padre (perchè padre di lei non può essere, com'è chiaro, che il suo autore medesimo), certo come suo grande antenato lo Hegel, e, più remoto e non meno venerando, il Vico' (63).
3 Bertrando Spaventa, *La filosofia italiana nelle sue relazioni con la filosofia europea*, ed. G. Gentile (Bari: Laterza, 1908). Cf. also G. Vacca, *Politica e filosofia in Bertrando Spaventa* (Bari: Laterza, 1967).
4 The history of these debates in post-Risorgimento Italy – a period to which Gentile devoted protracted meditation – was eloquently sketched by Eugenio Garin in his introduction to Giovanni Gentile, *Storia della filosofia italiana*, ed. E. Garin (Florence: Sansoni, 1969), I, xiv–li).
5 Cf. Giovanni Gentile, *Rosmini e Gioberti*, in G. Gentile, *Storia della filosofia italiana*, 705–898.
6 The history of the polemic between Croce and Gentile is treated by Augusto Del Noce, *Giovanni Gentile: Per una interpretazione filosofica della storia contemporanea* (Bologna: Il Mulino, 1990), 398–417.
7 I follow the edition Benedetto Croce, *La filosofia di Giambattista Vico* (Bari: Laterza, 1962).
8 Giovanni Gentile, 'Studi vichiani,' in *Storia della filosofia italiana*, a cura di Eugenio Garin, I (Florence, 1969), 444. The English translation of the sentence is mine.
9 On the whole issue, see Claes G. Ryn, *Democracy and the Ethical Life: A Philosophy of Politics and Community* (Baton Rouge: Louisiana State University Press, 1978); cf. also Folke Leander, 'Irving Babbit and Benedetto Croce,' in C.G. Ryn and G. Panichas, eds., *Irving Babbit in Our Time* (Washinton, DC: Catholic University of America Press, 1986), 75–102.

10

The Impact of Croce's *Aesthetics* of 1902 and Today's Revolt against Modernity

EDMUND E. JACOBITTI

The Crisis of Positivism and the Crisis of Modernity

Benedetto Croce came to prominence at the turn of the present century in an Italy torn by cultural and political crises and searching for new direction. For many intellectuals, very many in fact, that new direction came from Croce. According to Eugenio Garin, Croce's work, particularly in aesthetics, 'rendered an entire generation Crocean' (rese crociana una generazione intera).[1] To grasp the reasons for his enormous influence, one must understand the nature of the dramatic dislocations that marked *fin-de-siècle* Italy.[2]

These dislocations had many dimensions but were understood by many intellectuals to be rooted in the 'crisis of positivism'[3] – that sudden loss of faith in a scientific method that had insisted that humanity and nature could and *should* be described in the same 'value-free' scientific terms. It is now evident, however, that this great seismic readjustment was not restricted either to Italy or to the fin-de-siècle: it was but the first stages of a much greater and enduring event that we today call 'the crisis of modernity,'[4] the metaphysical flame-out of a tradition that had animated Western culture since the time of the ancient Greeks. Croce, in short, along with many other intellectuals, was a pioneer in a crisis that has now overwhelmed our own present fin-de-siècle and that began that 'incredulity towards metanarratives' that Lyotard has described.[5]

At least since the time of Plato and Aristotle, the Western intellectual tradition has been based on the philosophical side of 'the ancient quarrel between philosophy and poetry' (*Republic* 607b). Although the rationalist tradition has various dimensions, common to all of them are the beliefs that local poetic tradition is inferior to truth that conforms to the universal *logos* and that knowledge of humanity, nature, God, the *subjectum*, or Being, could be obtained – but at a price. That price was the suspension of belief in the opinions of one's received tradition and the expunging of them from serious philosophical and scientific language.

Against this reverence for the *logos*, there has been a constant underlying protest from poetry, religion, ordinary language philosophy, and theorists of rhetoric. This opposition argued, and argues today, that suspending belief in the values of one's culture leaves one lost in a moral abyss. For these thinkers, it is precisely the bracketing off of moral values – the unification of human and natural science in value-free positivism – that has led us into a situation 'so disastrous that,' as MacIntyre puts it, 'there are no large remedies for it.' Likewise, Robert Bellah holds that it is because we have removed poetic values from reason and made philosophy value-free that 'we are hovering on the very brink of disaster.' To Francis Fukuyama, our disparagement of traditional non-rational values has paved the way for a 'future [that] is more likely than not to contain new and unimagined evils, from fanatical dictatorships and bloody genocides to the banalization of life through modern consumerism.'[6] To all these thinkers, and many more, only through a return to poetry can there be a moral redemption of the West.

By poetry then, these figures clearly mean a rather wide – though hardly unprecedented[7] – number of things that, since Plato's exile of poetry from *The Republic*, have generally been taken to be quite opposed to philosophy. According to this point of view, poetry was not only the first speech of pre-reflective humans as they fled their bestial origins, it was the language that first imposed order and morality on society. The poets were the true founders of society, Vico argued, because they unconsciously created the gods who in turn tamed humanity. No doubt, such poets had to be also men of exceptional courage and physical strength, 'armed prophets' such as the Moses, Cyrus, Romulus, and Theseus of Machiavelli's *The Prince*. These figures, celebrated in works of epic poetry such as the *Iliad* and the *Odyssey*, Exodus, *Le Chanson de Roland*, and the *Niebelungedlied*, were the poet-founders whose legends provided the models of moral virtue, courage, honour and strength to which later generations could look for guidance – if the philosophers did not expunge the record. Poetry was therefore the ethnic and local code of particular people; and the virtues celebrated in this poetry were therefore insular – of the tribe, the village, and later the *polis*. A universal virtue or morality would necessarily have to oppose such particular and local tradition. And, unless a universal morality could be grounded in something as firm as poetic tradition – some as yet undiscovered rational, universal law of nature – the ideal of universal morality could only fuel scepticism about a people's local tradition.

Thus poetry is not a form of expression in verse but the *sensus communis*, the *petit recits* that permeates the various individual societies. It is in short *vivere civile*, a way of life or what Francesco De Sanctis called 'culture': 'What does culture mean in this case? It means undoubtedly a coherent, unitary ... conception of life and of man ... a philosophy that has become precisely "a culture," that is, it has generated an ethic, a mode of living, a civil and individual conduct.' (Ma cosa significa 'cultura' in questo caso? Significa indubbiamente una coerente, unitaria ... 'concezione della vita e dell'uomo', una 'religione laica', una filosofia che sia diventata appunto 'cultura', cioè abbia generato un'etica, un modo di vivere, una condotta civile e individuale.)[8]

The *Aesthetics* of 1902 and the Rebirth of Culture

In this equation of poetry and traditional culture one can easily see how a defence of poetry could become the vehicle for an attempt to refound a society and how mere empirical observation and scientific reason would appear as obstacles to such a rebirth. Positivism and empiricism, in short, leave people without a sensus communis, wandering and rootless in the open-ended world and longing for spiritual direction and awakening. It was such an awakening that Croce meant to inspire by his rejection of Enlightenment rationalism. For the Encyclopaedists, the ideal was 'natural man' in an abstract 'state of nature,' unsituated, unobligated, and undirected by a culture. Such an ideal undermined the local values that had given Italy a culture, a way of life, and had inspired the Risorgimento. Against positivism, Encyclopaedism, and the Jacobin ideals of the rights of abstract 'man,' Croce aimed the ideals of Machiavelli, the patriot who, in the last chapter of *The Prince*, had called for an Italian Moses to unite the country and establish the rights and culture of Italians. Positivism or 'the Masonic mentality used to be called Encyclopaedism and Jacobinism in the eighteenth century' (La mentalità massonica si chiamo ne secolo decimottavo enciclopedismo), explained Croce, 'and it can be said that the entire Italian Risorgimento developed as a reaction against that French, Jacobin, Masonic direction' (si puo dire che tutto il moto del risorgimento italiano si sia svolto come reazione a quell'indirizzo francese, giacobino, massonico).[9]

A poetic reawakening would have to be *against* this scientific mentality. Thus, in an essay of 1908 entitled 'The Cultural Awakening of Italy' (Il risveglio filosofico e la cultura italiana), Croce announced that

the heroes of the mental world no longer appear, as they once did, as poets, philosophers, [and] historians; but rather ... as physiologists, physicists, zoologists ... These new directors of social life are entirely insensitive to art; they ignore history; they sneer like drunken bumpkins at philosophy; and they satisfy their religious needs ... in masonic lodges and electoral committees. The philosophical reawakening ... will have to put the naturalists and doctors, physiologists and psychiatrists, in their place and put a brake on their arrogance. [Gli] eroi del mondo mentale non appaino più, come un tempo, i poeti, i filosofi, gli storici ... ; ma a esclusione di costoro, i fisiologi, i fisici, gli zoologi ... Questi nuovi direttori della vita sociale sono affatto insensibili all'arte, ignorano la storia, sogghignano, come villanzoni ubbriachi, innanzi all filosofia, e soddisfano, se mai, il bisogno religioso in quei sacri luoghi, che sono le logge massoniche e comitati elletorali. Il risveglio filosofico ... dovrà riabbassare all 'ufficio, che è loro proprio, naturalisti e medici, fisiologi e psichiatri, e infrenare la loro arroganza.)[10]

As early as 1902, Croce had seen from his reading of Vico[11] that poetic thought was the imaginative, creative imposition of a moral *mythos* on an unruly world. Poetic myth, Vico had argued in the eighteenth century, was the originary source of order, culture, and sensus communis. This meant to Vico that poetry – not philosophy – had been the original language of humanity. It also meant that a re-emergence of culture would have to obliterate the anti-humanist mentality of scientific philosophy. To assert such heresy in the heavenly city of the Enlightenment, where orthodoxy held that society had originated when *rational* men assembled in the forest primeval and signed a social contract, was enough to make Vico a marginal figure. But in the twentieth-century revival of poetry and scepticism about positivism, it could not help but attract the attention of Croce.

Like Vico, Croce meant to establish the primacy of poetry over reason. Unlike Vico, Croce had the fortune to appear at precisely the time when, throughout Europe, the rational order had begun to unravel. Nietzsche, Freud, and many others had all turned *away* from the logos and towards the creative, imaginative, individual constituents of human behaviour. In that atmosphere, Croce's *Estetica* of 1902 burst like a bomb[12] on the positivists and naturalists, catapulting Croce into the position of 'lay Pope' (papa laico) of Italy, as Gramsci so nicely put it.[13]

'It must never be forgotten,' wrote Eugenio Garin, 'that the essential impact of Croce upon the Italian culture was largely that of the *Estetica* of 1902 ... For nearly two decades ... philosophical Italy ... remained tied to a book ... that rendered an entire generation Crocean.' (non andrebbe mai dimenticato, il peso essenziale del Croce nella vita della cultura italian fu lungamente il peso dell'*Esteica* del 1902 ... Per circa due decenni ... l'Italia filosofica ... rimase legata a un libro ... che rese un generazione intera crociana.)[14]

The opening passages of the *Aesthetics* were revolutionary and stressed the 'liberating and purifying function of art' (funzione liberatrice e puraficatrice).[15] There were, Croce argued, *two* forms of knowledge: imaginative and conceptual. Imagination or intuition provided knowledge of the particular (the fact, the incident, the object, the individual), while conceptual knowledge was of the universal (logical and natural relations, laws, abstractions). In an era that held firmly to the idea that thought was conceptual or it was not thought, asserting that imagination/intuition was a form of knowledge independent of conceptual thought was a startling idea. And Croce did not stop there. Not only, said Croce, was art independent of conceptual knowledge, it was the primary form of knowledge, on which and from which all other knowledge depended and derived.[16] Works of prose, philosophy, history, and even science were first poetic: 'Every work of science is at the same time a work of art ... Poetry is "the mother language of humanity"; the first men "were by nature sublime poets."' (Ogni opera di scienza e insieme opera d'arte ... la poesia e 'lingua materna del genere umano'; i primi uomini furono da naturua sublimi poeti').[17]

The aim of the *Aesthetics* was to liberate aesthetic knowledge from all other forms of knowledge – aesthetic imagination 'has no need of parents; it does not need to rest on anything' (non ha bisogno di padroni; non ha necessita di appoggiarsi ad alcuno) – and defend it against psychologists, positivists, and philosophers who dismissed it as dabbling, entertainment, or a form of neurosis: 'Art is independent of science, practical matters, and morality' (L'arte è indipendente così dalla scienza, come dall'utile e dalla morale).[18] By making conceptual knowledge depend on art, the intuition of the particular (how could one have a concept or universal without having first a particular?), Croce had made rational thought merely derivative.

Moreover, with art freed from the control of scientists and moralists, moral virtue acquired (or perhaps regained) a grounding in prereflective aesthetic intuition. While positivists composed their empirical sociology, and rationalists engaged in vain quests for a 'rational' morality or simply dismissed moral values as mere preferences, Croce showed that morality derived, like conceptual knowledge, from the poetic imagination. The pure unreflective morality of the Risorgimento that had been undermined by positivists was now rescued. A moral view was legitimate because it was a poetic intuition. One need no longer apologize to philosophers for defending morality, and one need not tolerate immorality: 'We propose,' Croce wrote in introducing his journal *La critica* in 1903, 'to maintain a *determinate point of view*. Nothing is, in fact, more dangerous to the healthy development of scholarship than the misunderstood sentiment of tolerance, which is, in fact, indifference and scepticism.' (in questa publicazione ci proponiamo di sostenere *un determinato ordine di'idee*. Niente è, infatti, più dannoso al sano svolgimento degli studi di quel malinteso sentimento di tolleranza, che è infondo indifferenza e scettcismo.)[19]

The fundamental equation of the first *Aesthetics* was between intuition and expression or language: 'Every true intuition or representation is at the same time expression. What is not objectified in expression is not intuition or representation, but sensation or naturalness. The spirit does not intuit except by making, forming, expressing. Whoever separates intuition from expression will never succeed in rejoining them.' (Ogni vero intuizione o rappresentazione è, insieme, espressione. Ciò che no si oggettiva in un'espressione non è intuizione o rappresentazione, ma sensazione e naturalità. Lo spirito non intuisce se non facendo, formando, esprimendo. Chi separa intuizione da espressione, non riesce mai più a ricongiungerle.)[20] Aesthetic intuition was not therefore the private preserve of the professional artist. It was the primary language of a people: 'It cannot be asserted that the intuition that is generally called artistic differs from ordinary intuition ... The principle reason that has prevented aesthetics, the science of art, from revealing the true nature of art, its real roots in human nature, has been its separation from general spiritual life, having made of it a sort of special function or aristocratic club.' (Non si può ammettere che l'intuizione, che si dice di solito artistica, si diversifichi da quella comune ... Perché l'avere staccato l'arte dalla comune vita spirituale, l'averne fatto non so qual circolo aristocratico o quale funzione singolare, è stata tra le principale cagione che hanno impedito all'Estetica, scienza dell'arte, di attingere la vera natura, le vere radice di questa nell'animo umano.)[21]

It followed from this stance that all language was poetic or aesthetic and that whatever a person expressed was therefore art: 'If an epigram be art, why not a simple word? If a novel be art, why not the jottings of new journalists? If a landscape, why not a topographical sketch? The teacher of philosophy in Moliere's comedy was right: "Whenever we speak we create prose."' (Un epigramma appartiene all'arte: perche no una semplice parola? Una novella appartiene all'arte: perche no una nota di cronaca giornalistica? Un paesaggio appartiece all'arte: perche no uno scizzo topografico. Il maestro di filosofia della commedia di Moliere aveva ragione: "sempre che si parla, si fa della prose."')[22]

According to Croce then, the principle characteristic of language as expression was that it was part of a people's 'common sense,' its 'general spiritual life.' This extraordinary equation of language with aesthetics and aesthetics with skills such as map-making foreshadowed, as we see below, our own contemporary emphasis on the paradigm, the *Ge-Stell*, and *Wirkungsgeschichte*. For the moment, let us observe only that one effect of the equation of aesthetics and spiritual life was to warn a people that *abandoning* their common language for value-free scientific discourse would mean surrendering their spiritual values.

Croce's unhorsing of conceptual knowledge, like that of Heidegger's later, had the effect of challenging all forms of transcendence – the Greek *logos*, Enlightenment naturalism, the Hegelian *Weltgeist* – and emphasized instead humanity's grounding in language, in particularity and concreteness: 'Historical intellectualism has given birth ... in the last two centuries ... to a philosophy of history, an ideal history, a sociology, a psychological history (all of which claim) to extract universal laws and concepts from history ... Laws and concepts of history? ... A law of history, a historical concept ... are contradictions in terms ... History means concreteness and particularity; the law and the concept [mean] abstraction and universality.'[23] It was in short the beginning of an immanentism that would lead to what Croce later called 'absolute historicism' (storicismo assoluto).[24] To describe humanity accurately required, he said, 'the negation of positivism and with it the negation of every form of transcendence and belief' (la negazione del positivismo, e insieme la negazione di ogni form di trascendenza e di credenza).[25]

The initial impact of the *Aesthetics* was, not surprisingly, on the young intellectuals bored with positivism and searching for a legitimation of moral action. Mario Vinciguerra, later editor of *La nuova Europa*, remembered the day when, at the age of fifteen, he bought the book: 'I clutched it to my chest and raced home, and unmindful of anything else, I dove within it. I do not evoke this faraway memory out of autobiographical vanity ... It was not the case of a boy of acute sensitivity; it was rather the

spiritual disposition of a great part of our generation ... who received at
the outset, in its original form, the inspirational (*innovatrice*) word
launched by that book.'[26] The text seemed not only to have filled a
kind of spiritual gap but to have presented an entirely new system for
viewing the world. Thus, as Vinciguerra put it, the book was 'the
"open sesame" not only of the world of art, but of the world as art.'[27] To
paraphrase what Boileau said of Malherbe, *Enfin Croce vint*: for a generation, the arrival of Croce transformed and ordered its vision of the
world.[28]

'It seemed to me,' wrote the young Luciano Anesceschi, later co-
editor with Enzo Paci of *Orpheus*, 'that I had come into the possession of
a golden key' (Mi sembrava, allora, di esser guinto in possesso di una
chiave d'oro).[29] Giuseppe Prezzolini summed it up: 'In Italy! This is our
fortune: To have Croce. His merit ... is precisely in the fact that he has a
system. See how he is right, see how his figure dominates. See how he
could do what Bergson could not do ... Croce [has given] ... *a total
impulse* to our culture and to the thought of our nation ... I am a Crocean.
Many are more Crocean than I ... It is the security, it is the certainty, it is
the substance of faith that I find in Croce and that matters to me.' (Ma in
Italia! Questa è la nostra fortuna: di avere il Croce. Il merito suo è ... proprio quello di avere un sistema. Vedete come è diritto, come la sua figura
domina. Vedete come egli può quello che il Bergson non può ... Il Croce
[ha dato] *un impulso totale* alla coltura e al pensiero del nostro paese ... Io
sono un crociano (tanto lo sono più di me ... È la sicurezza, è la certezza,
è la sostanza di fede che trovo nel Croce, che mi importa.)[30] And in the
wake of the book's success, a somewhat startled Croce rocketed into
prominence: 'Even I have become a follower of myself' (anch'io comin-
cio a diventare sequace di me stesso), he wrote to Karl Vossler.[31] Prezzolini was correct in his view that Croce had given the Italian culture a
'total impulse' – that he had, as Vinciguerra observed, restored the
'world *as* poetry' or as moral force.

It is this determination to root morality, language, and culture in
aesthetic and poetic myths of a people that led Croce to Sorelian Marxism. In the late 1880s and early 1890s, Italian socialism had begun to
transform itself from a disparate and desperate collection of Mazzi-
niani, anarchists, idealists, Hegelians, and positivist reformers into a
political party. In 1892, the group expelled the anarchists and formed
the Italian Socialist Party (PSI). For the next decade and a half the party
was torn apart by an internal dispute between the positivist reformers
– Filippo Turati, Claudio Treves, and Leonida Bissolati – and the Sore-

lian syndicalists. Though the reformers held the leadership until 1912, it was always a tenuous command challenged by Sorel – and soon by Croce.[32]

Through his uncle, Bertrando Spaventa, Croce became acquainted in 1884 with Antonio Labriola[33] and through Labriola with Georges Sorel. In Marx, Croce had seen the potential for a poetic Marxism, a moral vision that scorned the positivism and vegetarian socialism of Turati and the reformers: For Croce, Marx was not a scientist of historical materialism, but the poet-hero, the Roland, Siegfried, or 'Machiavelli of the proletariat' (Machiavelli del proletariato). Thus Marx seemed to Croce to recall 'the best traditions of Italian political science ... firm principles of strength, struggle, power, and satirical caustic opposition to the insipidities of anti-historical and democratic natural law and the so-called ideals of 1789' (migliori tradizioni della scienza politica italiana, ... la ferma asserzione del principio della forza, della lotta, della potenza, e la satirica e caustica opposizione alle insipidezze giusnaturalistiche, antistoriche e democratiche, ai cosidetti ideali dell'89).[34]

Croce's vision of Marx as the 'Machiavelli of the proletariat,' the visionary saviour, established a *point de reunion* with Sorel. As early as 1899, Croce had recommended Sorel to Gentile: 'He is a man of powerful and lucid genius ... I am amazed at how he has seen so many question so accurately ... Sorel, who is not a philosopher by profession like Labriola, always has clear and determined thought and does not get muddled in words nor make [logical] leaps as Labriola unfortunately does. Moreover, he is a man of great intellectual loyalty – better, of morality.'[35]

By 1907, Croce had become convinced that Sorel's *Reflections on Violence* should become the Bible of authentic socialism, for Sorelian syndicalism was a movement that set the *Aesthetics* to socialist music: According to Sorel, Marxism was a poetic myth like the ancient Christianity that had overcome the Roman Empire: convinced that Jesus would return in their lifetime and that the world would then end, the Christians had tossed out their worldly goods and dashed into the lion's den with such enthusiasm that the pagans began to believe that these martyrs were really 'on' to something – and the conversion of the West was the result. The blood and enthusiasm of martyrs, propelled by poetic myth, had produced a change in social reality. What difference did it make that the 'second coming' never materialized?[36] Thus in 1907 Croce wrote a flattering introduction to the *Reflections* and had his friends at the Laterza press in Bari publish it.[37] As Antonio Gramsci noted later,

Croce's endorsement of Marxism as ideological/poetic hegemony helped to shift the entire focus of Italian Marxism away from materialist positivism and towards the power of poetry, ideas, and culture.[38]

Croce and Contemporary Thought

Croce's hostility to materialist Marxism and its deterministic 'philosophy of history,' however, not only led to new directions within Marxism and elsewhere in contemporary culture, they foreshadowed other developments in our own era that point to the shaping force of language in philosophy and science. Like Vico, Croce had seen that language was an expression of a people's spiritual life. This powerful insight indicated that it was not empirical reality or abstract truth that governed science and philosophy, but rather that language governed the way in which empirical reality and truth were seen – or created. Language, as a manifestation of spiritual life, provided the categories through which truth and reality passed in order to be processed as information. They therefore prefigured what information a people found important and what it dismissed as mere background noise. Without the prefigurative power of poetic 'common sense,' the world would be an open-ended abyss of choices, 'a bloomin' buzzin' confusion,' as William James put it.

Like Vico and Nietzsche,[39] but years before Heidegger's study of the *Gestell*,[40] Gadamer's 'prejudice,'[41] Foucault's *episteme*[42] or Kuhn's notion of 'the priority of paradigms,'[43] Croce had seen that at the base of all explanation there lay an arbitrary poetic and prefigurative insight: every work of science, as he put it, was first a work of art. Thus where today Kuhn has brought to light the way in which the scientist learns and must learn to conform to the standards of the scientific community's aesthetic intuition, its common sense – 'there is no standard higher than the assent of the relevant community'[44] – Croce's *Aesthetics* had shown that it was a culture's originary poetic shaping of the formless world into a common sense that determined its interpretation of reality.

As a result of all this limitation, knowledge of the sort sought by philosophers from Aristotle to at least Hegel and Marx seems hopelessly out of the question. The more we look at it, the more knowledge of the world and even of our own human nature seems to be simply a reflection of the inner world established by originary poetic language: 'Far more clearly,' wrote Kuhn, 'than the immediate experience from which they in part derive, operations and measurements are paradigm-determined.'[45] It was this imprisonment in the paradigm that led a science writer such as Briggs and a physicist such as Peat to refer to the universe as a 'looking glass'[46] – and directed Croce (and years earlier, Vico) to the conclusion that all knowledge was poetic, an imaginative sorting mechanism directed on a multidimensional world.

Croce's Aesthetic and Modern Science

One result of Croce's emphasis of the idea of prefiguration was the realization that the scientific viewpoint was merely, as Nietzsche put it, 'a point of view.' The second was that since human history itself passed through the same sorting mechanism, it was poetic and could not be encapsulated in anything as exotic as a 'philosophy of history.'

A brief examination of how the imaginative or poetic prefiguring of data into an orderly or logical form – an arbitrary exclusion of the disorderly and singular – shaped the scientific perspective reveals how prescient Croce's ideas were. Much earlier than Heidegger's attack on the *logos* in *Being and Time* and *Early Greek Thinking*, or Foucault's critique of the *episteme*,[47] Croce had seen that the basis for any classification of natural phenomena into like and unlike was arbitrary. A so-called natural classification varied according to which factor one chose as the ground of taxonomy.[48] 'To be able,' Croce said, 'to *choose* this or that basis of division (the organs of nutrition, or reproduction, etc. or this or that particular part of the organs or functions) is precisely the arbitrary element and hence the extraneous (element) that is introduced (by science).' (Potere scegliere uno o un altro fondamento di divisione [gli organi di nutrizione o di riproduzione ecc, e una o un'altra parte di questi organi e funzioni], sta per l'appunto l'elemento arbitrario, e quindi estraneo, che s'introduce.)[49]

Croce had understood that scientific conviction rested on a series of arbitrary choices and further on the arrogant assumption that though nature might be complex it was understandable, an equation or riddle with an answer that would provide the key to the universe. Although most people would put the goal line farther off than Max Born did back in 1928, the scientific mind proceeds with the same cheery swagger as the Nobel Prize winner did when, having just seen Dirac's equations for the electron, he announced to an audience at Göttingen University that 'Physics, as we know it, will be over in six months.'[50] The idea that nature could be explained by simply finding the root equations reduced physics to a pedestrian matter of filling in the blanks in the so-called Grand Unified Theory (GUT).[51] What Croce had understood was that the latest GUT itself – the assumption that nature obeyed human mathematical convention – was a whistle-in-the-dark.

In fact, in the history of science this assumption was quite recent and, as Croce could see from reading Vico's *On the Most Ancient Wisdom of the Italians*,[52] quite arbitrary. It was only with the birth of algebraic geometry and classical mechanics in the seventeenth century that it seemed really possible (in principle, anyway) to write the necessary equations for the description of all natural movement. But for all its elegance, classical mechanics – we know today – applied only in a limited area of the spectrum. When events occur over long distances or when things begin to move at near-relativistic speed – as a good deal of the universe does – the laws of classical physics break down, and chance again rears its mighty head. Thus in the subatomic world of quantum wave mechanics that followed Bohr's 1913 papers, exact pinpointing of tiny particles moving at relativistic speeds was no longer possible.[53]

Certainly, given enough particles, really freakish events are unlikely because large numbers of particles can be put into probabilistic equations. It is always necessary, however, to recall that such equations are, like maps or words, simplified poetic or metaphorical descriptions[54] written over a much more complex reality. In short, they confirm Croce's observation that what we know – what we can describe without tropic expression – is not the world but the poetic equation that we have made. This is all the more evident in contemporary chaos theory.

Chaos theory investigates turbulence or the far-from-equilibrium systems that we see all over the world – in meteorology, demographics, open-ended chemical systems, vortices (even traffic patterns, running water, stock-market gyrations), and so on – where feedback loops and other such phenomena make complete knowledge impossible. If Heisenberg's and Schrodinger's quantum electrodynamics demonstrated that there were at least *two* different dimensions of (and two different forms of mechanics to describe) reality – chaos theory reveals a *multi*dimensional reality where the laws at one level are incommensurate with those at another level: atomic, molecular, biological, and sociological systems all operate according to their own *local* laws.[55]

In short, the physical universe may not *be* ruled by universal laws but may well be composed – as Croce suggested of human cultures – of competing forces whose principles are in constant flux and require the use of non-linear differential equations to be explained. Such equations are at best poetic attempts to round up stray variables, any one of which could unleash cascades of unexpected consequences.[56] One can sense in the new style of scientific metaphor the uneasiness or hopelessness of using a language that claims precise calculation to describe events that are in principle indescribable, if not downright unimaginable. Thus metaphors such as 'strange attractors,' 'feedback loops,' 'fractals' (infinite variation in finite space), and 'pitchfork bifurcations' have come to replace tamer tropes such as 'inertia,' 'equilibrium,' 'mechanics,' Galilean or Lorentzian 'transformation,' 'survival of the fittest,' or even 'relativity.' In the new tropes, a host of unnerving forces seem to maraud through our theoretical apparatus and reveal our lack of knowledge.[57]

The limits of poetic constructs in science are severe and require a different more modest kind of physics, according to the Nobel Prize–winning physicist of chaos, Ilya Prigogine. What fascinates Prigogine is that up until recently physics has always been a laboratory science. And the more one leaves the artificial environment and ventures into the real or natural world, the more one sees that Croce's observation that science is first art is necessarily true. 'Our universe has a pluralistic, complex character,' wrote Prigogine. 'Structures may disappear, but also they may appear ... The artificial may be deterministic and reversible. The *natural* contains essential elements of randomness and irreversibility. This leads to a *new view of matter* in which matter is no longer the passive substance described in the mechanistic world view but is associated with spontaneous activity. This change is so profound that ... we can really speak about a new dialogue of man with nature.'[58] In short, in the complex systems of the real world the spontaneous behaviour of nature requires a much more humble view of what we can know.

Croce and Contemporary Historiography

The second area where Croce's ideas foreshadowed contemporary thinking is in the human world of history. As science has discovered that its paradigms often hide many of the chaotic random events that spontaneously develop in physical systems and alter their course, the discipline of history has begun to see that its philosophy of history hides the spontaneous, human, and contingent factors that alter the course of human history.

Philosophy of history is a paradigm that postulates the framework or parameters within which historical events transpire. It concerns the 'engine' of history and provides the link between cause and effect that permits historical explanation. But like the differential equation, this linking of cause and effect is often arbitrary, certainly poetic, and always over-simplified. Without a philosophy of history, one has no mechanism for explaining historical change. With a philosophy of history, history loses its spontaneity and its human subjects lose their freedom.

It was precisely this loss of freedom that Croce addressed in his attack on philosophy of history. And in this, as in the physical sciences, he anticipated much of the current ferment in historical studies. That ferment issues from the realization that 'scientific' historical explanation allows no room for the real craziness of the world – the fact that momentous events can result from a pedestrian character flaw, a train wreck, a stupid political blunder, or a freak bulls eye. Scientific history, philosophy of history, leaves no room for such factors. Indeed, it does not *like* such factors. What historical text would mention, let alone emphasize, that if George Washington had drowned in the Delaware, if Louis XVI had simply been a more forceful reformer in the spring of 1789, or if Jesus had died in the desert, then the United States, Europe, and the entire West, respectively, would be different places? As the biologist/palaeontologist Stephen Jay Gould put it, we do not like to believe that something as serious as history or evolution could, because of some freak event, just as well have produced a world ruled by dinosaurs.[59]

The current debate in historiography[60] arises precisely because of a determination no longer to sweep the contingent under the philosophical rug. It is not that anyone doubts that the French Revolution *occurred* or that the American Civil War actually *happened*, but that we are not sure of the *causes* of even such huge events. Philosophy of history attempts to eliminate this lack of knowledge by stringing together the flotsam and jetsam of contingent events to fit a preconceived causal philosophy. In so doing, it puts the cart before the horse: To assign a *cause* to the events of empirical history, we need to know what to look for, what counts as a cause. In short, it seems necessary *already* to have – before looking at the events – knowledge of the engine of history.

Philosophy of history has its focus on the why of events before the events themselves occur.[61] It therefore presents history from 'outside history,' from the impartial, scientific perspective that gives the narration of events the appearance of objectivity. From the 1860s to the late 1960s, the reigning causal narrative was, of course, Marxist materialism. And it was Croce's attack on materialist Marxism in favour of Sorelian syndicalism that led him to reject philosophy of history.

It was because Croce found cause and effect so difficult to line up that as early as the spring of 1893 he began to sketch out the artistic or poetic nature of historiography. In 'History Brought under the General Concept of Art,' Croce argued that writing history was an 'artistic production that aims at capturing (ha per oggetto della sua produzione) what really happened.'[62]

This 'what really happened' could not be elicited from some philosophy of history that prefigured the data, for, on its own, 'historical movement can only be reduced to a single idea, that of development' (sviluppo).[63] 'Philosophy of history' reduces history to a matter of filling in the blanks in the already imagined grand theory: 'The idea of philosophy of history surrenders the autonomy of historiography to abstract philosophy. Wherever such a claim is made, one seems to hear bells tolling the death of history ... [Serious] historians rebel with violence when anyone talks to them of philosophy of history ... Before Hegel seeks the facts, he knows what they must be.'[64]

Likewise, history could not, Croce argued,[65] be Ranke's *Historie wie es eigentlich gewesen*, the passionless retelling of events 'for the sheer pleasure of recounting them' (per il solo piacere di raccoglierli) for history was not a mindless (and impossible) foraging among documents[66] in order to recapitulate names, dates, and battles, but the imaginative reconstruction of the spiritual life of a people or peoples, as Croce did in histories such as *The History of the Kingdom of Naples*, the *History of Europe in the Nineteenth Century*, and *The History of Italy (1871–1915)*. These were what Croce called 'ethico-political history,' 'moral history,' or 'history as the story of liberty.' Such history presents the spiritual life of a people, its 'struggle against evil' (la lotta contro il male), in its quest to establish a moral identity. Unlike Hegelian history, 'ethico-political history does not stand over or above other histories, nor does it resolve them into itself; yet it penetrates into all these and obtains its own concrete character.' (Storia etico-politica non sta sopra le altre storie ne le risolve in se, ma tutte competrandole, riceve da esse la sua propria concretezza.)[67]

This kind of writing, which resonates with the 'thick description' associated with figures such as Michael Sandel, Cornel West, and Clifford Geertz, escapes both the amoral Rankean positivism and the *Aufhebung* of the *Weltgeist*. It presents human history from within where the adventure and the drama can never be known in advance or judged from outside history, but can only be imagined through art.

Every era has a framework that establishes what counts as 'explanation.' By prefiguring the historical narrative, that framework or philosophy of history narrows down an open-ended world, where infinite causes can produce infinite effects; but it also pre-empts the spontaneous, human, and contingent factors that really produce historical development.

Croce's attack on philosophy of history aimed precisely at removing such blinders and allowing us to see that 'concrete knowledge and true [knowledge] are always historical,' rooted in the current stage of spiritual life, from which there is no escape to Cartesian certainty. Only by accepting Croce's rejection of historical inevitability are we able to see how miraculous history really is and how important the individual is.

NOTES

All translations from the Italian are my own, unless otherwise noted

1 Eugenio Garin, *Cronache di filosofia italiana* (Bari: Laterza, 1966), I, 226.
2 For more detailed analysis, see Robert Wohl, *The Generation of 1914* (Cambridge, Mass.: Harvard University Press, 1979); H. Stuart Hughes, *Consciousness and Society* (New York: Vintage, Random House, 1958); A. William Salamone, *Italy in the Giolittian Age* (Philadelphia: University of Pennsylvania Press, 1960); Alexander De Grand, *The Italian Nationalist Association and the Rise of Fascism in Italy* (Lincoln: University of Nebraska Press, 1978); and Edmund E. Jacobitti, *Revolutionary Humanism and Historicism in Modern Italy* (New Haven, Conn.: Yale University Press, 1981).
3 See Giovanni Marchesini, *La crisi del positivismo e il problema filosofico* (Turin: Einaudi, 1898); Ludovico Limentani, 'Il positivismo italiano,' *Logos* 7 (1924), 33ff; Croce, 'À proposito del positivismo italiano,' now in *Cultura e vita morale* (Bari: Laterza, 1955), 41–6.
4 See, for example, David Roberts, *Benedetto Croce and the Uses of Historicism* (Berkeley: University of California Press, 1987).
5 Jean-Francois Lyotard, *The Postmodern Condition: A Report on Knowledge*, trans. Geoff Bennington and Brian Massumi (Minneapolis: University of Minnesota Press, 1984), xxiv.
6 MacIntyre, *After Virtue: A Study in Moral Theory* (Notre Dame, Ind.: University of Notre Dame Press, 1981), 4; Robert Bellah et al., *Habits of the Heart: Individualism and Community in American Life* (New York: Harper and Row, Perennial Library, 1985), 114–15, 284, 295–6; Fukuyama, *The End of History and the Last Man* (New York: Free Press, 1992), 3.
7 For discussion of some of the extended meanings of poetry, see Eric Havelock, *The Liberal Temper in Greek Politics* (London, 1957); *Preface to Plato* (Cambridge: Harvard University Press, 1963); *The Literate Revolution in Greece and Its Cultural Consequences* (Princeton, NJ: Princeton University Press, 1982);

190   Edmund E. Jacobitti

Werner Jaeger, *Paideia*, 3 vols., trans. Glibert Highet (New York: Oxford University Press); George Kennedy, *The Art of Persuasion in Greece* (Princeton, NJ: Princeton University Press, 1963); Walter J. Ong, SJ, *Orality and Literacy: The Technologizing of the Word* (New York: Methuen, 1982); and Brian Vickers, *In Defense of Rhetoric* (Oxford: Clarendon Press, 1990).

8   De Sanctis, as quoted in *Antonio Gramsci: Quaderni del carcere*, ed. Valentino Gerratana, 4 vols. (Turin: Einaudi, 1975), III, 2185–6.

9   'Due conversazioni,' in *Cultura e vita morale*, 145.

10 'Il risveglio filosofico e la cultura italiana,' now in *Cultura e vita morale* (Bari: Laterza, 1955), 22–3.

11 In 1902, Croce had published 'Giambattista Vico, First Discoverer of the Science of Aesthetics,' in *Flegrea*. This was later reworked and published as part of the so-called first aesthetics. On the early version, see Giovanni Gullace, 'Introduction,' to *Benedetto Croce: Poetry and Literature*. For Croce's remarks on Vico, see *Estetica come scienza dell'espressione e linguistica generale* (Bari: Laterza, 1908), 249–65.

12 Scirocco, *Croce: la vita, l'itinerario, il pensiero: La religione della liberta* (Milan: Edizione Academia, 1973), 22–3.

13 Gramsci, *Quaderni del carcere*, II, ed. Valentino Gerratana (Turin: Einaudi, 1975), 867, 1306.

14 Garin, *Cronache di filosofia italiana* (Bari: Laterza, 1966), I, 226; my translation.

15 *Aesthetics come scienza dell'espressione e linguistica generale*, 3rd ed. (Bari: Laterza, 1908), see, for example, 4, 24, 58, 61.

16 Ibid., 27ff.

17 Ibid., 30–1; although Croce uses quotes, he does not say that the quotes are from Vico.

18 Ibid., 61.

19 *La critica* 1 (1903), 3.

20 *Estetica*, 11.

21 Ibid., 16–17.

22 Ibid., 17.

23 Ibid., 47

24 In Croce's view, historicism was *not* 'philosophy of history,' the Hegelian vision of humanity as a mere creature of history, but humanity in the Nietzschean abyss, unable to grasp the whole with metaphysics. See, *Ciò ch'e vivo e ciò ch'è morto della filosofia di Hegel* (Bari: Laterza, 1906). And, as he later saw it, even Vico's *corsi e ricorsi* was a philosophy of history: See *La filosofia di Giambattista Vico*, 6th ed. (Bari: Laterza, 1962). 'I ... had acquired,' Croce wrote in his autobiography, 'a sort of unconscious immanentism, not being interested in a world other than the one in which I was actually living and not feeling directly or even at all the problem of transcendence.' See 'Contributo alla

critica di me stesso,' in *Etica e politica* (Bari: Laterza, 1967), 343.

25 Croce, 'Per la rinascita dell'idealismo,' now in *Cultura e vita morale*, 3rd. ed. (Bari: Laterza, 1955), 33ff.

26 Mario Vinciguerra, 'Il primo e l'ultimo Croce,' in *Croce: ricordi e pensieri* (Naples: Vajaro, 1957), 27.

27 Vinciguerra, 'Il grande solitario,' in *Croce: ricordi e pensieri* (Naples: Vajaro, 1957)

28 See Sergio Solmi, 'Croce e noi,' *La rassegna d'Italia* 1 (Feb.–March 1946), 262.

29 'Lettera privata per un'omaggio,' ibid., 226.

30 'Io devo ... ,' *La voce* 4 (Feb., 1912), 756.

31 See Eugenio Garin, *Cronache di filosofia italiana*, (Bari: Laterza, 1966) I, 226.

32 S. Massimo Ganci, 'La formazione positivista di Filippo Turati,' *Rivista storico del socialismo* 1 (Jan.–June 1958), 56–68.

33 Luigi Dal Pane, *Antonio Labriola nella politica italiana* (Turin: Einaudi, 1975), especially 447–75.

34 *Materialismo storico ed economia marxistica*, 1st paperback edition (Bari: Laterza, 1968), xiii and 104.

35 Letter of 15 Sept. 1899 in 'Lettere di Benedetto Croce a Giovanni Gentile,' *Giornale critico della filosofia italian* (1969), 85.

36 *Reflections on Violence*, trans. J. Roth and T.E. Hulme (New York: Collier, 1961), 126.

37 See my 'Labriola, Croce, and Italian Marxism,' *Journal of History of Ideas*, 36 no. 21 (April–May 1975), 297–318, as well as my 'Hegemony before Gramsci,' *Journal of Modern History* (March 1980), 66–84. Sorel's book did not fall on deaf ears. Mussolini reviewed it enthusiastically in *Il popolo* of Trent. See Laura Fermi, *Mussolini* (Chicago: University of Chicago Press, 1966), 75.

38 Certainly they contributed to *Gramsci*'s doubts about the scientific method. See my 'The Religious Vision of Antonio Gramsci,' *Italian Quarterly* 25 nos. 92–8 (summer–fall, 1984), 101–32. See also Enzo Santarelli, 'La revisione del marxismo in Italia nel periodo della seconda internazionale,' *Rivista storica del socialismo* 1 (Oct.–Dec. 1958), 381–404. 'Come nacque e come morì il marxismo teorico in Italia (1895–1900),' in Croce, *Materialismo storico ed economia marxistica*, 1st paperback edition (Bari: Laterza, 1968), 253–94. It is rather a common assumption on the left that Croce was largely responsible for the destruction of Marxism in Italy. See, for example, Michele Abbate, *La filosofia di Benedetto Croce e la crisi della società italiana* (Turin: Einaudi, 1965).

39 See, for example, his observation that we are 'spiders' who sit in our own net and who 'catch nothing at all except that which allows itself to be caught in precisely *our* net.' *Daybreak* 73, trans. R. J. Hollingdale (Cambridge: Cambridge University Press, 1982).

40 *Being and Time*, trans. John Macquarrie and Edward Robinson (New York:

Harper and Row, 1962), 191: 'In every case interpretation is grounded in something we see in advance.' From this derived his conviction that humans can know only what, from their own fallen state, they project (*entwerfen*) – that nearly unpackable German word linking together 'to throw' (*werfen*) and 'thrownness' (*Geworfenheit*), with their implications of meaningless arrival in the 'always already,' and 'to project' (*entwerfen*), with its implications of projecting shadows on the wall of the cave and taking them for real.

41 *Truth and Method* (New York: Crossroad Press, 1984), 239 and *passim*: 'The recognition that all understanding inevitably involves some prejudice gives the hermeneutical problem its real thrust.'

42 *Power/Knowledge: Selected Interviews and Other Writings (1972–1977)*, ed. Colin Gordon, (New York: Pantheon Books, 1980), 132: 'By truth I do not mean "the ensemble of rules according to which the true and the false are separated and specific effects of power attached to the true" ... but ... the status of truth and the economic and political role it plays.'

43 'Operations and measurements are paradigm-determined.' Thomas Kuhn, *The Structure of Scientific Revolutions* (Chicago: University of Chicago Press, 1962), 43–51 and passim 125. To say nothing of the implications of the so-called anthropic principle in cosmology. The principle holds in effect – in the words of one who applauds it – that 'the laws of nature are explained if it can be established that they must be as they are in order to allow the existence of theoretical physicists to speculate about them.' See Freeman Dyson, *Infinite in All Directions* (New York: Harper and Row, 1989), 296.

44 Kuhn, *Structure*, 93 and 112.

45 Ibid., 125.

46 John Briggs and F. David Peat, *Looking Glass Universe* (New York: Simon and Schuster, 1984).

47 See *Being and Time*, trans. Macquarrie and Robinson; *Early Greek Thinking*, trans. David Farrell Krell and Frank A. Capuzzi (New York: Harper and Row, 1984); also consider Foucault's taxonomy set out in a 'certain Chinese Encyclopedia, in Michel Foucault, *The Order of Things* (New York: Vintage, 1973), xvi–xvii

48 This is of course more obvious and more complex today. Using morphology, one produces one taxonomy. Thin-cell analysis, however, can move the taxon to another station, DNA analysis to still another; and base-pair analysis of the double helix to yet another. Species thus bounce between different kingdoms, phyla, classes, and so on. So what is a species?

49 See 'Il risveglio filosofico e la cultura italiana,' in *Cultura e vita morale* (Bari: Laterza, 1955), 22–3. See also 'Il professore De Sarlo e il problema della logica

filosofica,' *La critica* 4 (1907), 165–9. See too 'Una seconda risposta al professore De Sarlo,' *La critica* 4 (1907), 243–7.

50 See Stephen Hawking, *A Brief History of Time* (New York: Bantam, 1988),
156.

51 'I bring this particular matter to your attention,' the late Nobel Prize-winning
physicist Richard Feynmann explained to his students, 'because it illustrates
that when a law is right it can be used to find another one ... If we had not
known the Law of Gravitation we would have taken much longer to find the
speed of light ... This process [of using one law to find others] has developed
into an avalanche of discoveries, each new discovery permits the tools for
much more discovery, and this is the beginning of the avalanche which has
gone on now for 400 years in a continuous process, and we are still avalanch-
ing along at high speed.' Feynman, *The Character of Physical Law* (Cambridge,
Mass.: MIT Press, 1986), 23.

52 See chap. 1 on the *verum ipsum factum*, trans. L.M Palmer (Ithaca, NY: Cornell
University Press, 1988), 46

53 To establish the position of a particle, we have to shine a light on it. In the
macro world of our ordinary lives, this is of course insignificant. We shine
light on things all the time, and nothing odd happens. But 'in the quantum
world this is not the case. Light [is] energy [and] arrives in lumps[;] and making a measurement necessarily gives a significant jolt to the object on which
we are making the measurement. Furthermore, there is no way that we can
reduce the jolt to zero, even in principle. The laws of quantum mechanics,
therefore, entail fundamental and unavoidable limitations in measurement
and exact knowledge is no longer possible. Particles, therefore, are considered "indeterminate" and Heisenberg's indeterminacy principle required
that in place of certain knowledge we use *probability* distributions.' Tony Hey
and Patrick Walters, *The Quantum Universe* (Cambridge: Cambridge University Press, 1987), 16. See also Feynman, *The Character of Physical Law*, 127–48.

54 Heisenberg's equation and Schrödinger's equation both imply approximation. Thus in Heisenberg's formula it is necessary to write = as ≠ (i.e., approx-
imately) and in Schrödinger's to use the Greek Δ to imply probability.

55 Moreover, these systems – retroviruses, for example – are not stable; they
evolve, break down, reconstitute themselves, and generally misbehave in
incalculable ways. Titanic changes issue from random microscopic additions,
order magically rises out of disorder, autocatalytic systems feed on themselves and then turn into something else. David Bohm, *Causality and Chance
in Modern Physics* (London: Routledge & Kegan Paul, 1957); *Wholeness and
Implicate Order* (New York: Routledge and Kegan Paul, 1980); Ilya Prigogine,
From Being to Becoming: Time and Complexity in the Physical Sciences (San Fran-

cisco: W.H. Freeman and Co., 1980). 'In a linear system a small change in an interaction will produce a small change in a solution. This is not the case with a nonlinear differential equation. The solution may change slowly as a parameter in the equation is varied and then suddenly change to a totally new type of solution. This change of behaviour is *dramatic and unpredictable.'* Briggs and Peat, *Looking Glass*, 174.

56 Some, such as Jacques Monod – *Chance and Necessity*, trans. A Wainhouse (New York: Knopf, 1971) – attribute nearly *everything* to chance.

57 See, for example, James Gleick, *Chaos: Making a New Science* (New York: Penguin, 1989).

58 *Order Out of Chaos* (New York: Bantam, 1984), 9, emphasis added. See also Briggs and Peat, *Looking Glass*, 174. 'Not all systems are linear, however – in fact, very few real ones are.' James Gleick, *Chaos* (New York: Penguin, 1987), described the way in which chaos theory permeated the essential understanding of demography, biology, physics, chemistry, and so on.

59 Stephen Jay Gould, *Wonderful Life: The Burgess Shale and the Nature of History* (New York: Norton, 1989), 318. The entire book, with its debunking of the idea of the survival of the fittest and its defence of the idea of the survival of the *luckiest*, is a hymn to contingency in history.

60 One need only read through journals such as *History and Theory* or *New Literary History* to see how dramatically history has changed since 'philosophy of history' fell apart. The works of figures such as Martin Heidegger, Dominick LaCapra, Hayden White, Michelle Foucault, and Simon Schama have paved the way here. Perhaps the best examples of the *application* of the new approach to history can be found in the new interpretations of the French Revolution carried out by the 'political culture school.' The leading works and scholars here – to name but a few – are *The French Revolution and the Creation of Modern Political Culture* (vol. I, *The Political Culture of the Old Regime*, ed. Keith Michael Baker; vol. II, *The Political Culture of the French Revolution*, ed. Colin Lucas (Oxford: Pergamon Press, 1988); vol. III, *The Transformation of Political Culture (1789–1848)*, ed. Francois Furet and Mona Ozouf (Oxford: Pergamon Press, 1989); Keith Michael Baker, *Inventing the French Revolution: Essays on French Political Culture in the Eighteenth Century* (Cambridge: Cambridge University Press, 1990), Carol Blum, *Rousseau and the Republic of Virtue: The Language of Politics in the French Revolution* (Ithaca, NY: Cornell University Press, 1986); Robert Darnton, *The Business of Enlightenment: A Publishing History of the 'Encylpédie' 1775–1800* (Cambridge, Mass.: Howard University Press, 1979); William Doyle, *Origins of the French Revolution* (Oxford, 1980); Patrice Higgonet, *Sister Republics: The Origins of French and American Republicanism*; Lynn Hunt, *Politics, Culture, and Class in the French Revolution*

(Berkeley: University of California Press, 1984); Ronald Paulson, *Representations of Revolution (1789–1820)* (New Haven, Conn.: Yale University Press, 1983); 'Revolution and the Visual Arts,' in R. Porter and M. Teich, eds., *Revolution in History* (Cambridge: Cambridge University Press, 1986); 240–60.

The spotlight here, however, is largely on Francois Furet, for it has been largely his work, especially *Penser la Revolution française* (Paris: Gallimard, 1978), translated as *Interpreting the French Revolution* (Cambridge, Mass.: Harvard University Press), that has come to dominate the array of plausible explanations for 1789 that appeared after the Marxist demise. Beginning in 1965, Furet began to provide a whole new interpretation of 1789 based not on socio-economic factors or on historical metaphysics but on a rereading of Tocqueville and a renewed appreciation for the nineteenth-century historian's brilliant insights and predictions.

61 See, for example, 'Identita del giudizio del fatto con la conoscenza della gennesi,' *La storia come pensiero e come azione* (Bari: Laterza, 1966), 138–41.

62 'La storia ridotta sotto il concetto generale dell'arte,' in *Primi saggi* (Bari: Laterza, 1927), 35–6.

63 'Sulla forma scientifica del materialismo storico,' in *Materialismo storico ed economia marxistica*, 3, 4, 9, 15.

64 *Ciò che è vivo e ciò che è morto nella filosofia di Hegel* (Bari: Laterza, 1907), 132–5.

65 'Ranke,' in *La storia come pensiero e come anzione*, 75 and passim.

66 See, for example, 'Documenti e testimonianze,' in *La storia come pensiero e come anzione*, 101–7.

67 See the entire essay entitled 'Storia come pensiero e come azione,' in *La storia come pensiero e come anzione*, 7–51, especially, 45ff.

11

History as Thought and Action: Croce's Historicism and the Contemporary Challenge

DAVID D. ROBERTS

A New Croce?

Benedetto Croce was once well known – as a "neo-Hegelian," as a philosopher of art, as a philosopher of history, as a partisan of liberty against fascism. A long-time antagonist, the émigré scholar Giuseppe Antonio Borgese, found him 'the most famed Italian abroad, at least in the scholarly world, since the days perhaps of Galileo.'[1] But by the mid-1940s, near the end of his long life, Croce found himself on the defensive even in Italy, and after his death in 1952 his legacy gradually fell from view all over the Western world.[2]

The reaction against Croce stemmed partly from the contingencies of the post-fascist challenge in Italy, but some of those outside Italy who seriously confronted his work pinpointed features that suggested his thinking was simply passé. In the 1950s, Patrick Romanell charged that Croce's tendency to denigrate the natural sciences had led him to a debilitating ignorance of some of the most exciting currents in contemporary thought.[3] And certainly Croce's mode of argument, especially his talk of 'the spirit,' sometimes suggested discredited metaphysics in its most ethereal and futile form.[4] Two decades later, Hayden White, though initially a Croce partisan, portrayed Croce as the sterile culmination of nineteenth-century historiographical traditions, a thinker who – ironically, in light of his claims to have renewed historical understanding – ended up eviscerating historical knowledge for conservative purposes.[5]

But the intellectual agenda has changed notably in the half-century since Croce began falling from view. Especially since about 1960, when thinkers from Thomas Kuhn to Hans-Georg Gadamer raised new questions about the place of the sciences, an international discussion in the humanities has gathered force, posing very large questions about the present cultural situation and the possibilities that it affords us. Much – from foundationalist philosophy to modernity to history itself – has been said to be ending, but what possibilities open if the world lacks the metaphysical ordering that we used to take for granted?

Prominent among the ensuing attempts at cultural reassessment have been Gadamer's philosophical hermeneutics, Richard Rorty's neo-pragmatism, and the quite different forms of post-structuralist decon-struction represented by Michel Foucault and Jacques Derrida. But the principals in this discussion routinely invoke an array of figures from roughly Croce's period, both to characterize the present situation and to understand its historical sources. Nietzsche and Heidegger have been the most influential of those earlier thinkers, but Rorty draws especially on the American pragmatist John Dewey, while the French intellectual Gilles Deleuze, seeking to reconceive the space for selfhood within a moving or temporal totality, has turned to Henri Bergson.

Working in the pivotal period between Nietzsche and Heidegger, Croce addressed many of the issues prominent in recent humanistic dis-cussion. During his own lifetime he was often compared with Dewey and Bergson. He was as rigorously anti-metaphysical and anti-subjectiv-ist as the most influential of our contemporary humanistic intellectuals. Such a thinker might be expected to come up as a matter of course in current discussion, yet somehow he has not. René Wellek, the distin-guished historian of criticism, has recently noted that in movements influential at various points since Croce's death – from Russian formal-ism and structuralism to hermeneutics and deconstruction – Croce 'is not referred to or quoted, even when he discusses the same problems and gives similar solutions.' And for Wellek this is anomalous in the extreme, for Croce had been arguably the most erudite and wide-ranging figure in the history of criticism.[6]

Occasionally, and very tentatively, some have suggested that the Ital-ian intellectual tradition entails special features, particularly a radical immanence, that might equip it to offer a distinctive contribution, help-ing to counter a certain extravagance in the French way of positing our cultural situation.[7] Vico, in particular, has seemed central to that Italian tradition, and the larger discussion has entailed a renewed appreciation of him in the non-Italian world. Croce claimed his mantle, insisting that only in our time, with the eclipse of metaphysics, could we begin to appreciate what Vico had been up to.[8] But rather than reconnect with

Croce, contemporary Vichians routinely lament Croce's alleged idealist deformation of Vico, based on their assumption that Croce, as a Hegelian, had afforded privilege to conceptual thought.[9] So the recent prominence of Vico, rather than fostering renewed interest in Croce, has tended to confirm the sense that Croce remains part of the problem, exemplifying approaches that the new humanistic thinking seeks to overcome – or bypass.

To be sure, Croce had a moment of systematic philosophy, and because of our longstanding tendency to privilege any such moment, he has long been viewed as a neo-Hegelian idealist. Yet his repeated attacks on philosophical system-building and any pretence of definitive philosophy are among the most striking features of his thought.[10] He explicitly rejected the neo-Hegelian label and even concluded that the very term 'idealism' ought to be abandoned altogether.[11] As an alternative he characterized his own framework as absolute historicism, but 'historicism' is surely as problematic as idealism. Croce distinguished his position from the tradition of German historicism encompassing such figures as Ranke, Dilthey, and Meinecke, so the label hardly serves to place him.

Even granting that Croce may be ripe for revival, it is not clear where to start, how to bring his thinking together with the cultural challenges that have become central during the last several decades. It was never easy, even for Italians, to grasp the centre of gravity of his thought. His ideas were frequently misrepresented, even caricatured, and it was hard to understand the connections among them.[12]

Croce remains elusive partly because, in propounding an absolute form of historicism, he was fastening most fundamentally on 'history.' But since its hypertrophy in the nineteenth century, history has become perhaps the most elusive, and suspect, of categories. Some view any historical approach as still-metaphysical, as justifying the victors. It is arguable, however, that an effort to understand ourselves as historical creatures – which entails a conception of the totality of the human world and the modes of individual experience possible within it – has been central to the developing discussion in the humanities.[13]

In a recent contribution to that discussion, the American literary scholar Brook Thomas characterized central aspects of the present cultural challenge in terms of the incompleteness of the earlier historicist revolution, associated with Germans from Ranke to Meinecke.[14] But, typically, Thomas did not engage Croce. The influential American neopragmatist Richard Rorty showed how the eclipse of foundationalist philosophy yields 'historicism' and forces a reassessment of cultural priorities on that basis, but he too had no encounter with Croce.

Croce's approach to historiography made him exciting, even provocative, to innovative historians such as Carl Becker and Charles Beard in the United States by the later 1920s. And the discussion that has followed from Peter Novick's *That Noble Dream* over the past decade suggests that the issues Croce addressed three-quarters of a century ago are more current than ever, in light of the continuing erosion of the notion that the historian copies or represents some stable past.[15] Novick ended up somewhat resigned about what is left, yet, though devoting much attention to Becker and Beard, he hardly mentioned Croce, to whom Becker and Beard were explicitly indebted, and who claimed to offer a way out of precisely the uncertainties that troubled Novick.

But Croce had his limits. Even in those spheres – aesthetics and historiography – in which he earlier seemed to have most to say, his approach is in some respects genuinely outmoded, unable to account for much of what has proved most exciting in art and historical writing in this century. To apprehend what proves most living in his thought today, we must pull back from the delimited concerns of historiography, or aesthetics, or even philosophy, to understand the overall cultural framework and strategy that he offered. Croce's always-evolving thinking responded to an underlying, broadly religious challenge, which inevitably had implications for cultural priorities and modes of individual experience. Feeling this challenge as historically specific, Croce portrayed it as the task of his generation to replace the old religion, with its mythological underpinnings.[16] Indeed, he took it for granted that the transcendent God that Vico had bracketed had by now fallen away altogether. With the dissipation of transcendence, we also realize that there is no natural law specifying 'values' and no 'philosophy of history' showing us what to do or enabling some to claim privilege for their particular critique of the present world. Nor does study of the natural world afford some key to the way things really are, apart from human being. Croce insisted that science, though essential in its sphere, comes up simply with rough-and-ready generalizations, in response to the questions that people ask.

But how do we characterize the world that is left to us as so much falls away, and what modes of cultural response and individual experience open in such a world? Croce was a pioneer in the ongoing effort to think through the human situation with the end of metaphysics, the loss of foundations or transcendence. The challenge, from his perspective, was to do without much that had long sustained humanity but without overreacting into nihilism, irrationalism, or self-indulgent subjectivism.

Vico had provided the key two centuries before, as he reacted against Cartesianism and sought to head off the developing cultural hegemony of the natural sciences. How strange, said Vico, that scholars had come to place such premium on the study of nature, which only God could truly know – because it was He who had made it. What we human beings can know, and what ought to provide our focus, is the world of civil society that is for ever being built up through human response over time, in history.[17] During the first decade of the century, Croce offered a Vichian recasting of Hegel – a way of understanding reality as history, and history as totality, without Hegel's metaphysical and teleological framework, without any master thread given a priori by what spirit *is* on some level.[18] Vico's way of bracketing nature leaves only the concrete human world, which results and grows as human beings respond through their imaginative language to what has resulted so far.

To characterize the totality of such a world, Croce adapted the term 'spirit' from the idealist tradition, but in his hands the concept became radically concrete and immanent. In one sense, the spirit is nothing but us; it does not operate apart from us historically specific, differentiated human beings. Each individual is a finite embodiment of the spirit, and, as such, each is a participant in the creative process through which our world endlessly comes to be, over time, as history. Each individual is creative, but only in interaction with others, and only in response to the outcome of history, or the total activity of the spirit so far. In this sense, the creation of the world in history is a supra-personal task; the agent is the universal spirit immanent in all individuals.[19] But because we collectively respond to the world that has resulted from the activity of spirit so far, the spirit is in another sense history itself. Although 'spirit' initially sounds abstract, or worse, to those reared in Anglo-Saxon traditions, it stands up as a radically immanent, even post-metaphysical way of understanding individuality and totality in tandem. The world is a single creative happening, a particular history, that we belong to, that we *are*.

Certain cultural priorities followed. Croce summed them up as 'history as thought and action,' a strategy with implications for knowing, evaluating, and acting, for personal experience and political interaction. The key to reassessing Croce is to grasp the web of themes that comprised this strategy. The interconnections are crucial, making sense of categories that, taken in isolation, may seem extravagant – or vacuous.

As a response to a post-metaphysical world, Croce's historicist strategy fruitfully contrasts with such more recent orientations as Rorty's neo-pragmatism and Gadamer's philosophical hermeneutics.

Historical Inquiry and Understanding

As the assault on Croce gathered force during the 1940s, critics charged that he offered a doctrine of passive understanding, of conservative acceptance of whatever has resulted from history.[20] It was thus in part that Gramsci supplanted Croce in major respects in Italy during the 1940s, for Gramsci apparently offered a practical strategy, an opening for action based on study of the real terrain. In fact, however, Crocean historicism was not a warrant for passive acceptance but a call to action, the action through which the world is endlessly remade in history. It was simply a more general framework for action, or practice, than the Marxist tradition offered, and it had room for more radical forms of politics than Croce himself, as one political agent, chose to pursue.

To orient ourselves for action, we need to know or to understand the world in some sense. In a world without foundations, history becomes the fundamental form of knowing; though historical inquiry, we can come to understand how the present world, or some particular situation within it, has come to be as it is. Thus Croce wrote history himself, but he also turned repeatedly to historiography, or the philosophy of history, throughout his career. For historical knowing was problematic, bristling with questions about purpose, method, focus, and truth-value that he had to address.

Croce anticipated aspects of the philosophical hermeneutics that Hans-Georg Gadamer, adapting Heidegger, forged in response to Dilthey. Yet from today's perspective, the contrasts between Croce and Gadamer are also illuminating. For each thinker, the point is not method, which proves secondary at best, but what historical understanding entails and how it serves the ongoing building up of the world. The key for both is that history becomes culturally central as we retreat from foundationalism and put the sciences in new cultural perspective.

For Croce, as later for Gadamer, this more central role means that, in opposition to the commonplace notion that history deals with the past *as opposed to* the present, historical inquiry focuses on some process to the present, not on 'the past for its own sake' – not even 'the past on its own terms,' taken as an exclusive proposition, an end in itself. Precisely because historical understanding has vital implications for present action, Croce found it fundamental that genuinely historical inquiry, as opposed to mere antiquarianism, is not disinterested but is energized by some contemporary concern. Anticipating part of Gadamer's later assault on Dilthey, Croce accused Ranke of settling for 'the fine art of embalming a corpse.'[21] And one of Croce's best-known dicta proclaimed that 'all history is contemporary history.'[22]

By the early 1930s, Croce's extreme presentism made him exciting – and controversial – to practising historians in the United States. Seeking answers to questions that seemed to open with the advent of pragmatism, major historians such as Carl Becker and Charles Beard embraced Croce's thinking, but somewhat warily, for his presentism raised troubling questions about truth and relativism.[23] To be sure, Croce claimed to show how to answer – or sidestep – those questions, but few grasped the terms of his argument, which could pass into today's historiographical controversies with virtually no recasting.

Partly because his early Vichian aestheticism seemed to invite irrationalist excess, Croce sought, in his philosophical works of 1908–9, to balance the creative, imaginative dimension of our response to the world with a cognitive dimension. We seek to make cognitive sense of the particular world that has resulted from history because we are never satisfied but rather want to go on remaking it. And for Croce, as for Vico, we can know the world because we have made it. To put it in Gadamerian terms, we are vehicles for the happening of truth. There is not much more that can be said – or needs to be said.

But we have other defining characteristics as well, and other attributes of the human spirit may impede or distort the happening of truth as we inquire into history. Thus the various contraries of truth may – indeed, to some extent inevitably will – turn up in the historical accounts that result. So how do we distinguish attributes of the human spirit that serve the happening of truth from those that impede or distort it? And how can we distinguish among historical accounts – and understand more generally how the culture winnows out some provisional but true understanding from the aggregate of the historical accounts that are offered? Croce, again anticipating Gadamer, posited ways of doing so, based on the complex interaction of the ethical, the cognitive, and the useful.

The scope for truth is bound up with action, for our inquiries stem from our need for orientation for action. Moreover, because we want to shape what the world next becomes, we seek to influence the understanding of others as well. Turning the tables on pragmatism, Croce insisted that truth is possible precisely because of the practical stakes of our historical inquiries.[24] We need genuinely to learn if we want to act effectively, responding to a world that, as a result of our history so far, has become some particular way.

For truth to emerge, the inquirer must be willing to be challenged, must desire to learn, must genuinely seek to know. So in the last analysis it is the ethical dimension of what we are that leads us to relate to the world in such a way that truth becomes possible.[25] But the relationship between the ethical and historical inquiry is hard to characterize. Croce distinguished moralistic, hortatory accounts from the genuine history that we need to orient ourselves for action, so how does ethical response relate to truth-seeking or openness to learning? Moreover, Croce always insisted that whereas historical understanding can 'prepare action,' affording us orientation, it cannot determine action – cannot tell us what we ought to do. That remains the province of the autonomous ethical side of what we are. But at a time when we speak routinely of a 'crisis of values,' we are bound to ask about the basis of the ethical capacity.

Ethical response does not rest, as it long seemed to, on suprahistorical values, to be invoked from some transcendent sphere. In this sense, there are no 'eternal values.' Responding just after the war 'to my friends who seek the "transcendent,"' Croce argued that each of us has not some heavenly searchlight but only a portable lantern – but this is sufficient, enabling each of us to go on responding ethically to the world, taking responsibility for it.[26] Like our capacity to know, our ethical capacity is built in, a defining characteristic of human being. And it comes into play not only in our delimited interpersonal situations but in our response to the wider world, in the public dimensions of our actions. To be sure, we do not *always* respond ethically; our actions may be merely useful or self-serving. But in some of our moods we feel a wider responsibility for what the world becomes, so we respond in a way that is not merely personally advantageous. When we, as differentiated, historically specific embodiments of the spirit, act in that mode, we establish what is right, or good, or just in that particular situation, thereby adding to what those ethical categories have come to encompass so far.

So although values cannot be considered 'transcendent,' they are eternal in a crucial sense. As ethical agents, we human beings will continue to evaluate, to judge – and will endlessly re-establish the good, or the right, or the just as we do so. But the key for Croce was the other – historicist – side of the coin. The eternal dimension is empty; there is nothing prescriptive. Until we, with our portable lanterns, have responded ethically, there is no way to know what the good, or the right, or the just will next entail.

To the extent that we feel responsibility for the world, we want to affect what it becomes. And to do so requires precisely truth – a certain mode of openness to the actual world – as opposed to one of the contraries of truth that results in so far as the useful underpins the historical account. Thus we can distinguish even among the practical concerns that underlie the production of a work of history. In constructing genuine histories, we do not settle for entertaining fantasy or edifying fiction. We are content neither with political propaganda to buttress an a priori position nor with moralistic exemplification – with history as 'oratory,' intended to inspire action. Nor do we settle for personal advantage, which can include anything from the mere laziness that leads us to settle for received opinion to the ambition that leads us to curry favour with editors and reviewers. Rather, we seek to open ourselves to the truth-happening mode – to truth.

Thus for Croce, the scope for truth and the scope for ethical response intertwine, and together they are bound up with action. It is crucial to do justice to all facets of the relationship. Because historical understanding can only prepare action, not determine it, we look to the ethical, but it is equally important to realize that ethical response undisciplined by historical understanding is inadequate – a mere gesture of authenticity. So the ethical leads us not simply to act but to question first, in order that we might gain the preparation that only historical understanding can afford.

The vogue of Croce among innovative historians by the early 1930s raised questions concerning the relativistic implications of his radically historicist conception. And renewed concerns about relativism have recently afflicted historiography as it has embraced innovations from the wider humanistic discussion. In an influential study published in 1938, Maurice Mandelbaum sought to surmount Croce, Dilthey, and Karl Mannheim, whom he took to be the central modern relativists.[27] But Croce had claimed as early as 1915 to have shown why relativism dissolves once we understand how radically we are bound up with the endless growth of the world in history.

Relativism afflicts us, Croce insisted, only if we assume that we must apprehend a stable 'thing-in-itself' back there in the past.[28] But there is no such thing – no past 'as it actually happened' that might be discovered and rendered once and for all. Indeed, there is no distinguishable 'past' at all, but only the history that is generated as we make some present sense of the the documents – and of the present outcome of all the previous attempts to understand how some part of our world came to be. So the bite of relativism dissipates as we come to understand that each instance of genuinely historical inquiry participates in the ongoing coming to be of a particular, more or less true, historical understanding. At any one moment, that understanding is conflicted, tension-ridden, provisional, incomplete – and thus invites further questioning. But it is also sufficient to prepare action – again, as the essential rational supplement to the ethical stimulus for action.

Writing in 1971, Gadamer made almost exactly Croce's point about the dissolution of relativism. For Gadamer, too, a kind of relativism is undeniably inherent in our cultural situation, but we experience it as a problem only in so far as we continue to think in terms of 'the standard of an absolute knowledge,' which suggests that there is some vantage point from which definitive and complete knowledge might be possible.[29] We abandon any such standard as we accept history as the only reality. And Gadamer, much like Croce, accented the open-endedness of the tradition that is endlessly being built up, that endlessly changes and grows, partly through our historical inquiries.

Indeed, by adapting a major theme in Heidegger concerning concealment, or holding back, as the other side of coming to be in history, Gadamer offered a deeper conception of what we can learn through historical inquiry, overcoming limits that critics have long noted in Croce.[30] The objective for Croce was to understand the present in its historical genesis, the better to be able to act on it. What matters in any past moment are the seeds of the next – for us, whatever has resulted in our present world. What is lost, forgotten, or 'held back' simply 'is not,' so the present moment embodies all that remains living of the past. But this aspect of Croce's approach has made his histories – most notoriously his treatment of the Baroque – seem one-dimensional or monological.

By accenting the interplay between 'becoming actual' and holding back, Gadamer pointed beyond Croce's way of restricting the historiographical focus to what in fact became actual. Concealment accompanies every disclosure, yet what is concealed, though it is hidden and forgotten, is not lost altogether. The fact that every actualizing has entailed a holding back means that whereas we are the resultants of the whole past in one sense, we are not in another – because that whole past includes the absences, the 'unthought,' the 'other' of coming into being or becoming actual. Thus Gadamer pointed beyond Crocean monologue to genuine dialogue, and thus to a deeper, more productive relationship between the present and what came before.

But aspects of Gadamer's thinking reflected metaphysical residues and even his own personal conservatism, which kept him from featuring the openness that his conception seemed to invite. He sometimes implied that the point of historical inquiry is to get at the real nature of things, as opposed to preparing action to change what has come to be so far. And he often accented the authority of tradition, as opposed to the ever-renewed tension that invites historical inquiry, criticism, and action.[31] When we encounter these dimensions in Gadamer, we come better to appreciate the value of Croce's way of conceiving the human relationship with a merely historical world.

Although he had much to say about how historical understanding occurs, Gadamer never asked as explicitly as Croce why we ask historical questions in the first place. But Gadamer seems to have been reluctant to link such questioning to ongoing making, to constructing the world, so that history is thought serving action. Echoes of Heidegger's hostility to anthropocentric objectification and the attendant concern for letting things be, apart from human purposes, are evident in Gadamer's quasi-metaphysical statements.[32] So rather than connect historical understanding with action, Gadamer suggested that through a dialogical approach to history we might attend to the dimension forgotten with the advent of such objectification and reconnect with – or at least get closer to – being itself. But this premium on letting some essence of things come to light mixes uneasily at best with Gadamer's historicist emphasis on the growth of tradition through an endless fusion of horizons.

Gadamer also emphasized that, even as horizons move, we are endlessly involved in a process of coming to agreement, of reaching a consensus, of building up a common world.[33] Ragged though the tradition always is, provisional though every agreement is, the ongoing fusing of horizons brings human responses – criticisms, disagreements, conversations – back to the tradition as that tradition itself grows. But though this conservative accent can easily be balanced by a radical or critical one from within his own framework, Gadamer's way of emphasizing coming to agreement and the authority of tradition sometimes seems *prejudicially* conservative. He was so concerned with 'the rehabilitation of authority and tradition' that he played down, or seemed to preclude, that radical or critical moment.[34]

Gadamer's conservative and essentialist tendencies have led critics such as John Caputo to assume that the truth that he found embodied in the tradition is a form of metaphysical truth – that the tradition is a vessel of some completed truth that we might glimpse.[35] More generally, the ambiguity in Gadamer's way of linking truth to tradition has made it easy for critics to conflate *any* reference to truth with a claim to metaphysically grounded authority.

Although Croce was less radical in expanding the range of historical questioning, he afforded more scope than Gadamer for the crucial element of creative tension with the particular tradition. That tension leads us first to question history in an effort to learn, but it also affords the possibility of responding critically to the present on the basis of what we learn. From a Crocean perspective, Gadamer was never clear enough on what motivates historical inquiry. Given his emphasis on a fusion of horizons, he, like Croce, had to rely on some present concern. But where does any such impetus come from? For Croce, an inchoate dissatisfaction with the outcome of history so far leads us to probe some aspect of the process from past to present, seeking illumination to enable us to respond to the outcome by changing it. And because each of us is a bit different, each of us brings out something different through that creative encounter with the past. With Croce's conception, critical tension and the scope for disagreement are more obviously inherent in the overall framework. In other words, Croce was more attuned to the endless raggedness of the merely historical world, so he, more explicitly than Gadamer, showed that we do not settle for the provisional outcome at any one time. Rather, the world is a continuing invitation to ask anew and to respond in action partly on the basis of the new understanding that results.

Although their accents were not fully compatible, Croce and Gadamer each invited a radical expansion of the range of historical questioning. As we come to conceive ever more of what we experience as the resultant of nothing but history, the array of potential subjects expands to infinity. Yet especially with the advent of the new social history, when everything from dress through nutrition to child-rearing practices has come to seem worthy of the historian's attention, traditionalist historians have worried about 'levelling,' or the dissolution of standards of significance, as a corollary of relativism. With all these new strands competing for attention, the old, largely political master narrative appears suspect, even elitist and authoritarian. Yet with the focus fragmenting, the wider public may well tune out or follow merely antiquarian interests, so that history fails to play the more central cultural role that seems necessary. Although Croce was hardly a practitioner of the new history, his presentism, stemming from his absolute historicism, suggested that anything at all might be subject to historical inquiry. So how do we know what is most worthy of our attention? What basis is there for saying that one line of inquiry is more important than another?

As a practising historian, Croce answered explicitly through a series of four full-scale histories, from *Storia del Regno di Napoli* (1925) to *Storia d'Europa nel secolo decimonono* (1932). These were exercises in what he called ethical-political history, which reacted against historical determinism by tracing the thread of response by those who set the agenda for public, collective action. Although this approach tended to be overtly elitist and to preclude analysis of the structural factors conditioning the responses of ethical-political agents, it remains useful as a check on reductionism, especially the still-widespread tendency among historians to take socio-economic class as privileged. Although he had plenty of room for the immediate practical interests that might channel an individual response, Croce's accents demand that we approach *every* historical actor as a free, creative moral agent, that we look for the thread of creative moral response as we seek to understand what happened.[36]

But whatever their value against reductionism, Croce's histories seem bloodless, one-dimensional, and elitist when compared with the most innovative historiography of the past half-century, which has moved beyond politics and articulated ideas to focus on ordinary people and everyday experience. But Croce's wider historicist framework yields a more convincing response, inviting more openness and variety than his own practice as a historian manifested.

Whereas for Hegel we discover the privileged content of history after making it, for Croce there is no a priori form determining a privileged content. But the absence of a priori criteria of significance does not force us to go from one extreme to the other – to levelling, to the absence of articulation, so that no one strand is more worthy of attention than any other. Although reaction against the old, restrictive basis for establishing hierarchies of significance has bred confusion and overreaction, we can find a kind of middle ground. Depending on what we of the present deem important, *any* historical strand may be taken as more significant than any other – for now. We collectively are always establishing a provisional hierarchy of importance as we choose to focus on this and not that and seek to convince others that our accounts are more valuable than those competing for attention.

To be sure, individual historians may refuse to make any such determination or even concentrate on disrupting whatever hierarchy in fact results from this competitive interaction. Such responses are deleterious because they compromise the role of historical inquiry in preparing action. But even if such responses become part of the process, there will be some particular consensus, or master narrative – the resultant of the competitive interaction among historians. This interaction is part of the ongoing history through which the world is built up, but the resulting consensus, or master narrative, is always ragged, conflicted, provisional. At the same time, the contest becomes more heated as we understand, if only implicitly, that the stakes of historical inquiry are increasing. So the issue of historiographical interaction leads to questions about broader societal practice and ultimately about the political implications of Croce's conception.

Rethinking the Bases of Liberalism

From the critiques of Mosca and Pareto to the posthumous vogue of Gramsci, Italy from the 1880s to the 1940s was the scene of an extraordinarily instructive debate about the possibilities of modern politics.[37] Croce was central to that debate, though his explicitly political categories were problematic, and any relevance to our contemporary discussion is not obvious. But we have not adequately probed the degree to which our contemporary belief in liberal democracy rests no longer on categories that we associate with earlier thinkers such as Locke and Mill, but on the troubling – devastating – historical experience of this century, as a phase in our ongoing political experiment. Thus there may be greater interest than first appears in the recasting of liberalism that Croce offered in response to fascist totalitarianism.

With his denial of transcendence and hostility to the natural law tradition, Croce never had any use for the liberal ideas of 1789, which he found flaccid and sentimental. He eschewed the appeal to individual rights and, for all his emphasis on human freedom, placed little premium on 'negative' freedom for the individual vis-à-vis the state. In fact, he was initially satisfied to relegate politics to the realm of the useful, distinguishable from the ethical; politics had a certain autonomy as power, or the quest for effectiveness. Put off during the First World War by pro-French propaganda that trumpeted conventional democratic ideas, Croce went out of his way to laud first Treitschke, for his realistic conception of the state, and then Marx, for having undercut the moralistic liberal myths of humanity and justice.[38]

Once the totalitarian direction of fascism was clear by early 1925, Croce unequivocally repudiated Mussolini's regime. But in light of his longstanding denigration of the conventional justifications for liberal democracy, there were those who claimed that he was 'a fascist without the black shirt.'[39] Even after the fall of fascism, some insisted that it had not been significant matters of philosophy that had deflected Croce from fascism, but merely contingent, less-than-noble personal concerns.[40] Others charged that Croce's thinking had fostered the relativism, and the worship of success, that had undermined democracy and fed fascism and totalitarianism.[41]

The challenge of fascism persuaded Croce that he had to think more deeply about the political sphere – but not that the conventional understanding of liberal democracy, based on Enlightenment or utilitarian categories, had been right after all. He concluded that it was not individual rights, resting on the outmoded natural law tradition, but his recasting of historicism that afforded the basis for a modern liberal politics. Croce was responding partly to the ethical-state ideas of Giovanni Gentile, who had been his junior partner for over a decade before the First World War, and who was arguably the most significant European fascist thinker.[42] Indeed, Gentile drew on both idealism and historicism to give the totalitarian impulse its purest expression – and he explicitly attacked Croce in doing so.[43] Although the cleft between the two thinkers was as instructive as any in modern intellectual history, its political implications have not been adequately probed.

The nasty political split emerged early in 1925, but it had been foreshadowed in subtle differences in philosophical emphasis that became public in 1913. While Croce kept making distinctions – between theory and practice, knowing and doing, politics and ethics – Gentile sought to bring things together, to find deeper unities or identities. During the First World War, this philosophical difference began to have implications for the practical orientation of the two thinkers as Italians called on them to explain the meaning of Italy's idiosyncratic war experience. Whereas Croce adopted a circumspect, 'agnostic' position, Gentile was arguing by 1918 that the Italian cultural self-assertion at work in the war could give rise to a new, post-liberal form of politics.[44] In fact, the situation was such that Italy could leapfrog over the apparently more advanced liberal democracies and point the way for the West. This was true partly because of the special features of the nation's war experience, but especially because of the distinctive intellectual tradition that Croce and Gentile themselves had renewed before the war, bringing it to the forefront of modern thought. Gentile's postwar political conception, based nominally on an extreme version of philosophical idealism, was extravagant and abstract, but it proved exciting to intelligent, idealistic young Italians, some of whom would help give fascism its direction.[45] And Gentile himself viewed fascism as the vehicle for the totalitarian ethical state that he came to advocate.

As Gentile began playing the role of civil educator late in the war, it became clear that he was responding not simply to abstract philosophical concerns but to what seemed the mutually reinforcing problems of Western liberal culture and idiosyncratic Italian mores. On the one hand, he worried about contemporary tendencies towards cynicism, indifference, and narcissism, which he attributed to liberal, and generally positivist, distinctions between subject and object, inner and outer, public and private. On the other hand, he lamented what he took to be the characteristic Italian vices going back to the late Renaissance – rhetoric, most obviously, but ultimately the frivolously sceptical and detached mode of life that spawned rhetoric and that Francesco De Sanctis had lamented in a famous lecture of 1869, 'L'uomo del Guicciardini.'[46]

Both the modern liberal problem and the special Italian vice rested on separation – of words from actions, of ideals from commitments, of humanity from reality – which could too easily be talked about without genuine commitment and the action that follows from it. To posit unity as an antidote was to suggest that to think something – *really* to think it – is to believe it, to want others to believe it, to commit oneself to it, to conform one's actions to it, to seek to shape the world in accordance with what one thinks. In so far as knowledge, character, and action form this fundamental unity, we take life seriously – and take responsibility for the world.[47]

In response to the inadequacies of modern liberalism and, more fundamentally, to the erosion of the religious foundations of our culture, Gentile found it necessary to reconceive the relationships among power, freedom, rationality, responsibility, and participation. As faith in a transcendent sphere dissipates and we adjust to a historicist perspective, the world comes to seem *our* responsibility in a way that it never quite did before. As a historicist then, Gentile accented not simply obedience to the state as the incarnation of rational will, but participation in collective, history-making action.

Individuals' sense of their own freedom and ethical capacity draws them into the national political sphere, for it is there that they have built institutions that concentrate power in such a way that they collectively may exercise that responsibility in action. Indeed, because their sense of responsibility grows in a world of radical immanence, they seek ways to bring the national community together in more cohesive ways to assume the ongoing task of shaping the world. And they seek to expand the scope for power, or the political sphere, because to expand the state is to increase their freedom to act, to exercise their responsibility. The state becomes all-encompassing, totalitarian, to enable the community consciously, even rationally, to make history.

Thus for Gentile concentration of power and expansion of the state do not limit freedom but enable people to exercise it more extensively and responsibly. Moreover, the totalitarian state does not stand opposed to the freedom of differentiated individuals, as we tend to assume it must, but rather values individuation and the resulting difference of perspective. Individual commitments will differ, but all these free, differentiated individuals are to identify their lives as responsible moral agents with the public world. There was no place in Gentile's order for contemplative withdrawal, or self-cultivation, or alienation. People are genuinely free only in so far as they together can be genuinely responsible for the world, and this requires that knowing, willing, and doing come together as people endlessly remake the world.

What Gentile envisioned was more general than the remaking posited in the Marxian tradition, based on class struggle and at least some measure of historical materialism and economic determinism. As Gentile's conception proved ever more inadequate with the unfolding of the fascist experiment, the flaws in his thinking helped Antonio Gramsci develop his more differentiated though still-Marxian conception of the formation of a collective will. But in continuing to embrace a largely Marxian notion of human ends, Gramsci was not quite historicist, despite the efforts of his apologists to proclaim his openness. Croce drew different lessons, which now seem still more worthy of a place in the ongoing conversation in the light of the questions that have come to surround even Gramsci's version of Marxism.

Although Croce caricatured Gentile, and though after the fact he did not probe fascism as imaginatively as his conception of historiography would seem to require, he had good reason for rejecting fascism and, more important, for proposing a new understanding of liberalism in response to totalitarianism. What followed from the more radical historicism that had emerged uniquely in Italy was not the totalitarian inflation of politics that Gentile proclaimed but a new understanding of human limits – and thus a new grounding for conventional liberal procedures and institutions.

To grasp the wider significance of their ultimate divergence, it is crucial to note how far Croce and Gentile travelled together away from the conventional understanding of liberal democracy. Even as a fascist, Gentile believed that the free individual, not the state, is the source of the world's ethical capacity; in this sense, he was as much an individualist as Croce was. Conversely, Croce had no more room than Gentile for individual self-affirmation as an end in itself. Nor was Croce any more concerned with protecting the private individual by restricting the state; he was as explicit as Gentile in criticizing the conventional liberal effort to limit the reach of the state.[48] For both thinkers, it was not enough simply to embrace the sociological tradition stemming from Durkheim and to understand the individual as bound up with some particular society. Rather, the individual is bound up with history, the growing whole. More specifically, both thinkers unified the individual with the totality through history-making action. At any one moment, every individual embodies part of the potential of the world, and the political system needs to invite the committed responses of everyone to the present situation. For both Croce and Gentile, we are all collaborators in the coming to be of some particular world in history.

Turning on the *form* of collective, world-making action, the divergence between Croce and Gentile reflected emerging differences over the scope for freedom and power. Until faced with Gentile's new collective will and totalitarian hypertrophy of politics, Croce had not quite put the elements in proportion – the place of freedom, the scope for political action, and the relationship between individual ethical response and politics.

More specifically, Gentile's categories – both the initial aspiration and the undeniably negative outcome – forced a deeper understanding of both freedom and rationality. In a sense inadequately pondered, Gentile's fascism offered a far more thoroughgoing 'religion of liberty' than Croce's neo-liberalism to a world without a transcendent God. But Gentile's insistence on a unified culture transcending Croce's distinctions between thought and action, public and private, did not do justice to the original, idiosyncratic quality of individual moral response.[49] So Gentile's emphasis prompted Croce to insist still more explicitly on his distinction between theory and practice – and thereby to think more deeply about individual political action.[50]

To say, with Croce, that knowing and doing never quite come

together makes practice free – *necessarily* free – in a lonely, creative sense, whereas freedom for Gentile required that knowing, willing, and doing coalesce, so that people know what they do and do what they know. Croce's 'religion of liberty' meant only that liberty is irrepressible, because free creative human response is built in, an attribute of human being. No matter how much people concentrate power, and no matter how successfully they require everyone to participate in that power, they are *not* free collectively to shape the world in some rational way. From Croce's perspective, Gentile's conception, because it went overboard in assuming that the world was rational, or could be made rational, was not compatible with the real conditions of individual moral response.

Croce admitted that, as a result of the essential distinctions, the ongoing remaking of the world has an element of blindness to it. And because individuals cannot know what is happening as they act, there is a sense in which only history itself is the agent of the world; people collaborate blindly in its agency.[51] But this meant that even as he reaffirmed certain of his longstanding distinctions against Gentile, Croce was insisting on an alternative totality, as opposed to repairing to the sort of individualism that was becoming fashionable with existentialism. Finding existentialism a self-indulgent overreaction to the political excesses of the age, Croce sought to show that, though Gentile badly misconstrued the mechanisms, the responses of each human being do indeed participate in the growth of the world in history.

Seriously to engage the contrast between Croce and Gentile forces us to deepen our categories and, more specifically, to question the binary dualisms in any discussion informed by the extremes of the twentieth-century political experience. In suggesting that history itself is the agent of the world, Croce was not submerging individuals, as critics long charged, but positing a relationship between individuality and the totality-as-history that yields a premium on humility and tolerance. That conception had implications for political forms, inviting liberal democracy. And though in a crucial sense the fascist Gentile was more 'rationalist' than the neo-liberal Croce, the point is not that Croce was thus an 'irrationalist.' In fact, as we have seen, Croce offered an important element of rationalism in insisting on the scope for historical understanding to prepare action.[52]

From a Gentilian perspective, Croce's distinctions left the culture not merely with loneliness and humility, but with melancholy and indifference. Without a unified culture, the world runs out of control, and people cannot feel – and seize – their responsibility for it. But the outcome of fascism and the other totalitarian experiments of this century suggest that humanity is *not* free and responsible, that it *cannot* know what it is doing, or what is happening, in the grandiose way that Gentile envisioned. The challenge then becomes precisely Croce's: to show that though people act collectively, and though there are no a priori limits to the reach of the state, and though the world continually changes through the aggregate of individuals' actions, humility, pluralism, and tolerance balance our individual commitments.[53] But, at the same time, Croce had to show why his more humble conception did not have to generate the sense of futility, the political indifference, that Gentile associated with it. And hence the deepened emphasis on the enduring weight of what people do, on action as history-making, that we see in comparing Croce with Richard Rorty in the next section.

But Croce's neo-liberalism, though it inspired the movement against fascism, proved controversial even as Italy sought political renewal during the 1940s. Quite apart from the wider charge of passive acceptance, Guido Calogero and others criticized Croce for ignoring the distorting impact of socio-economic inequality and injustice.[54] Croce's accent on individual freedom was too abstract, for what did freedom mean – and what good was it – in a situation of socio-economic injustice? Moreover, Croce's emphases betrayed an inadequate grasp of the realities of modern mass politics.

Croce was not trying to limit the role of the state in pursuing justice; he was not even ruling out the Marxist critique of capitalism. In accenting the priority of freedom, he had in mind free interaction in the ongoing pursuit of justice, as opposed to an a priori claim to know what justice is – and on that basis to dismiss opponents. We cannot say that, until we have achieved justice, freedom is confined to the elect, that those whom we deem the victims of injustice are not free – and thus count only in anticipation. Rather, freedom pertains to all of us now, and we collectively, through interaction, seek continually to overcome what we take to be injustices in historically specific circumstances.

Croce's emphasis on the individuality of political decision was hardly to submerge the individual in some totalizing process, as one set of critics argued. Yet because he insisted that one start with free individuals, with the level of individual freedom, Croce was subject to criticism from the other, more down-to-earth side. For critics from Calogero to Arcangelo Leone de Castris, Croce's way of starting with individual freedom was old-fashioned, in light of the realities of modern mass politics. As so often, Croce was attacked from two conflicting sides. But although he had nothing to say about central dimensions of modern politics, the implications of his argument pointed beyond both lines of criticism, in ways we can still usefully ponder. At issue is why everybody counts – and as individuals, not as a mass – even in an incomplete world in which injustice limits freedom.

However, we worry about certain of the questions that Croce did not address, especially those concerning 'communicative competence,' or the quality of the process of interaction, in the ongoing quest for justice among these abstractly free individuals. Although he had treated Marxism with flexibility and a measure of sympathy earlier in his career, Croce became vehemently anti-Marxian during the ideologically charged debates of the 1940s. Explicitly denigrating the concept of ideology, he did not consider the possibility of coercion, and thus systematic sources of distortion, in the interaction through which a particular provisional notion of justice gets hammered out.[55] In this respect, Croce seems to pale before the Frankfurt School, particularly as extended in recent decades by Jürgen Habermas. But of course Habermas too has drawn criticism – from, among others, Hans-Georg Gadamer, in a celebrated polemic, and Richard Rorty, who measured his own neo-liberal efforts partly against Habermas. A Crocean perspective can contribute even to this dimension of the ongoing conversation, for Croce points beyond the antithesis between Habermas and Gadamer.

Responding especially to Gadamer's emphasis on tradition, Habermas worried that a traditional consensus, or any present societal self-understanding, may embody the effects of compulsion and coercion. If we are to avoid the tyranny of received opinion, we need a 'general criterion,' based on 'the meta-hermeneutic awareness of the conditions for the possibility of systematically distorted communication,' to enable us to determine when such distortion is at work.[56] In fact, he argued, something of the sort has been implicit in human interaction all along. We inevitably presuppose a 'theory of communicative competence,' including what undistorted communication would entail. And what we now need, in light of the relativistic tendencies abroad in the culture, is explicitly to articulate such a theory, connecting 'the process of understanding to the principle of rational discourse, according to which truth would only be guaranteed by *that* kind of consensus which was achieved under the idealized conditions of unlimited communication free from domination.' We come to understand, in other words, that what binds us together, making genuine dialogue possible, is not simply the particular tradition, as Gadamer's emphases suggested, but the ideal of undistorted communication and the anticipation of 'unforced universal agreement,' to be realized in the future.[57] Habermas thus invited ongoing criticism and change, whereas Gadamer seemed too content to settle for the authority of tradition, of whatever has come to be.

Up to a point, Gadamer's counterattack against Habermas recalls Croce's themes from decades earlier, although Gadamer does not seem to have recognized the intellectual kinship. At the same time, the fact that he had to respond directly to Habermas led Gadamer to offer more pointed arguments than Croce's. In their different ways, Croce and Gadamer both recognized that sometimes we must repair to a higher, more theoretical level and consider the rules, the criteria, or what counts as free, rational, and undistorted. But the insight to be gained on that level is itself historically specific and provisional. Debate over criteria, over the rules of the game, over how we make the rules, is itself part of the historically situated hermeneutic dialogue, and, as Croce always insisted, history itself is the only judge – though an endlessly provisional judge. Gadamer found Habermas too quick to climb to some 'meta-hermeneutic' level, as if the 'general criterion' or 'principle of rational discourse' was outside the realm of hermeneutic discussion.[58] In Gadamer's terms, the ongoing process of coming to agreement takes the place of some universal framework derived through rational reflection; it affords an adequate framework for further discussion and disagreement.

In his polemic with Habermas, Gadamer made the same point that Croce had made in accenting liberty against Calogero during the early 1940s. It is crucial that everybody counts, despite the temptation to believe that there are rational, enlightened experts who, by means of purified theoretical reflection, can climb to a higher level, transcending the finitude and historical specificity of everyone else, and specify decision procedures or what counts as undistorted communication.[59] Though I may find distortion in the views of my adversaries, I must respect them enough to take them seriously. Indeed, as Croce liked to insist, even if I could be dictator of the world and impose my own view, I would prefer to rely on the judgment of history – the outcome of my interaction with those who disagree with me.[60]

Although Gadamer criticized Habermas in terms that recall Croce's historicism, Gadamer sometimes seemed to delimit or undermine the scope for action, to make history a matter of incorporation into a pre-existing tradition *as opposed to* extending that tradition through history as action. For Gadamer, there is 'coming to agreement' as a new consensus emerges, but Croce makes it clearer that that consensus is always provisional. The process of producing a new consensus encompasses criticism and disagreement, and the criticism and disagreement continue, just as does the coming to agreement. Moreover, it is clearer in Croce than in Gadamer that renewing the consensus entails concrete changes in societal practice. So Croce's historicism is more consistently an invitation to ongoing criticism and action and thus at least complements Gadamer's way of countering Habermas.

With his emphasis on the ongoing struggle to free up human creativity, Croce could surely accept much of what Habermas had in mind in positing a regulative principle of undistorted communication. Old-fashioned though it appears, Croce's dictum that history is 'the story of liberty' is similar in major respects to Habermas's notion that history is wound around an ongoing effort to free human communicative competence from present distortion.[61] Knowing ourselves to be partial and incomplete, we seek to learn from those sharing this particular world with us. Thus, just as Habermas insisted, we have a common interest in undistorted communication.

But from a Crocean perspective, Habermas makes tradition more overbearing and restrictive than it is, and thus he overplays the need for some suprahistorical theory or regulative principle to counter 'the authority of tradition.' Conversely, Habermas's way of conceiving the alternatives proves too limited to encompass Croce's historicist conception of human interaction. Because the truth of the tradition is tension-ridden and incomplete, the present entails a built-in invitation to criticism – on the basis not of some abstract principle, but of the ongoing ethical capacity of finite, historically specific human beings. We can choose to criticize what we will, but what that will be – or ought to be – cannot be specified in advance. And the basis of our interaction is our desire to learn about this particular world from our need to act within it, not the ideal or goal of actually achieving that undistorted communication, so that definitive agreement becomes possible.

Rather than positing an image of completeness, Croce emphasized that obstacles and distortions recur endlessly. At each moment we are hammering out what freedom is, and requires, in light of historically specific circumstances. As we overcome ever-new obstacles, our capacity for freedom expands. So there is nothing anomalous about the fact that we *still* need to address distortions, that the ideal has not been reached. In contrast, Habermas implied that present distortion is anomalous; to undercut it is to be in touch with the ideal – and to merit privilege. Hence the lurking tendency to 'go transcendental and offer principles' that critics such as Rorty continued to find in Habermas, even as his thought became ever more liberal and historicist.[62]

We have seen that to care for the world is to discipline moral response with a rational element, but reason for Croce is immanent and weak. It entails simply historical questioning that seeks to learn, to understand the particular situation. There is neither room for, nor need for, enlightened status or Habermas-style 'Reason.' So Croce invited ongoing criticism and action more consistently than Gadamer, yet without relying on the 'rational critique,' with its implicit claim to privilege, that Habermas emphasized.

The Weight of What We Do

Gentile assumed that if Croce was right in denying the scope for a unified culture, humanity will drift into melancholy and indifference. Croce's challenge was to show why, and how, we can proceed with a modicum of confidence and rationality even in a world that is indeed more 'melancholy' than Gentile's in important respects, but that has increasingly come to seem, as the modern political experiment has proceeded, the only world we have. To understand Croce's neo-liberalism, we must understand the very delimited 'faith in history' that he posited at once to underpin and to complement the element of rationality that he continued to invite. The package stands opposed to an array of responses, from Albert Camus's gesture of authenticity to Richard Rorty's emphasis on edification and self-creation, that have been prominent in recent culture.[63]

Although the divergence between Croce and Rorty proves more instructive than the similarity, it is striking how closely Rorty's influential recasting of liberalism paralleled Croce's. Finding 'historicism' the outcome of the erosion of foundationalist philosophy, Rorty insisted that what we are is hammered out in history.[64] And he conceived almost exactly as Croce did the mechanisms whereby the world grows. We all want our modicum of novelty, our creative response in language, to be carried into the future, becoming part of the aggregate that will be taken as literal truth.[65] And the mechanism – interaction and persuasion – through which some particular response most shapes the future is precisely congruent with Croce's. Like Croce a half-century earlier, Rorty held that we cannot specify in advance what counts as undistorted, or ideological, or true, or good; all we can do is set up free, pluralistic, democratic institutions and trust in the ever-provisional outcome of the resulting interaction.[66] In interacting, we are seeking an ever-renewed yet always provisional consensus within a tolerant, broadly liberal framework. Moreover, Croce had already explained the historicist humility that Rorty found crucial to such broadly liberal interaction.

But Rorty, adapting categories from the literary intellectual Harold Bloom, ended up stressing irony, personal autonomy, and edification. And he invited a cultural premium on 'fictions' as opposed to 'history,' both as an autonomous mode of inquiry and as a way of embracing the wider 'public' world. Rorty was assuming a place in a current that can be traced back to Nietzsche and early literary modernists such as Gide, Joyce, Eliot, and Musil and that explored the new uncanniness that attached to individual experience as foundations seemed to erode and transcendence dissipate. In a sense, the world seemed to reduce to nothing but history – to the world of Croce's absolute historicism. But the modes of personal experience that become possible in such a world are disparate indeed, as are the modes of response to that world, each entailing a particular relationship between human being and history. The impermanence of a purely historical world could yield a sense of weightlessness; the apparent impossibility of escape could yield a sense of suffocation. In accenting capriciousness, absurdity, or irony, thinkers from Nietzsche through Camus to Rorty pointed away from the cultural orientation that Croce pioneered in response to the same loss of foundations and transcendent guideposts.

The broadly political experience of this century, in which human beings seem tragically to have overreached themselves, intensified the sense of blankness or uncanniness that cultural pioneers had explored for a generation before the First World War. As the world spins out of control, our actions seem futile or have unintended – and deleterious – consequences. For Camus, even broadly political action tends to become a gesture of self-assertion, defiance, almost to spite history, which simply confronts us with one plague after another.

Although Croce too was shaken by the epoch of fascism and world war through which he had lived, his response was to reaffirm and refine the historicist orientation that he had gradually elaborated over more than four decades. Indeed, that orientation seemed more relevant than ever in the light of the cultural tendencies of the 1940s – to retreat to Marxism or even the natural law tradition or to overreact into existentialism. Croce outlined a way of experiencing ourselves and understanding what we do that contrasts usefully with the whole array from Nietzsche through Camus to Rorty.

In denying transcendent values and in highlighting the loneliness of free individual response, Croce had much in common with existentialism, but he and Italian existentialists such as Nicola Abbagnano became bitter antagonists. Whereas Abbagnano accused Croce of playing down subjective personal experience, Croce found existentialism morbid and self-indulgent.[67] Even while emphasizing that individual experience in a historicist world is closer to tragedy than to idyll, Croce emphasized the sufficiency of this world, the scope for individuals to fulfill themselves within it by meshing with it, embracing a vocation, and acting to help shape what it becomes. So rather than dwelling on personal anxiety, we should do what we take to be our duty and look to the consequences. But to accent the place of the individual in an all-encompassing history did not mean submerging the individual in some overarching, providential process, as Abbagnano charged. The new understanding that Croce offered entailed a much weaker relationship between individuality and totality.

Although the world is ever provisional, and although a sense of slippage and impermanence sometimes threatens to overwhelm us, our actions are 'for keeps' because, taken in the aggregate, in their complex interaction, they produce the next moment, which becomes the basis for all subsequent moments. Hence Croce's emphasis on 'the immortality of the act,' the cumulative weight of our actions in the endless coming to be of this particular world.[68]

Although some individuals have a disproportionate influence in certain spheres, we are *all* historical actors, making some small contribution to the ongoing growth of the world. None of us can foresee the outcome, which always transcends the intention of any one actor. Thus, as we saw above, Croce sometimes found it necessary to insist that the maker of the world is ultimately the whole spirit – that the spirit is the only agent.[69] But this does not mean that we individual actors are but shadowy manifestations of spirit, as critics have long charged.[70] It is simply to say that the individual is bound up with the growing whole and to emphasize the 'public' implications, the enduring weight, of everything that we do.

To be sure, any individual can choose simply to sit back and await the outcome at every moment, but even such a choice for passivity is a form of action with wider, public consequences. In so far as we care for the world and feel responsibility for it, we want what we do to last, affecting what the world becomes. In this sense, we experience what we do as history-making, as having enduring weight. And thus it is not enough that action be authentic, or self-creating. At the same time, however, we operate in a dual mode, understanding that the growth of the world rests on the creative responses of individuals, but also that no individual, even the 'greatest,' is sufficient. Thus Croce posited not irony or self-preoccupation but humility. And we understand that action is fraught with risk, for we can never be sure of the outcome.

However, the sense of humility and risk can give way to a sense of futility, which undercuts any sense of enduring weight – and thus any emphasis on the immortality of what we do. As a result, we may come to emphasize self-creation, authentic defiance, or playful disruption instead. But as Croce pursued his thinking about action, he developed themes that suggested antidotes to these tendencies.

In the light of the uncertain consequences of present actions, we require a measure of faith to sustain us as we act. Yet all that is left to us is a mere faith in history – history stretched thin, with no implication of providence, deliverance, or even direction. In a world of absolute historicism, history entails simply what Gadamer called 'gathering' – the coherence that brings actions together to produce a next moment that builds on the present, even if in ways that are never totally foreseeable. But this is enough for us to feel that it matters what we do, to engage our sense of responsibility.

At the same time, we understand that our world has resulted from the sum of the actions of all who came before us, that we have fallen heir to their collective legacy. This sense of kinship stimulates each of us to do our part, to pick up and transform, through our own present action, the world that they bequeathed to us. As their collaborators, we feel ourselves under obligation to use their legacy well.[71]

We have seen that a sense of responsibility for the world fuels a need to know. And the scope for knowing means that we need not simply act and hope for the best; faith in history is not blind or irrational. Through truth-seeking historical inquiry we can gain the understanding that prepares action, increasing the likelihood of effectiveness. Thus what we need for action in a neo-liberal mode is not edifying fiction but truth-seeking historical questioning. To the extent that some form of amoral utility compromises the effort to learn, the resulting deficiencies in understanding may undermine the effectiveness of action, even render it futile. As we saw above, such amoral utility may even stem from moralistic good intentions, although it may also result from a premium on self-cultivation or edification.

But even in so far as we have sought to understand the present historically, we cannot know what will happen to what we do. So no matter
how responsibly we have acted to transform the legacy of the past for
the future, we feel anxiety about how our actions will enter history. We
entrust what we do to the strangers of the future, uncertain what they
will make of it. Thus, again, in our darker moments our faith wavers
and our efforts seem futile, or worse, because we risk the capriciousness
of history.

Croce never neglected the troubling dimensions of the individual's
relationship with history – the sense of slippage and impermanence, of
risk and futility – but he continually sought to show how we endlessly
surmount them. As early as 1908, concluding his *Philosophy of the Practical*, he noted that the philosopher labours knowing full well that his or
her work will promptly be superseded, but faith in history overcomes
the resulting feeling of futility: 'Every philosopher, on completing some
piece of research, discerns the first uncertain lines of another, that he
himself, or someone who comes after him, will undertake. And with this
modesty, which stems from the nature of things and not simply from my
own personal sentiment – with this modesty, which is also faith in not
having laboured in vain – I end my work, offering it to the well disposed
as an instrument of labour.' (Ogni filosofo, alla fine di una sua ricerca,
intravede le prime incerte linee di un'altra, che egli medesimo, o chi
verrà dopo di lui, eseguirà. E con questa modestia, che è delle cose
stesse e non già del mio sentimento personale, con questa modestia che
è insieme fiducia di non aver pensato indarno, io metto termine al mio
lavoro, porgendolo ai ben disposti come strumento di lavoro.)[72]

Rorty's very different sense of the possibilities at work in our relationship with history led him to eschew any premium on knowing the
world as history or experiencing what we do as history-making. History
is at once suffocating and capricious. Thus Rorty worried about our tendency to 'worship corpses' – to take some past creative 'metaphor,' or
creative use of language, as today's literal truth. And he noted the
uncertainty and risk inherent in entrusting acts to the capricious
future.[73] Our relationship to history is fundamentally ironic, and the
appropriate response is a cultural premium on literature as opposed to
history, on personal autonomy, redescription, and edification, as
opposed to the 'seriousness' of history-making action.[74] In showing the
scope for a different, 'reconstructive' way of experiencing ourselves as
actors, Croce's orientation stands as a 'non-ironic' alternative within the
same post-metaphysical framework.

Although he grasped the basis for the sense of impermanence and risk that fed more extreme responses, Croce emphasized 'history as thought and action' to establish a new cultural middle ground, showing how we can still operate in a constructive spirit – yet without lapsing back into some authoritarian claim to privilege. Conversely, even as we abandon the 'metaphysics' that might warrant such a claim, we are left with history, the world endlessly coming into being over time. And we can find a way of meshing with that world sufficient to avoid the various forms of overreaction that have tempted us for a century and more. For Croce, each of us is only a collaborator, but it is crucial that there is scope for such collaboration and that the world is endlessly remade as the result of what we do.

NOTES

1 Giuseppe Antonio Borgese, *Goliath: The March of Fascism* (New York: Viking, 1937), 295–6.
2 For a gloomy assessment by a distinguished Crocean, see Raffaello Franchini, *Intervista su Croce* (Naples: Società editrice napoletana, 1978). On Croce's fortunes in the United States, see David D. Roberts, 'Croce in America: Influence, Misunderstanding, and Neglect,' *Humanitas* 8 no. 2 (1995), 3–34. This article adapts and expands the sections on Croce in my 'La fortuna di Croce e Gentile negli Stati Uniti,' in *Croce e Gentile un secolo dopo*, a special issue of *Giornale critico della filosofia italiana* 73 nos. 2–3 (May–Dec. 1994), 253–81.
3 Patrick Romanell, 'Romanticism and Croce's Conception of Science,' *Review of Metaphysics* 9 (March 1956), 505–14.
4 For example, the distinguished intellectual historian H. Stuart Hughes found as one of the most dubious features of Croce's thought 'its insistence on the pervasive role of a quasi-deity called "the spirit,"' essentially derived from Hegel. See Hughes's *Consciousness and Society: The Reorientation of European Social Thought, 1890–1930* (New York: Random House, Vintage Books, 1958), 208; see also 26.
5 Hayden White, 'The Abiding Relevance of Croce's Idea of History,' *Journal of Modern History* 37 (June 1963), 109–24; Hayden White, *Metahistory: The Historical Imagination in Nineteenth-Century Europe* (Baltimore: Johns Hopkins University Press, 1973), chap. 10; see especially 378–9, 397–400.
6 René Wellek, *History of Modern Criticism* (New Haven, Conn.: Yale University Press), vol. VIII, *French, Italian, and Spanish Criticism, 1900–1950* (1992), 187, 189; see also vol. VI, *American Criticism, 1900–1950* (1986), 63.
7 Giovanna Borradori argues along these lines in her introduction to *Recoding*

Metaphysics: The New Italian Philosophy (Evanston, Ill.: Northwestern University Press, 1988), an anthology intended to acquaint an English-speaking audience with recent Italian thinking, from Vattimo and Rovatti to Gargani and Perniola. She finds value in the specifically Italian hermeneutic tradition, not derived from German sources, that ran from Vico through Croce and the Italian existentialists on up to the present.

8 In addition to Croce's *La filosofia di Giambattista Vico* (1911), see his *Filosofia e storiografia*, first pub. 1947 (Bari: Laterza, 1969), 353–4, for a much later example of his continuing insistence on the centrality of Vico.

9 See especially Donald Phillip Verene, *Vico's Science of Imagination* (Ithaca, NY: Cornell University Press, 1981), 23, 68–9, 217; and Michael Mooney, *Vico in the Tradition of Rhetoric* (Princeton, NJ: Princeton University Press, 1985), xi, 26–9.

10 See, for example, Croce's 'Troppo filosofia' (1922), now in his *Cultura e vita morale* (Bari: Laterza, 1955), 248–53; see also 262–3, 279–80, and 292–300 for further examples, and David D. Roberts, *Benedetto Croce and the Uses of Historicism* (Berkeley: University of California Press, 1987), 90–8, for fuller discussion of this issue.

11 Benedetto Croce, *Discorsi di varia filosofia*, 2 vols., first pub. 1945 (Bari: Laterza, 1959), II, 15–17.

12 Discussing Croce's fortunes in the United States, Frederic Simoni in 1952 concluded without exaggeration that 'reference to Croce in current literature constitutes a comedy of errors.' See Frederic S. Simoni, 'Benedetto Croce: A Case of International Misunderstanding,' *Journal of Aesthetics and Art Criticism* 11 (Sept. 1952), 7–14; quoted passage from 9.

13 I have made this argument more fully in David D. Roberts, *Nothing but History: Reconstruction and Extremity after Metaphysics* (Berkeley: University of California Press, 1995); chap. 5 treats Croce in this connection.

14 Brook Thomas, *The New Historicism and Other Old-Fashioned Topics* ((Princeton, NJ: Princeton University Press, 1991), 16, 31–2, 35, 215–16.

15 Peter Novick, *That Noble Dream: The 'Objectivity Question' and the American Historical Profession* (Cambridge: Cambridge University Press, 1988).

16 Benedetto Croce, 'Frammenti di etica,' in *Etica e politica* (Bari: Laterza, 1967), 167–8. See also Croce, *Cultura e vita morale* (1908), 35, and (1911), 166–7; and Benedetto Croce, *Ultimi saggi*, first pub. 1926 (Bari: Laterza, 1963), 223–4.

17 Giambattista Vico, *The New Science*, trans. Thomas Goddard Bergin and Max Harold Fisch (Ithaca, NY: Cornell University Press, 1984), 96 (no. 331).

18 For Croce's mature sense of his own relationship to Hegel, see especially *Il carattere della filosofia moderna* (Bari: Laterza, 1963), 38–53. See also Raffaello

Franchini, *Croce interprete di Hegel e altri saggi filosofici*, 3rd ed. (Naples: Giannini, 1974), 3–51.

19 See, among many examples, Croce, *Filosofia e storiografia* (1947), 250–5; Croce, *Carattere*, 209–10; and Benedetto Croce, *Teoria e storia della storiografia* (Bari: Laterza, 1973), 93–8.

20 Even Guido de Ruggiero, a major intellectual long within Croce's orbit, came to level such charges, insisting that there was a void at the heart of Croce's conception. See Guido de Ruggiero, *Il ritorno alla ragione* (Bari: Laterza, 1946), 13–16. See also Elio Vittorini, 'Una nuova cultura,' *Il politecnico*, 29 Sept. 1945, 1, for an example from a different quarter.

21 For Croce's critique of Ranke, see *La storia come pensiero e come azione* (Bari: Laterza, 1966), 65–7, 73–88. See also Croce, *Teoria e storia della storiografia*, 304–5.

22 See especially Croce, *Teoria e storia della storiografia*, 4–7, 10–12, 16, 99–106, for the overall argument. See also Croce, *Cultura e vita morale* (1924), 265, and Croce, *La storia*, 11–12.

23 Becker and Beard each relied heavily on Croce in their presidential addresses to the American Historical Association – which remain two of the best-known ever delivered. Of special note on the relationship between Croce and these American historians are Ellen Nore, *Charles A. Beard: An Intellectual Biography* (Carbondale, Ill.: Southern Illinois University Press, 1983), especially 156, 158–62, 165, and 192; and Cushing Strout, *The Pragmatic Revolt in American History: Carl Becker and Charles Beard* (New Haven, Conn.: Yale University Press, 1958), especially 50–5. For a fuller discussion, and reference to the key sources, see Roberts, 'Croce in America,' 18–22.

24 Croce, *Carattere*, 176. See also Roberts, *Benedetto Croce*, 153–4.

25 See especially Croce, *Filosofia e storiografia* (1947), 169–70, for the notion that historical inquiry is moral when it is genuinely open to truth. See also Croce, *Carattere*, 114–16, 223–5, on the relationship between ethics, cognition, and the scope for truth. For discussions of Gadamer's thinking along the same lines, see Georgia Warnke, *Gadamer: Hermeneutics, Tradition and Reason* (Stanford, Calif.: Stanford University Press, 1987), 40–1, 87, and 89; and David Couzens Hoy, *The Critical Circle* (Berkeley: University of California Press, 1978), 52–3, 67–8.

26 Croce, 'Agli amici che cercano il "trascendente"' (8 May 1945), now in *Etica e politica*, 378–84.

27 Maurice Mandelbaum, *The Problem of Historical Knowledge: An Answer to Relativism* (New York: Liveright, 1938). See especially 54–7 for the core of his case against Croce. Croce responded in a critical review, now in his *Nuove pagine sparse*, 2 vols. (Bari: Laterza, 1966), II, 59–60. A generation later, Jack W.

Meiland proved better able than Mandelbaum to grasp Croce's generally constructivist orientation and the basis of his claim to have sidestepped historiographical relativism. See Meiland's *Skepticism and Historical Knowledge* (New York: Random House, 1965), especially 11–38, 42, 62, and 81.

28 Although he made the argument repeatedly, Croce offered his classic statement about relativism in 1915 in his 'Contributo alla critica di me stesso,' now in *Etica e politica*, 350. See also Croce, *Teoria e storia della storiografia*, 43–8; and Croce, *La storia* 122.

29 Hans-Georg Gadamer, 'Replik,' in Karl-Otto Apel et al., *Hermaneutik und Ideologiekritik* (Frankfurt: Suhrkamp, 1971), 299. See also Warnke, *Gadamer*, 130.

30 Hans-Georg Gadamer, *Reason in the Age of Science* (Cambridge, Mass.: MIT Press, 1981), 104–5, 166–7; *Philosophical Hermeneutics* (Berkeley: University of California Press, 1976), 203, 208, 226. For a fuller discussion of this theme and the relationship between Croce and Gadamer, see Roberts, *Nothing but History*, 158–79.

31 Hans-Georg Gadamer, *Truth and Method* (New York: Seabury Press), 265, 272.

32 See Gadamer, *Philosophical Hermeneutics*, 71–2, for an example of such essentialism; the Heideggerian sources of the tendency are especially evident here. See also Gadamer, *Truth and Method*, 253–8.

33 Gadamer, *Reason in the Age of Science*, 166; Gadamer, *Truth and Method*, 158.

34 The conservative accents were not compatible with Gadamer's dominant emphasis on the change, novelty, and growth that follow from ongoing response and dialogue. See Gadamer, *Truth and Method*, 245–53, especially 249, for a key statement of that theme. Georgia Warnke stresses that Gadamer's conservatism is a kind of overlay that need not follow from his recasting of hermeneutics; fusion of horizons can include disagreement and 'distantiation.' See Warnke, *Gadamer*, 136–8.

35 According to John D. Caputo, for example, Gadamer's conception remains essentially metaphysical, for although Gadamer put the maximum of movement into it, what he offered was still a philosophy of eternal truth. See Caputo, *Radical Hermeneutics* (Bloomington: Indiana University Press, 1987), 111–14.

36 The freedom of the spirit means that the sources of the commitments that underlie action cannot be pinned down. Croce argued in 1923, for example, that each of us will respond to a given situation differently, according to our temperament, our hopes and fears, the situation we feel within us, the commitments to which we feel tied, and the faith that we have in certain people and certain things. See Croce, *Cultura e vita morale*, 250.

37 In addition to the invaluable works of Norberto Bobbio over many years, I mention Domenico Settembrini's polemical but often brilliant *Storia dell'idea*

antiborghese in Italia, 1860–1989 (Rome and Bari: Laterza, 1991). In English, Richard Bellamy's *Modern Italian Social Theory: Ideology and Politics from Pareto to the Present* (Stanford, Calif.: Stanford University Press, 1987), offers useful insights on the principal figures but seeks to force a simplistic overall argument and, in the final analysis, does not do justice to the richness of the Italian political discussion.

38 Benedetto Croce, *L'Italia dal 1914 al 1918: Pagine sulla guerra* (Bari: Laterza, 1965), 95, 107–12, 235–8; Benedetto Croce, 'prefazione,' to the third (1917) edition of *Materialismo storico ed economia marxistica* (Bari: Laterza, 1968), xiii–xiv.

39 Giovanni Gentile, *Che cosa è il fascismo* (Florence: Vallecchi, 1925), 153–61; Gioacchino Volpe, *Guerra dopoguerra fascismo* (Venice: La Nuova Italia, 1928), 293–9.

40 See especially Ulisse Benedetti, *Benedetto Croce e il fascismo* (Rome: Giovanni Volpe, 1967), 93–4, 158. Croce adopted a stance of haughty superiority when he looked back on his 'relations or non-relations with Mussolini' in 1944; see *Nuove pagine sparse*, 1, 80–95.

41 See especially Borgese, *Goliath*, 23, 295–302. See also Chester McArthur Destler, "Some Observations on Contemporary Historical Theory," *American Historical Review* 55 (1950), 504, 517.

42 Among the notable recent studies in Italian are Giuseppe Calandra, *Gentile e il facsismo* (Rome and Bari: Laterza, 1987); Gabriele Turi, *Giovanni Gentile: Una biografia* (Florence: Giunti, 1995); and Danilo Veneruso, *Gentile e il primato della tradizione culturale italiana: Il dibattito politico all'interno del fascismo* (Rome: Studium, 1984).

43 For example, Giovanni Gentile, *Fascismo e cultura* (Milan: Fratelli Treves, 1928), 57–8.

44 For a fuller discussion, see David D. Roberts, 'Croce and Beyond: Italian Intellectuals and the First World War,' *International History Review* 3 no. 2 (April 1981), 201–35.

45 Norberto Bobbio noted in 1974 that even in Italy Gentile's philosophy seemed not only dead, but literally incomprehensible. Yet Bobbio also observed that not so long ago, intelligent, idealistic young Italians found Gentile's thinking exciting, inspiring. Bobbio's characterization is cited, and endorsed, in Maurizio Ferraris, 'Il Gentile di Garin,' *Aut Aut*, n.s. no. 247 (Jan.–Feb. 1992), 26. Along similar lines, the distinguished historian of philosophy Eugenio Garin, no partisan of Croce and Gentile, has emphasized that, if we refuse to take their ideas seriously, 'we risk not understanding the position of so many young people who, at the time of the First World War, found in Croce and Gentile two incomparable teachers' who seemed to show

these young Italians 'how the course of history might converge with their ideals.' See Eugenio Garin, *La cultura italiana tra '800 e '900* (Rome and Bari: Laterza, 1976), 183–4.

46 Now in Francesco De Sanctis, *Scritti critici* (Bari: Laterza, 1969), III, 1–25. Note also 'La scienza e la vita,' 161–82 in the same volume, on the need to unify culture and life.

47 Gentile, *Fascismo e cultura* (1918), 1–15.

48 See, for example, Croce, *Ultimi saggi*, 310–11.

49 Croce, *Etica e politica*, 147–8, 188, 190–1, 293–4; Croce, *Cultura e vita morale*, 301–2.

50 See especially Croce, *Cultura e vita morale* (1923), 244–7, and (1923), 250.

51 Croce, *Filosofia e storiografia*, 143–4, 253–5.

52 See Jane Caplan, 'Postmodernism, Poststructuralism, and Deconstruction: Notes for Historians,' *Central European History* 22 (Sept.–Dec. 1989), 274–8, for some indications of the scope for adapting the insights of deconstruction to deepen our approach to the problem of fascism. This would entail letting the binary oppositions at work in the discussion of fascism – rational/irrational, for example – themselves be at issue, so that we might open the standard dichotomies, questioning their positive terms.

53 For Croce's repeated insistence on world-historical modesty, see 'Frammenti di etica,' in *Etica e politica*, 151–3; *Carattere*, 209–10; and *Discorsi di varia filosofia* (1942), I, 297.

54 Guido Calogero, *Difesa del liberalsocialismo ed altri saggi*, new ed. (Milan: Marzorati, 1972), 34, 78–80, 102–3, 257–61. See also Roberts, *Benedetto Croce*, 224–37.

55 Benedetto Croce, *Terze pagine sparse* (Bari: Laterza, 1955), (1950), I, 280–1; Croce, *Nuove pagine sparse*, II, 210–11, 265–6.

56 Jürgen Habermas, 'The Hermeneutic Claim to Universality,' in Joseph Bleicher, ed., *Contemporary Hermeneutics: Method, Philosophy and Critique* (London: Routledge and Kegan Paul, 1980), 181–211, particularly 191, 202–9. See Gadamer, *Philosophical Hermeneutics*, 26–38, 41–2, for examples of his critique of Habermas.

57 Habermas, 'The Hermeneutic Claim to Universality,' 202–3, 205, 206–7.

58 Gadamer, *Philosophical Hermeneutics*, 31. See also Hans-Georg Gadamer, 'Hermeneutics and Social Science,' *Cultural Hermeneutics* 2 (1975), 314–15.

59 See, for example, Gadamer, *Philosophical Hermeneutics*, 41–2, 93. See also Warnke, *Gadamer*, 127, for an excellent discussion of Gadamer's anti-elitism in the context of his debate with Habermas.

60 Croce, 'Frammenti di etica,' in *Etica e politica*, 151–3; Croce, *Carattere*, 209–10; Croce, *Discorsi di varia filosofia* (1942), I, 297.

61 See, for example, the well-known passage in *La storia come pensiero e come azione*, 225, in which Croce links liberty to the human ethical capacity, which seeks to free up the human creativity necessary for the ongoing growth of the world.

62 The phrase is adapted from Richard Rorty's characterization in *Consequences of Pragmatism: Essays (1972–1980)* (Minneapolis: University of Minnesota Press, 1982), 173. See also Richard Rorty, *Philosophy and the Mirror of Nature* (Princeton, NJ: Princeton University Press, 1979), 380–3, 385, for this line of criticism against Habermas.

63 I compare Croce and Camus in Roberts, *Benedetto Croce*, 189–98. I offer a fuller discussion of Rorty in Roberts, *Nothing but History*, chap. 9.

64 See, for example, Rorty, *Philosophy and the Mirror of Nature*, 327–31, on the working out of the modern concept of rationality at the time of Galileo.

65 Richard Rorty, *Contingency, Irony, and Solidarity* (Cambridge: Cambridge University Press, 1989), 42; see also 61. For a few of Croce's many statements along these lines, see *Cultura e vita morale* (1916), 206–9; (1917) 210–11; and *Filosofia e storiografia* (1945), 64–5.

66 See especially Rorty, *Contingency*, 84.

67 See Nicola Abbagnano, *Critical Existentialism* (Garden City, NY: Doubleday Anchor, 1969), 1–18, for a good example of such critical characterizations of Croce's thought. See also Antonio Santucci, *Esistenzialismo e filosofia italiana* (Bologna: Il Mulino, 1959), 17–23, 68–77, 160–227; and Roberts, *Benedetto Croce*, 187–98.

68 Croce, 'Frammenti di etica,' in *Etica e politica*, 22–3, 25, 99–101, 123. See also Roberts, *Benedetto Croce*, 174–82.

69 Croce, *Filosofia e storiografia* (1946), 144.

70 The distinguished student of historicism Pietro Rossi, whose work has been widely published in English, is a prominent example. Rossi made the charge, yet again, in his essay 'Max Weber and Benedetto Croce,' in Wolfgang J. Mommsen and Jürgen Osterhammel, eds., *Max Weber and His Contemporaries* (London: Allen and Unwin, 1987), 459–64.

71 Croce, *Ultimi saggi* (1930), 263–4.

72 Benedetto Croce, *Filosofia della pratica: economia ed etica* (Bari: Laterza, 1963), 406.

73 Rorty, *Contingency*, 21, 40–1.

74 Rorty, *Consequences of Pragmatism*, 87–8.

12

Croce's *Taccuini di lavoro*

RITA MELILLO

I taccuini di lavoro are working diaries that Croce began writing in 1906 and continued until just two years before his death in 1952. Collected in six volumes, these notebooks were published in a limited edition by the Croce Institute in Naples and are available at the John P. Robarts Research Library in the University of Toronto. There is only one critical study of the diaries – Gennaro Sasso's *Per invigilare me stesso: I taccuini di lavoro di Benedetto Croce* (Bologna: Il Mulino, 1989). Sasso's title quotes the words that Croce used to explain why he wrote the notebooks. Literally they mean 'to keep an eye on myself,' by which Croce implied not only keeping track of his own work, but making sure that he worked and had something to account for every day. In fact, the notebooks are mainly a record of Croce's daily work: the essays and books he planned, wrote, published, or re-edited, the readings he did, the correspondence he kept. At times entries also include personal reflections on historical or political events, as during the fascist years, or afterward. Thus the *Taccuini* are neither diaries in the normal sense of the word nor a work of autobiography. As Sasso remarks, Croce did not want to appear in these notebooks as an individual or a person to be assessed or analysed, rather (60), 'as an activity, an energy, a task, which if realized in this act [of writing], and only in this act, the individual would realize himself' (come un'attività, un'energia – come un compito che, se fosse realizzato in questo atto, e solo in questo, l'individuo si realizzerebbe). Croce always shied away from the 'vanity,' as he called it, of speaking or writing about himself, preferring, as Sasso tells us (60), to narrate 'the story of his intellectual development such as it was' (la storia del suo qualsiasi svolgimento intellettuale).

'They aren't a diary of my sentiments and thoughts, but simply the account of my days, something I did *almost to keep an eye on myself;* and at the same time, they record the chronology of my works and their preparation.' (Non contengono già un diario dei miei sentimenti e pensieri, ma semplicemente il resoconto delle mie giornate, che *quasi per controllo di me stesso* sono stato solito di fare; e, insieme, segnano la cronologia dei miei libri e della loro preparazione.)[1] Croce describes the progress of his work in philosophy, poetry, history, and literary criticism; he speaks primarily of his works, what went into their preparation and how long it took him to complete them. The following is an example of this type of entry (I, 478): 'The year 1915 was spent primarily in revising and completing my previous works. I completed *La Storia della storiografia italiana nel secolo XIX;* I rewrote *I teatri di Napoli* ... The year 1916 will be devoted to reading various books to prepare some essays of mine on the XIXth century.' (L'anno 1915 è stato in gran parte speso a dar termine e assetto ai miei lavori precedenti. Ho terminato la *Storia della storiografia italiana nel secolo XIX;* ho riscritto *I Teatri di Napoli* ... L'anno 1916 sarà consacrato quasi tutto a letture svariate, di preparazione ad alcuni studii che intendo compiere sul secolo XIX.)

Croce kept an eye on himself to guard against wasting time, and his reflections make us aware that everybody's lifetime is too short to begin, let alone complete, all the projects that they would like to undertake. But if one compiles a daily inventory of what one has done or has left undone, as Croce did, one can accomplish much more than one otherwise might, for the simple reason that activities become programs. As we can see when studying Croce's *Taccuini,* when one knows how to realize an idea that one has in mind – knowing which tools one needs and which are available, and how much time it will take and how much time one has – then one no longer has a dream but rather has a project to carry out, and one can develop a precise program of study, writing, and action, a program of serious work of the kind that Croce in fact realized, though not, as the *Taccuini* reveal, without overcoming great difficulties.

Each day he records his intellectual work in the *Taccuini*: he has read such and such a book and taken notes on it, has written such and such an article or essay, which will eventually become part of a book. He organizes his time so that he can pursue several activities at once: first of all, carry on his studies, write, and revise his writing, but also publish single-handedly the journal *La critica,* direct a publishing company (Laterza), engage in serious political activity, travel throughout Italy and Europe to do research and attend congresses, and pay attention to the many people who constantly visit his house to seek advice or ask for assistance and so on.

Some of Croce's pupils have published accounts of how he lived and worked, including in their descriptions both amusing or interesting personal details and also showing what an example of dedication to scholarship he provided for the younger generation. In an essay by Alfredo Parente entitled 'How Croce Worked,' for example, we read that Croce, at work in his study, was sometimes annoyed by the loud bell of the church of Santa Chiara nearby or by his wife chatting with her friends near the main door open to the cold winter wind.[2] Parente also reports the constant visits of people wanting Croce to read their works – so many visits that Croce does not seem to have any time to concentrate on his own writing. Vittorio Enzo Alfieri, in contrast, in his book on Croce's pedagogy gives us the picture of a man not only busy with his studies but engaged in creating and maintaining a friendly relationship with a younger generation of scholars.[3] And Raffaello Franchini explains the ideal that guided Croce's political thought and behaviour.[4] This ideal is the principle of freedom, or the 'Religion of Liberty,' as Croce himself refers to it in an essay first published in *La critica* and then reprinted in *La storia d'Europa nel secolo XIX* (1932). Croce thinks of that principle in religious terms, in the sense that liberty has to be considered as a faith essential to humanity, as if it were breath, without which it perishes. That is why, as Franchini explains, Croce could not accept fascism or Marxism or any kind of totalitarianism, because for him any ideology that threatens freedom spells the destruction of humankind.[5]

The personal and social aspects of Croce's life as described in the *Taccuini* reveal much of his character – and especially of his dedication to his work. Many artists, poets, painters, and writers visit him daily at Palazzo Filomarino, his home in the heart of Naples. They come simply to meet the great man or to enlist his aid in some way. Perhaps he will read their works and give them some advice or encouragement. The surprising thing is that Croce always has time for everyone and never says no, even though in the *Taccuini* (VI, 62) he often calls these visitors 'scocciatori' (bothers): 'The dual flow of letters and persons continues: 1) of those who come to me confident that I can secure them a job of some kind; 2) of writers of poems who want me to put in writing my judgment whether (or rather that) they are poets.' (Ma continua la duplice processione, epistolare e personale: 1) di coloro che si rivolgono a me con sicura fiducia affinché procuri loro un impiego qualsiasi; 2) di scrittori di versi che vogliono un mio giudizio in iscritto che dica se [o piuttosto che] sono poeti.)

One finds notes of this sort not only in the latest volumes, composed when Croce was old and well-known the world over, but also from the start, in the first entries, when he was still relatively unknown. In volume I (65), on 21 August 1907, one reads: 'Forced to stay up late into the night (as for the three previous days) by that Italian chap from Brazil, who has got me working hard for several hours a day to correct his impossible verses.' (Incalzato fino a sera tardi [come nei tre giorni precedenti] da quell'italiano del Brasile, che mi ha fatto lavorare parecchie ore al giorno a correggere versi incorreggibili.) Annotations of this type, spread throughout the six volumes, not only provide a source of information about other scholars, the political situation of Italy, and so on, but also give us a vivid picture of Croce himself managing to carry on his daily life as a scholar and philosopher in spite of numerous interruptions and distractions.

Interference, however, did not always come from outside. Often Croce writes of the depression that he feels because of the political situation in Italy, the two world wars, the rise of fascism, and other events. He sometimes feels so desperate (IV, 140–1) as to want to die but always rejects the possibility of suicide: 'Waking up with the usual disgust and apathy towards life, I've found myself facing my usual dilemma: "either one dies, or one lives," with the usual conclusion that, not dying now, there is nothing left to do other than to resume life, that is, faith and hope.' (Svegliandomi con la solita ripugnanza e sfiducia a rientrare nella vita, mi sono ritrovato di fronte al solito dilemma: 'O si muore o si vive;' con la solita conclusione che, non morendo ora, non c'è da far altro che ripigliare la vita, cioè la fiducia e la speranza.) Often we find entries such as, 'Sadness. Did not work,' or 'Depression. Done nothing.' But he also writes (II, 452) that no matter how hard it is to accept the world and one's frustrations, 'it is impossible to die because of the duties that bind one to the family, to one's studies, to society. So one has to live: to live *as if* the world went according to our ideals.' (non è dato morire, pei doveri che legano alla famiglia, agli studii, alla società. Dunque, bisogna vivere: vivere *come se* il mondo andasse o si avviasse ad andare conforme ai nostri ideali.) Croce is often sad, desperate, and depressed, but he always succeeds in finding the strength to continue to live and so provides an extraordinary example for others. He is always aware of his duty, specifically of his work as a philosopher, through which, as the *Taccuini* show, he intends to make his principal contribution to the cultural and moral life of society.

Croce's tendency to depression often appears when he feels that the welfare – especially the liberty – of his country is threatened. On 27 October 1917, for example, he writes (II, 38) that news about the war has caused him 'a kind of mental block and severe nervous prostration' (una sorta di paralisi mentale e un grande abbattimento nervoso). On 11 April 1920, he reports (II, 153) that he is so depressed by the political situation in Rome that in the morning he cannot get to work without saying his 'prayer' ('recitare la mia preghiera').

From his description, it appears that his prayer consists of a kind of philosophical discipline – collecting his thoughts and meditating on the things that have distressed him. And the passages in the diaries that describe his sorrow and anger at the rise of fascism also show him employing philosophical discipline to overcome his tendency to depression. After a trip to Turin, where he observed the government's 'violent and hypocritical' suppression of the press, he comments that reflection on the situation there and in Italy as a whole would have left him depressed if he had not kept reminding himself that a philosopher should not give way to merely personal feelings of discouragement but should concentrate instead on what he ought to be doing, on his duty. When he did this, Croce reports (II, 441), 'it wasn't difficult for me to confirm my decision to continue doing what I am able to do, whatever may happen' (non mi è stato difficile rifermarmi nella risoluzione, che a me spetti continuare a fare quel che posso fare, qualunque cosa accada). Even when fascist thugs attacked his house in the middle of the night, breaking windows and cutting up pictures, he reveals that he was determined not to be put off his work. 'Next day,' Croce writes (II, 503), 'I resumed my historical readings and the notes from the books I had read and marked. But there was such a crowd of friends who wanted some news of the night before that I could hardly continue with my work, from which I had decided not to be distracted.' (A giorno, ho represo le letture storiche e gli appunti dai libri letti e segnati; ma c'è stata poi tale folla di amici, venuti a chiedere notizie dei fatti di stanotte, che ho potuto continuare a stento il lavoro, dal quale mi ero proposto di non distrarmi.)

For Croce, of course, his work – 'Doing what I am able to do' – meant primarily continuing to study and write. Indeed, the imperative that he felt to continue his philosophical work often awakened his fear that premature death would prevent him from tackling what he perceived to be the fundamental questions (a fear that perhaps can be traced to his experience in the earthquake of Casamicciola, when he lost his parents and his sister and nearly died himself). When in 1908 he completes the outline of his *Filosofia della pratica*, for example, he writes (I, 73) that he is afraid that he may die before he is able to complete it and thus 'not be able to give body to my thought, which in my notes remains unintelligible to anyone except me' (non poter dar corpo al mio pensier, del quale tra gli appunti non c'è nulla che riesca intelligible ad altri fuori di me). In a later passage, reflecting on his fear of premature death, he asserts (II, 33) his confidence that even if he were to die at that moment he would have demonstrated at least three important things: that philosophy is essentially method (metodo); that all true history is contemporary history; and that art is lyrical intuition (intuizione lirica). Only after he had written the works he considered indispensable to an understanding of the central points of his philosophy did he begin to be satisfied that he had done what he was able to do.

Croce always held philosophy to be his primary duty, and he never ceased to be wary of political activity that might carry him away from his studies and into a sphere of activity for which he feared he was little suited. After the Second World War, when many who sincerely cared for the future of Italy were asking him to be their leader, he confesses in the *Taccuini* that he doubts he is the right person (V, 250). And in 1946, when most politicians wanted him to be president of Italy, he writes (VI, 47): 'But I know myself and I know what I can and what I cannot do; and I know that for my part it would be as foolish as inconvenient to think that I can save Italy from the terrible consequences of defeat caused by fascism, thereby risking my reputation, such as it is, as a scholar and a man of science.' (Ma io mi conosco e so quel che posso e quel che non posso; e so anche che sarebbe da parte mia quanto sciocco altrettanto sconveniente pensare di poter salvare l'Italia dalle terribili conseguenze della disfatta provocata dal fascismo, facendo giocare il mio qualsiasi prestigio di uomo di studii e di scienze.)

Nevertheless, in spite of these frequently expressed reservations, the *Taccuini* also make clear that Croce was prepared to play a role in politics whenever he felt he could be effective in solving a crisis, furthering the cause of liberty, or aiding his country. He had accepted a life appointment to the Senate in 1910, and on 14 June 1920 he writes (II, 162):

While I was busy revising my work on Dante, a journalist from the *Tribune* came to ask me to go to Rome as soon as possible for political reasons. Knowing from the newspapers what it was all about, I was taken by a sort of mental *vortex*, thinking of how it would upset my projects and my life, and for the doubts I had about being a politician. It took me more than an hour to settle down, but I felt that in no way could I avoid my duties. I left for Rome at 5:30. (Mentre stavo lavorando all revisione del lavoro su Dante, è venuto da me il corrispondente della *Tribuna* a pregarmi ... di recarmi al più presto a Roma per cosa politica. Compreso, in relazione alla notizie apparse nei giornali, di che cosa si trattasse, sono stato preso come da un *vortice* mentale, per lo sconvolgimento che si annunziava nei miei disegni e nella mia vita, e pei dubbii che mi si sono ripresentati su me stesso e le mie attitudini politiche. Ho durato fatica, per qualche ora, a rassettarmi; ma ho sentito che non potevo, qualunque cosa accadesse, ricusarmi all'opera che da me sarebbe stata chiesta. Sono partito per Roma alle 17.30.)

Moreover, although he judged that it would be 'foolish' of him to think that he could save Italy from the consequences of its defeat in the Second World War, he was instrumental in bringing the parties that were fighting each other after the war to cooperate for the sake of the nation.

Throughout his life, Croce had tended to take a conciliatory position in politics, and this role became crucial between 1943 and 1945 when the major political figures of the time visited him (or, on rare and urgent occasions, Croce travelled to Rome to meet them) to discuss the political situation and ask for his advice regarding the best possible course of action.[6] The diaries of this period show him receiving even more visitors than usual, many of them very important people, conferring with them for hours, and answering the questions of foreign journalists. He does not turn away those who seek his advice. There are major problems to resolve. What kind of government should the country have after Mussolini's defeat? Is it convenient to have a regent, or would a regent only repeat the horrors of fascism? Who is the right person for such an important and delicate role? What kind of constitution is best for the reconstruction of the country? Which one will be most likely to produce liberty and peace? Croce is of the opinion that the king and the prince of Piedmont should retire (IV, 495) and that there must be a referendum to decide whether the nation will continue to be a monarchy or become a republic (V, 140).

Even in the middle of these political concerns, however, Croce managed to carry on with his work (VI, 68): 'Almost all day I had a series of political or quasi-political visits. Nevertheless, I've written the outline of another essay.' (Quasi tutta la giornata, sequela di visite politiche o semipolitiche. Malgrado ciò, ho fatto lo schema di un altro saggio.) That he was able to accomplish such feats must have derived ultimately from his firm sense that his philosophical work was the best way for him, given his abilities, to make a contribution to his country. What he says of the *Storia d'Italia dal 1871–1915* (History of Italy from 1871 to 1914), written in 1927 at the height of fascism, might be applied to all his writings. Although he found the book painful to write, he persevered (III, 28) because he understood it 'as the fulfilment of a duty towards my fellow citizens' (come dovere da adempiere verso i miei connazionali).

Thus the *Taccuini* present an image of a remarkably coherent life – a life all of one piece, with philosophical work as its immovable centre. And thus too the diaries help us to understand why Croce the philosopher became an extraordinary example to others by virtue of his determined intellectual and civic commitment. Because he understood the importance of providing guidance to the younger generation, he could become the teacher of a whole generation whose intellectual and civic values where shaped by his example. This example so profoundly marked the spirit of future generations that after his death his enormous success engendered a reaction against his legacy. But just as he overcame the petty annoyances and major crises of his life through philosophical reflection, so those who study his works today can put that reaction behind them and rediscover what is living both in his works and in his life.

NOTES

1 B. Croce, *Taccuini di lavoro*, from the dedication that Croce wrote for his daughters, July 1926, vol. I, 1, emphasis added.
2 In Alfredo Parente, *Croce per lumi sparsi: Problemi e ricordi* (Florence: La Nuova Italia, 1975).
3 V.E. Alfieri, *Pedagogia crociana* (Naples: Morano, 1967). See also *Maestri e testimoni di libertà* (Milazzo and Palermo: Sicilia Nuova ed., 1975).
4 R. Franchini, *Note biografiche di Benedetto Croce* (Rome: Edizioni Lubrensi, 1983).
5 R. Franchini, *Intervista su Croce* (Naples: S.E.N., 1978).
6 The entries for this period from July 1943 to June 1944 constitute a unique part of Croce's diary, published as B. Croce, *Quando l'Italia era tagliata in due: Estratto di un diario (luglio 1943–giugno 1944)* (Bari: Laterza, 1948).

Selected Bibliography

Croce's Works

Aesthetic as Science of Expression and General Linguistic. Trans. Douglas Ainslie. New York: Noonday Press, 1956.

The Aesthetic as the Science of Expression and of the Linguistic in General. Trans. Colin Lyas. Cambridge: Cambridge University Press, 1992.

Ariosto, Shakespeare e Corneille. 1920. 4th ed. Trans. Douglas Ainslie. Bari: Laterza, 1950. New York: Holt, 1920.

Benedetto Croce: An Autobiography. Trans. R.G. Collingwood. Oxford: Oxford University Press, 1927. *Contributo alla critica di me stesso.*

Benedetto Croce's Poetry and Literature: An Introduction to Its Critisism and History. Trans. Giovanni Gullace. Carbondale: Southern Illinois University Press, 1981. *La poesia: Introduzione alla critica e storia della poesia e della letteratura.*

Breviario de estetica. 1913. 15th ed. Bari: Laterza, 1966.

'Il Capasso e la storia regionale.' *Napoli nobilissima* 9 (1900), 42–3.

Il carattere della filosofia moderna. 1941. 3rd ed. Bari: Laterza, 1963.

'In commemorazione di un amico inglese, compagno di pensiero e di fede, R.G. Collingwood.' *Nuove pagine sparse*, vol. I. Naples: Riccardo Ricciardi (1948), 25–39.

Contributo alla critica de me stesso. 1951. Ed. Giuseppe Galasso. Milan: Adelphi, 1989.

Cultura e vita morale: Intermezzi polemici. 1914. 3rd ed. Bari: Laterza, 1955.

'Curriculum vitae' (dated 10 April 1902). *Memorie della mia vita. Appunti che sono stati adoprati e sostituiti dal 'Contributo alla critica di me stesso.'* Naples: Instituto Italiano per gli Studi Storici, 1966.

Discorsi di varia filosofia. 2 vols. 1945. 2nd ed. Bari: Laterza, 1959.

'Elementi di politica.' *Etica e politica.* Bari: Laterza, Edizione economica, 1967.

Essays on Literature and Literary Criticism. Trans. and intro. M.E. Moss. Albany: State University of New York Press, 1990.

The Essence of Aesthetic. Trans. Douglas Ainslie. London: Heinemann, 1921. Revised trans. of *Brevario di estetica.*

Estetica come scienza dell'espressione e linguistica generale: Teoria e storia. 1902. 10th ed. Bari: Laterza, 1958.

Etica e politica. 1931. Bari: Laterza, Edizione economica, 1967.

European Literature in the Nineteenth Century. Trans. Douglas Ainslie. London: Chapman & Hall, 1925. *Poesia e non poesia.*

Filosofia della pratica. Economia ed etica. 1909. 8th ed. Bari: Laterza, 1963.

La filosofia di Giambattista Vico. 1911. Bari: Laterza, 1962.

Filosofia e storiografia. 1947. 2nd ed. Bari: Laterza, 1969.

Filosofia, poesia, storia. 1951. Ed. Giuseppe Galasso. Milan: Adelphi, 1991.

Guide to Aesthetics. Trans. Patrick Romanell. Indianapolis: Bobbs-Merrill, 1965. *Breviario de estetica.*

Historical Materialism and the Economics of Karl Marx. Trans. C.M. Meredith. Intro. A.D. Lindsay. London: Latimer Ltd., 1914. *Materialism storico ed economia marxistica.*

History as the Story of Liberty. Trans. Sylvia Sprigge. New York: Norton, 1941. *La storia come pensiero e come azione.*

History: Its Theory and Practice. Trans. Douglas Ainslie. New York: Russell and Russell, 1960. *Teoria e storia della storiografia.*

History of Europe in the Ninenteenth Century. Trans. Henry Furst. New York: Harcourt, Brace & World, 1963. *Storia d'Europa nel secolo decimonono.*

History of the Kingdom of Naples. Ed. H. Stuart Hughes. Trans. Frances Frenaye. Chicago: University of Chicago Press, 1970. *Storia del regno di Napoli.*

Intorno alla critica letteraria. Polemica in risposta ad un opuscolo del Dr. Trojano. Naples: Pierro, 1895.

L'Italia dal 1914 al 1918: Pagine sulla guerra. 1919. 4th ed. Bari: Laterza, 1965.

'Leggende di luoghi ed edifizii di Napoli.' *Napoli nobilissima,* V (1896), 132–5, 172–5. Revised 'False leggende popolari.' *Curiosità storiche.* 2nd ed. Naples: Riccardo Ricciardi, 1921.

Logic as the Science of the Pure Concept. Trans. Douglas Ainslie. London: Macmillan, 1917.

Logica come scienza del concetto puro. 1905. Revised ed. 1908. Bari: Laterza, Edizione economica, 1967.

La mia filosofia. Ed. Giuseppe Galasso. Milan: Adelphi, 1993.

Materialismo storico ed economia marxistica: Saggi critici. 1900. Bari: Laterza, Edizione economica, 1968.

Nuove pagine sparse. 2 vols. 1942–3. 2nd ed. Bari: Laterza, 1966.

Nuovi saggi di estetica. 1920. 4th ed. Bari: Laterza, 1958.

Pagine sparse: Serie prima. Ed. Giovanni Castellano. Naples: Riccardo Ricciardi editore, 1919.

Philosophy of the Practical: Economic and Ethic. Trans. Douglas Ainslie. New York: Biblo & Tannen. 1967. *Filosofia della pratica: Economia ed etica.*

Philosophy, Poetry, History: An Anthology of Essays. Trans. Cecil Sprigge. London: Oxford University Press, 1966. *Filosofia-Poesia-Storia.*

La poesia di Dante. 1920. 11th ed. Bari: Laterza, 1966.

Poesia e non poesia: Note sulla letteratura europea del secolo decimonono. 1923. 7th ed. Bari: Laterza, 1964.

La poesia: Introduzione alla critica e storia della poesia e della letteratura. 1936. Ed. Guiseppe Galasso. Milan: Adelphi, 1994.

Poesia populare e poesia d'arte: Studi sulla poesia italiana dal tre al cinquecento. 1933. 5th ed. Bari: Laterza, 1967.

'"Premessa," to G. Mosca.' *Elementi di scienza politica.* 5th ed. Bari: Laterza, 1953.

Primi saggi. 1919. 3rd ed. Bari: Laterza, 1951.

Problemi di estetica e contributi alla storia dell'estetica italiana. 1910. 6th ed. Bari: Laterza, 1966.

Quando l'Italia era tagliata in due. Estratto di un diario (luglio 1943–giugno 1944). Bari: Laterza, 1948.

Saggi sulla letteratura italiana del seicento. 1911 3rd ed. Bari: Laterza, 1948.

Saggio sullo Hegel seguito da altri scritti di storia della filosofia. 1906. 5th ed. Bari: Laterza, 1967.

Scritti e discorsi politici (1943–1947). 2 vols. Bari: Laterza, 1963.

'Sommario critico della storia dell'arte nel napoletano.' *Napoli nobilissima* II (1893), 6–10.

La storia come pensiero e come azione. 1938. Bari: Laterza, Edizione economica, 1966.

Storia dell'età barocca in Italia: Pensiero – poesia e letteratura – vita morale. 1929. 5th ed. Bari: Laterza, 1967.

Storia del regno di Napoli. 1925. Ed. Giuseppe Galasso. Milano: Adelphi, 1992.

Storia d'Europa nel secolo decimonono. 1932. 7th ed. 1947.

Storia d'Italia dal 1871 al 1915. Bari. Laterza, 1929.

'La storia ridotta sotto il concetto generale dell'arte.' *Atti dell'Accademia Pontaniana,* 23 (1893), 1–32.

'Lo storicismo e l'idea tradizionale della filosofia.' *Quaderni della 'Critica'* 13 (March 1949), 82–7.

Storie e leggende Napoletane. 1919. Ed. Giuseppe Galasso. Milan: Adelphi, 1991.

I teatri di napoli dal rinascimento alla fine del secolo decimottavo. 1916. Ed. Giuseppe Galasso. Milan: Adelphi, 1992.

Teoria e storia della storiografia. 1917. Ed. Giuseppe Galasso. Milan: Adelphi, 1989.

Terze pagine sparse. 2 vols. Bari: Laterza, 1955.

Theory and History of Historiography. Trans. Douglas Ainslie. London: George G. Harrap & Co., 1921. Rev. American ed. *History: Its History and Practice.* New York: Russell & Russell, 1921. *Teoria e storia della storiografia.*

Ultimi saggi. 1935. 3rd ed. Bari: Laterza, 1963.

What Is Living and What Is Dead in the Philosophy of Hegel. Trans. Douglas Ainslie. New York: Russell & Russell, 1969. *Saggio sullo Hegel.*

Bibliographical Studies

Borsari, Silvano. *L'Opera di Benedetto Croce: Bibliografia.* Naples: Istituto Italiano per gi studi storici, 1964.

Brescia, Giuseppe. *Croce Inedito (1881–1952).* Naples: Società editrice napoletana, 1984.

Nicolini, Fausto. *L''edito ne varietur' delle opere di Benedetto Croce.* Naples: Biblioteca dell'Archivio storico del Banco di Napoli, 1960.

Ocone, Corrado. *Bibliografia ragionata degli scritti su Benedetto Croce.* Naples: Edizioni Scientifiche Italiane, 1993.

Secondary Works

Ajello, Raffaele. 'Benedetto Croce e la storia "ideale" nel Regno di Napoli.' *Archivio storico per le provincie napoletane* 110 (1992), 351–440.

Alfieri, V.E. *Pedagogia crociana.* Naples: Morano, 1967.

Benedetti, Ulisse. *Benedetto Croce e il fascismo.* Rome: Giovanni Volpe, 1967.

Borsari, Silvano. 'Scritti di storia napoletana di Benedetto Croce.' *Archivio storico per le provincie napoletane* 73 (1955), 495–500.

Brescia, Giuseppe. 'Benedetto Croce, studioso di storia locale.' *Nuovi studi politici* 8 (1978), 111–19.

– *Croce inedito (1881–1952).* Naples: Società editrice napoletana, 1984.

Boucher, David, Modood, Tariq, and Connelly, James, eds. *Philosophy, History, and Civilization.* Cardiff: University of Wales Press, 1993.

Boulay, Charles. *Benedetto Croce jusqu'en 1911.* Geneva: Droz, 1981.

Cantillo, Giuseppe, and Cavaliere, Renata Viti, eds. *La tradizione critica della filosofia: Studi in memoria di Raffaello Franchini.* Naples: Loffredo, 1994.

Caponigri, A. Robert. *History and Liberty: The Historical Writings of Benedetto Croce.* London: Routledge & Kegan Paul, 1955.

Caserta, Ernesto. *Croce and Marxism.* Naples: Morano, 1987.

– *Croce, critico letterario (1882–1912).* Naples: Giannini, 1972.

Corsi, Mario. *Le origini del pensiero di Benedetto Croce.* Naples: Giannini editore, 1974.

Franchini, Raffaello. *Croce interprete di Hegel e altri saggi filosofici*. Naples: Giannini, 1964.
– *Intervista su Croce*. Ed. A. Fratta. Naples: Società editrice napoletana, 1978.
– *Note biografiche di Benedetto Croce*. Rome: Edizioni Librensi, 1983.
– *La teoria della storia di Benedetto Croce*. Ed. Viti Cavaliere. Naples: Edizioni scientifiche italiane, 1995.
Galasso, Giuseppe. *Croce e lo spirito del suo tempo*. Milan: Mondadori, 1990.
Gentile, Giovanni. *Storia della filosofia italiana*. Ed. E. Garin. Florence: Sansoni, 1969.
Iermano, Toni. *Lo scrittoio di Croce, con scritti inediti e rari*. Naples: Fausto Fiorentino, 1992.
Jacobitti, Edmund E. 'Labriola, Croce, and Italian Marxism (1895–1910).' *Journal of the History of Ideas* 36 (April–May 1975), 297–319.
– *Revolutionary Humanism and Historicism in Modern Italy*. New Haven, Conn.: Yale University Press, 1981.
Moss, M.E. *Benedetto Croce Reconsidered: Truth and Error in Theories of Art, Literature, and History*. Hanover, NH: University Press of New England, 1987.
– 'The Crocean Concept of the Pure Concept.' *Idealistic Studies* 17 (1987), 39–52.
Milburn, Myra Moss. 'Benedetto Croce's Coherence Theory of Truth: A Critical Evaluation.' *Filosofia* 19 (1968), 107–16.
– 'Croce's Theory of Intuition Reconsidered.' *La rivista di studi crociani* 59–60 (July–Dec. 1978), 292–306.
Murray, Gilbert, et al. *Benedetto Croce: A Commemoration*. London: Istituto italiano di cultura, 1953.
Orsini, Gian N.G. *Benedetto Croce: Philosopher of Art and Literary Critic*. Carbondale: Southern Illinois University Press, 1961.
Parente, Alfredo. *Croce per lumi sparsi: Problemi e ricordi*. Florence: La Nouva Italia, 1975.
Piccoli, Raffaello. *Benedetto Croce: An Introduction to His Philosophy*. New York: Harcourt, Brace & Co., 1922.
Prete, Antonio. *La distanza da Croce*. Milan: Celuc, 1956.
Roberts, David D. *Benedetto Croce and the Uses of Historicism*. Berkeley: University of California Press, 1987.
– 'Croce and Beyond: Italian Intellectuals and the First World War.' *International History Review* 3 no. 2 (April 1981), 201–35.
– 'Croce in America: Influence, Misunderstanding, and Neglect.' *Humanitas* 8 no. 2 (1955), 3–34.
Romanell, Patrick. 'Romanticism and Croce's Conception of Science.' *Review of Metaphysics* 9 (March 1956), 505–14.

Russo, Luigi. 'De lineis et coloribus: Benedetto Croce e la pittura.' *Rivista di studi crociani* 4 (1967), 85–92.

Sasso, Gennaro. *Per invigilare me stesso: I Taccuini di lavoro di Benedetto Croce.* Bologna: Il Mulino, 1989.

Simoni, Frederic S. 'Benedetto Croce: A Case of International Misunderstanding.' *Journal of Aesthetics and Art Criticism* 11 (Sept. 1952), 7–14.

Vigorelli, Amodeo. 'Lettere di Robin George Collingwood a Benedetto Croce (1912–1939).' *Rivista di storia della filosofia* 4 (1991), 545–63.

Welllek, René. *Four Critics: Croce, Valéry, Lukacs, and Ingarden.* Seattle: University of Washington Press, 1981.

– 'La teoria letteraria e la critica di Benedetto Croce.' *Letteratura Italiana.* Vol. 4. *L'interpretazione.* Turin: Giulio Einaudi, 1985.

White, Hayden. 'The Abiding Relevance of Croce's Idea of History.' *Journal of Modern History* 37 (June 1963), 109–24.

– *Metahistory: The Historical Imagination in Nineteenth-Century Europe.* Baltimore: Johns Hopkins University Press, 1973.

Willette, Thomas. 'Bernardo De Dominici et le Vite de'pittori, sculturi ed architetti napoletani: Contributo alla riabilitazione di una fonte.' *Ricerche sul'600 napoletano.* Milan: Edizioni Lanconelli & Tognolli, 1986.